The Secre

IND
MAMMALS

KALYAN VARMA

VIVEK MENON

Wildlife
Trust
of India

hachette
INDIA

For the Awesome Seven,
cousins growing up together:
Sangeetha, Shruthi, Sudha, Shiva,
Anjali, Shasta and Sanjana

First published in 2017 by Hachette India
(Registered name: Hachette Book Publishing India Pvt. Ltd)
An Hachette UK company
www.hachetteindia.com

1

978-93-5195-115-5

Hachette Book Publishing India Pvt. Ltd
4th & 5th Floors, Corporate Centre
Plot No. 94, Sector 44
Gurgaon 122003, India

Printed and bound in India
by Manipal Technologies Ltd, Manipal

Contents

Contents

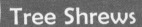

From the Wild Side!

Vivek Menon is a wildlife conservationist, author and photographer, with a passion for elephants. He is the Founder and Executive Director of the Wildlife Trust of India (WTI), an Advisor to the International Fund for Animal Welfare (IFAW) and its Regional Director (South Asia). He is the author of nine bestselling books on Indian wildlife, including *Indian Mammals: A Field Guide*.

'When exactly did you start observing nature and decide that this is what you want to do for life?' This question from Sir David Attenborough, the legendary naturalist and broadcaster, caught me by surprise. Instead of fumbling an inadequate reply, I asked him his moment of truth instead.

'Oh! Watching a pair of dragonflies mate in my father's pond at age eleven.' His answer was precise. I, on the other hand, still could not pinpoint that exact moment when nature beckoned me to its side for the rest of my life. Was it in Class IX when we were climbing Rohtang Pass and a bear decided to chase me through an apple orchard? Or was it later in Eravikulam, watching red dogs hunt a blue goat in an enveloping mist? Or was it. . .?

Nature calls out most to young people as it did to me. That inner urge to be in nature is primeval, inborn, irresistible. Mammals are some of the largest and best known forms of nature, and young people of all ages can enjoy watching not only tigers, elephants and primates but also the lesser known but equally fascinating mammals, such as hedgehogs, dugongs or bats.

This guide to the mammals of India was first written for adults but has been modified for young readers. Not much essential information has been left out other than that which is highly technical. The photographs remain the same although fewer have been used and in a larger format and more eye-catching design.

I hope all of this will help you, from GenNext, to grow up learning to love nature and use this book as a companion in your adventures into the wild. Happy mammal-hunting, boys and girls!

VIVEK MENON

FOUR OF INDIA'S NATIONAL SYMBOLS have a connection with mammals! The regality of the lion, the charisma of a tiger, the power of an elephant and the grace of a dolphin are celebrated, giving them a unique status.

VASUNDHARA KANDPAL

National Aquatic Animal
THE GANGES RIVER DOLPHIN was declared the National Aquatic Animal in October 2009 to save it from extinction.

सत्यमेव जयते

National Emblem
LION CAPITAL
Adapted from the Lion Capital of Ashoka at Sarnath, by Madhav Sawhney in 1950, this shows three lions, the fourth being hidden from view. The wheel appears in the centre of the abacus, with a bull on the right and a galloping horse on the left.

VIVEK MENON

National Heritage Animal
ELEPHANT
In October 2010, the Indian Government declared the elephant a National Heritage Animal.

VIVEK MENON

National Animal

TIGER

The tiger was given the status of National Animal in 1973, with the start of Project Tiger, a national tiger protection programme. Before this, the lion was the National Animal.

What are mammals?

I T'S EASY TO DISTINGUISH MAMMALS from other animals once you know the basic differences. Here a few pointers:

1   All mammals have a backbone (but we can't always see it).
2   All mammals have four limbs (yes, even bats and dolphins – but these limbs have been modified in these mammals.)
3   All mammals are warm-blooded; they can regulate their body temperature to stay in different climates (except the Naked Mole Rat).
4   All mammal females produce milk to feed their babies until the young are old enough to live on their own.
5   All mammals have body hair – even elephants and whales.
6   They have unique skeletal features, such as a different lower jaw, skull, and a middle ear with three bones (the malleus, incus, and stapes).
7   Teeth in a mammal do not get continuously replaced and are either lifelong or replaced just once.
8   Most mammals are adapted to a terrestrial life although aquatic cetaceans and aerial bats are also members of the Class Mammalia.
9   Most mammals are placental, i.e., they give birth to live young, except the Monotremes (like the platypus) that lay eggs.
10   All mammals have a large brain.

While creatures that looked like mammals appeared between the Lower and Middle Jurassic Period (i.e., 195–165 mya), the first placental mammals appeared only after the dinosaurs became extinct in the Paleocene Epoch. They flourished in the Cenozoic Era. There was mammalian life in the Indian subcontinent too when the split with Gondwanaland took place. Some evolutionary biologists have named India as the place of origin for all whales and dolphins.

One of the oldest living mammals in India are the Greater One-horned Rhinoceroses.

DUSHYANT PARASHER

RANJIT BASUMATARYINTI

Another ancient mammalian family history is that of the Chinese Pangolin.

Anatomy and characteristics

Relatively larger brain size

Specialized middle ear

Fur-clad body

Females have mammae

Infants are dependent on the mother for a relatively longer period

Bonnet Macaque and infant, Nilgiris

VIVEK MENON

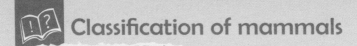

 PRIMATES (say *pri-MAY-tz*) Lorises, langurs, macaques, apes: *Front-facing eyes; shaped palms and soles; thumbs opposite to the fingers.*

 PROBOSCIDEA (say *PRO-boh-SID-e-ah*) Elephants: *Large size; long trunk; visible toenails; rough, thick skin with spiky hair.*

 PERISSODACTYLA (*per-RIS-so-DAK-ti-lah*) Rhinoceros, horses: *Hoofed herbivores with an odd number of toes; called odd-toed ungulates.*

 ARTIODACTYLA (*AR-te-o-DAK-ti-lah*) Antelope, camels, deer, cattle, sheep, goats: *Horned or antlered hoofed herbivores with an even number of toes; named even-toed ungulates.*

 CARNIVORA (say *kar-NIV-o-rah*) Wolves, bears, otters, cats: *Primarily meat eaters with enlarged canines and claws.*

 LAGOMORPHA (say *LAG-o-MOR-fah*) Rabbits, hares, pikas: *Herbivorous animals with four incisors in the upper jaw (not two as in rodents).*

 PHOLIDOTA (say *FOL-ee-doh-ta*) Pangolins: *Scaly, insectivorous animals with long tails, tubular snouts and strong claws.*

 SCANDENTIA (say *SKA-den-shee-ah*) Tree shrews: *Small, slender omnivores, with long tails and undeveloped canines and molars.*

 INSECTIVORA (say *in-sek-TIV-or-ah*) Moles, shrews: *Small insect-eating mammals with sharp teeth and long, pointed snouts.*

 ERINACEA (say *eri-NAY-see-ah*) Hedgehogs: *Spiny insectivores, with the ability to roll into a tight ball.*

 RODENTIA (say *ro-DEN-shee-ah*) Mice, voles, rats, squirrels, porcupines: *Small body size; enlarged top incisors; long, pointy snouts.*

 CHIROPTERA (say *ki-ROP-ter-ah*) Bats: *Large wings made of skin; claws; roost upside down; mostly nocturnal.*

 CETACEA (say *se-TAY-shee-ah*) Whales, porpoises, dolphins: *Water dwelling with fins; blowhole on upper body surface for breathing.*

 SIRENIA (say *si-RE-ne-ah*) Manatees, dugongs: *Marine herbivores with limbs adapted to water.*

THE BRANCH OF SCIENCE that deals with the classification of organisms is called *taxonomy*. All mammals belong to the Class Mammalia. They are then divided into three subclasses and about 26 Orders (biologists can't get to agree!) of related animals, of which 14 main ones are found in India.

All mammals are in the CLASS *Mammalia*	Mammals	
An ORDER is the next level of classification.	e.g., All carnivores including cats are in order Carnivora	
A FAMILY lies between order and genus.	e.g., All cats are in family Felidae	
A GENUS is a taxonomic rank between a family and a species.	e.g. lions, leopards and tigers are all of genus Panthera	
A SPECIES is generally a basic unit of taxonomy referring to a group of organisms that can interbreed and have fertile offspring. This is, however, a generalization and not applicable in all cases.	e.g. a tiger is *Panthera tigris*	

The following abbreviations, contractions and terms are used in the book:

cm	centimetre	TL	tail length
FF	forefoot length	TR	Tiger Reserve
g	gram	WLS	Wildlife Sanctuary
HAS	height at shoulder	WPA	Wildlife Protection Act
HBL	head-and-body length	Wt	weight
FA	forearm (length)		
IUCN	International Union for Conservation of Nature		
kg	kilogram		
km	kilometre		
m	metre		
mm	millimetre		
mya	million years ago		
NP	National Park		
RF	Reserve Forest		

A few terms you might want to know:

Digit: finger or toe

Dorsal: upper side or back

Forage: food, or search for food

Gestation: time taken for a baby to grow and develop inside the mother's womb

Pelage: fur, hair or wool of a mammal

Venter: underside or front

Weaning: to accustom a young animal to food other than mother's milk

How mammals live together

THERE IS A DIFFERENT TERM to describe a group of each mammal, such as a pride of lions, a pod of dolphins, a troop of macaques, a sounder of pigs. Social living is a way of life for many mammals, as it is for humans!

A colony of bats cluster overhead in a cave.

KALYAN VARMA

A herd of Swamp Deer gathering in the plains for feeding or breeding is a common sight.

N.A. NASEER

M.K. RANJITSINH

A romp or pod of Smooth-coated Otters.

KALYAN VARMA

A troop of Bonnet Macaques huddle for warmth in the early morning.

ANIMALS IN THIS BOOK have been photographed using long lenses by professionals and the results have been then improved by magnifying and cropping the photo. However, out there in the field, visibility is quite different and you must remember this when going out to a National Park or Wildlife Sanctuary to see the mammals featured here. Use good binoculars, be prepared to walk and stalk (where permitted) and have tonnes of patience!

Species that live in tall grass are invisible if you drive through it, so going on elephant back is a good option for sighting them. Mountain ungulates can be shy and are in terrain that's hard to reach. Most Indian wildlife lives in forests, much of it thick and difficult to go through.

Viewing nocturnal species like the Leopard Cat through vegetation and low light is tough. Camouflage is key even for large, flamboyant animals, such as the tiger. Its stripes and colour merge into tall, dry grass, making it hard to sight. A forest is the natural home of wildlife, not a zoo for tourists to watch animals. Remember this when you visit a wildlife reserve.

KARMA SONAM

Bharal on the horizon.

GOUTAM NARAYAN

Pygmy Hog sounder in tall grass.

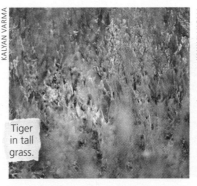

KALYAN VARMA

Tiger in tall grass.

KALYAN VARMA

Leopard Cat in the canopy.

What's for lunch? Herbivores

DEPENDING ON WHAT THEY EAT, most mammals can be grouped into two broad categories: carnivores (that eat flesh) and herbivores (that feed on plants). Omnivores can feed on both. Mammals can also 'specialize' in a diet: insectivores feed on insects, frugivores eat fruit, and piscivores mainly take fish.

Diet is a major factor that influences a mammal's body, and mammals have developed specialized aids to gather food and to feed. The powerful forelimbs of a tiger help it hunt, primates use the thumbs opposite their fingers to forage, the large molars of herbivores help them chew, while the complex stomach of leaf-eating species helps them in digestion.

GRAZERS: Deer, antelope, cattle and sheep are grazers, like this herd of Blackbuck (*above*) enjoying the juicy grass of Velavadar NP, Gujarat.

FRUGIVORE: Gibbons and some monkeys are frugivores, as are some bats. Here, a Lion-tailed Macaque rips out flesh from a jackfruit.

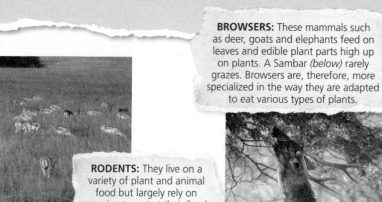

BROWSERS: These mammals such as deer, goats and elephants feed on leaves and edible plant parts high up on plants. A Sambar *(below)* rarely grazes. Browsers are, therefore, more specialized in the way they are adapted to eat various types of plants.

MANOJ DHOLAKIA

RODENTS: They live on a variety of plant and animal food but largely rely on gnawing to get at their food. Here, an Orange-bellied Tree Squirrel tackles a nut in Tawang, Arunachal Pradesh.

GOPINATHAN MAHESWARAN

VIVEK MENON

EXUDATIVORE: The Slow Loris is a unique example of a mammal that may feed mainly on plant gums and resins, besides a variety of insect species. Although gum and resins are not nutrient-rich, they are available almost year-round and may help lorises tide over periods when food is not easily available.

What's for lunch? Non-herbivores

LARGE CARNIVORES: Many carnivores living on the ground eat herbivores, such as this lion in the Gir. But large carnivores include the Killer Whales in the seas, the Brown Bear in the Himalayas and large wolves.

NIRAV BHATT

SMALL CARNIVORES: All carnivores are not dependent on large prey. This Indian Fox survives on small rodents, hares, birds and insects.

MANOJ DHOLAKIA

OMNIVORES: Omnivores, such as the bear, the macaque and the pig, eat both animal and plant matter. They may scavenge and hunt. They will, like most ungulates, also take minerals such as the rock salt being licked here by this Sloth Bear.

KALYAN VARMA

PISCIVORES: Otters are the only true fish-eaters among mammals. But in unique habitats such as the Sunderbans mangroves, even tigers take to eating fish.

DHRITIMAN MUKHERJEE

RADHIKA BHAGAT

INSECTIVORES: Some bats, such as this Lesser Mouse-tailed Bat *(below)*, pangolins, shrews, hedgehogs and moles are speciailized insectivores although they don't all belong to the order Insectivora.

MANOJ P.

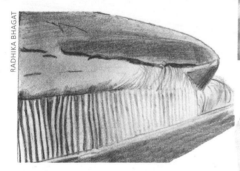

BALEEN FEEDERS: Baleen is a filtration structure *(left)* in the mouth of certain animals that replaces teeth. Made of keratin, it filters specific types of food. A number of marine species, especially whales, such as baleen whales, possess this. They mainly consume phytoplankton or zooplankton from ocean surfaces.

SCAVENGERS: Hyaenas can be powerful carnivores but also represent the scavenging world. They steal kills, or take over ones left by other carnivores.

KALYAN VARMA

SIXTEEN DIFFERENT FOREST TYPES exist in India: Wet evergreen, dry evergreen, semi-evergreen, moist deciduous, dry deciduous, littoral and swamp, thorn scrub, broadleaved, pine, dry montane subtropical evergreen, dry temperate montane, moist temperate montane, wet temperate montane, subalpine, dry alpine and moist alpine.

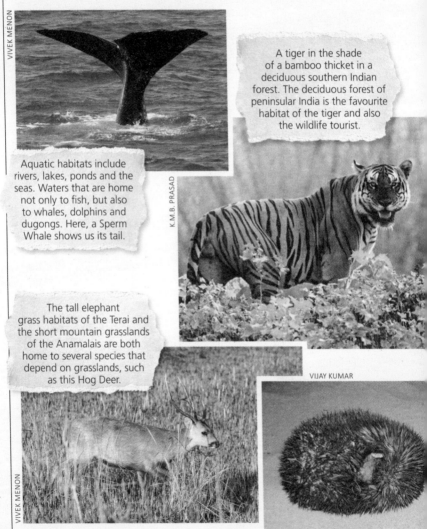

A tiger in the shade of a bamboo thicket in a deciduous southern Indian forest. The deciduous forest of peninsular India is the favourite habitat of the tiger and also the wildlife tourist.

Aquatic habitats include rivers, lakes, ponds and the seas. Waters that are home not only to fish, but also to whales, dolphins and dugongs. Here, a Sperm Whale shows us its tail.

The tall elephant grass habitats of the Terai and the short mountain grasslands of the Anamalais are both home to several species that depend on grasslands, such as this Hog Deer.

VIVEK MENON

K.M.B. PRASAD

VIJAY KUMAR

VIVEK MENON

A Nilgiri Langur in an evergreen forest: evergreen and semi-evergreen forests are teeming with many species of mammals.

KALYAN VARMA

The Himalayan marmots and many ungulates, including the wild ass, live on the open plateaus and cold deserts of the trans-Himalayas. Here, the marmot in Ladakh.

SOM B. ALE

A Tahr stands on a hilltop: Mount Everest looms in the background. The Himalayas are home to several wild goats and sheep.

PRAVEEN MOHANDAS

Mangroves, such as in the Sunderbans of West Bengal, are close to coastal areas. A number of species, including the Royal Bengal Tiger, live in these difficult habitats.

DHRITIMAN MUKHERJEE

The Thar in Rajasthan is the only true desert in India. Semi-dry lands and salt flats spread across western India. They seem lifeless at first glance, but a closer look shows an amazing variety of life, including a hedgehog.

Watching mammals
How their looks change and why

MAMMALS CHANGE COAT COLOUR and quality depending on climate, and this is striking in those that live in colder climates. In winter, the fur of many animals becomes thicker, while in summer it becomes lighter. In some cases, it changes colour too; for example, the Himalayan Stoat or Ermine goes from chestnut-brown in summer to pure white in winter. The look of an animal changes with age and place, as well as the seasons.

DHRITIMAN MUKHERJEE

The Red Fox in Ladakh changes from a furry winter beast *(right)* to a lightly furred one in summer *(bottom)*.

VIVEK MENON

Many males turn more colourful and spectacular during the breeding season. In the non-breeding season, stags may be antler-less or may have small velvet knobs that grow into antlers, but in the breeding season, they sport impressive headgear. Here, an adult Sambar stag in Ranthambore NP, Rajasthan, changes his velvet *(top left)* to hard antlers *(below left)*.

OTTO PFISTER

Albinos are animals that lack a skin pigment called melanin. Their skin is pale and eyes pink. However, a White Tiger is not an albino; it is a different gene that causes it. Here, an albino Gaur calf with a normal coloured female, Chinnar WLS, Kerala.

MOHIT AGGARWAL

SANJAYAN KUMAR

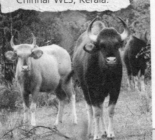

N.A. NASEER

Melanism (more melanin or dark-coloured pigment in the skin!) is the opposite of albinism. Black panthers are melanistic Common Leopards! Here, a rare melanistic Chital stands behind a normal one in Parambikulam WLS, Kerala.

Watching mammals
Are they really grinning at you. . .or angry?

Canines being shown in a primate can point to both fear or aggression. A combination of eyes and canines helps solve this mystery. Notice the shut-eyed threat display *(left)* and the open-eyed, fear-grin *(below left)* in a Bonnet Macaque.

The snarl of a big cat, mouth half open, nose wrinkling up, eyes open and ears pressed back on to the face, such as in the tiger at Ranthambore NP, Rajasthan *(above right)*, comes before a full-throated roar and perhaps a charge. Don't confuse it with a yawn: mouth fully open, eyes shut, ears normal and nose not as wrinkled, in Pench TR, Madhya Pradesh *(right)*.

Animals with spikes use them both for defence and offence, such as when a hedgehog curls up in defence in the desert sands of Rajasthan *(left)* while an Indian Porcupine bristles its spines at an intruder, Chhattisgarh *(bottom)*. The porcupine backs rapidly into its enemy and leaves its spines embedded in them.

VIJAY KUMAR

A jackal shows its canines and gums, eyes open and ears erect threateningly while at a kill *(below left)*, Keoladeo Ghana NP, Rajasthan, and it screams in fear, ears laid flat against body and tail between legs in Kolkata *(below right)*, West Bengal.

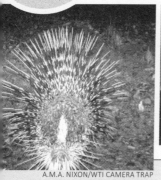

A.M.A. NIXON/WTI CAMERA TRAP

DHRITIMAN MUKHERJEE

MAYUKH CHATTERJEE (ABOVE & RIGHT)

G.S. BHARDWAJ

ANIRUDDHA MAJUMDER/ WTI

Watching mammals
Responding to threats

PRANAV CHANCHANI

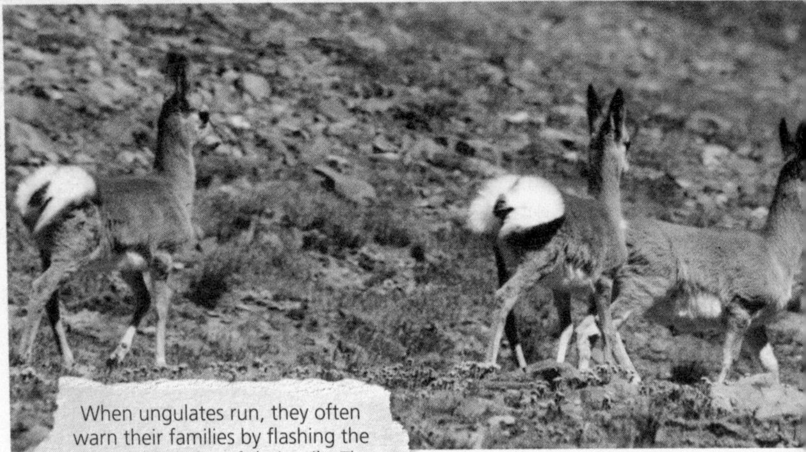

When ungulates run, they often warn their families by flashing the white undersides of their tails. The Tibetan Gazelle, especially, fans out its powder-puff tail when it takes to its heels. A flash of the tail, or walking on tiptoes, tells the predator that they are too healthy to pick for the kill.

When predators are in full view, such as these hyaenas in Velavadar, Gujarat, the prey – in this case, the Blackbuck – show high alert by raising their ears, muscles tightened and in most cases with their eyes focused on the source of alarm. Ungulates, unless used to it, do this even if humans approach.

VIVEK MENON

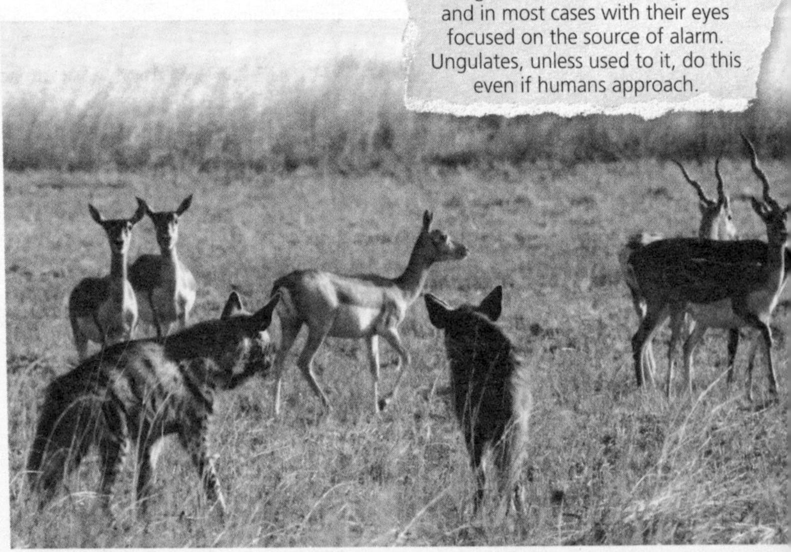

Watching mammals
Grooming, scratching, wallowing & dust bathing

SANDESH KADUR

N.A. NASEER

Many mammals scratch, when it itches, but if the animal cannot reach itself with its hands, it grooms others as these Bonnet Macaques are doing. Many mammals use vegetation for this. Grooming in primates is an elaborate social ritual, though, and is not just about removing parasites or scratching. Dominance levels decide who grooms whom and for how long!

An elephant rubbing up against a tree, such as this lone bull elephant, is a common sight.

Bath time, pesticide time: A Sambar takes a wet mud wallow in Ranthambore, Rajasthan, *(below)*, and a tusker dust bathes at Rajaji NP, Uttarakhand *(right)*: both methods help to remove pests from their bodies and cool down too.

ANIRUDDHA MOOKERJEE

G.S. BHARDWAJ

MALES FIGHT EACH OTHER by making aggressive gestures, or have actual physical battles to defend their territories and get close to females.

NIRAV BHATT

G.S. BHARDWAJ

MARK BIBBY

Most male–male aggression in the animal kingdom is subtle, where individual males evaluate each other's strengths through sounds (like roars) or show of strength. Physical fights are rare, and in most cases, end very quickly. Here, Swamp Deer males battle it out in water in Kanha, Madhya Pradesh *(above right)*; male Woolly Hares box *(left)* in Ladakh, Jammu & Kashmir, and two tired Khur stallions stand battered after a long bout of kicking and biting in the Rann, Gujarat *(top left)*.

Play behaviour serves as a splendid bonding mechanism between siblings, as well as a 'playground' to test hunting and fighting skills, needed later in life. Wolves in Velavadar NP, Gujarat *(bottom)*, and Desert Cats in Kutch, Gujarat *(below)* show such play.

Flehmen response is a behaviour in many mammals, especially cats (lioness in Gir, Gujarat, *below left*; tiger in Bandhavgarh, *below right*), where hormones received by the nose are pushed into an organ (the Jacobson's organ). This organ receives the molecules and interprets information such as who the other animal is.

KALYAN VARMA

G.S. BHARDWAJ

NIRAV BHAT

MANUEL RUEDI

G.S. BHARDWAJ

Behaviour between mother and infants among mammals involves a variety of caring gestures and calls. However, when it is time to take them off mother's milk, females can be quite harsh towards their offspring, although they rarely cause hurt. Here, a Sambar fawn raises its tail as it walks towards its mother in Ranthambore NP, Rajasthan.

NIRAV BHATT

PRABAL SARKAR

A macaque mother grooms its infant *(left)* at Turkeshwari Temple, Assam, and in a rare show of 'daddy' feeling, a male lion keeps watch over its cub in Gir, Gujarat *(above)*. However, many male cats, wolves, jackals, wild dogs and some primates (especially the langurs) kill and sometimes even eat their own offspring, to avoid later fights.

Watching mammals
Figuring out signs and clues

VIVEK MENON

VIVEK MENON

Animals leave behind more evidence than just footprints or tracks at their 'use sites'. You may also find body hair, which can help to figure out the exact species of animal. Some use sites may have nests as of the Pygmy Hog *(above right)* in Manas, Assam, or wallows of Wild Buffaloes, rhinos or Swamp Deer *(above)* in Kaziranga, Assam.

Elephants 'debarking' and pulling down branches and even whole trees while feeding is a major sign of their presence *(below right)*. This is different from the eating of the bark of a tree base by a porcupine *(below left)* or by squirrels where teeth marks can be seen *(below middle)*.

VIVEK MENON

SUMANTA KUNDU/WTI

K.M.B. PRASAD

Large carnivore kills attract vultures and are easy to spot as well as easier to detect as their smell carries far in the forest. Tigers *(below)* in Ranthambore and leopards ambush their prey and kill with a bite to the neck or throat. Dholes attack the belly and softer underparts of the animal. The Sambar is the size of animal favoured by the tiger; the Chital's size is more favoured by the leopard or the Dhole.

G.S. BHARDWAJ

Often, feeding signs such as broken termite mounds can help in determining who the predator or feeder was. For instance, Stripe-necked Mongooses often feed on freshwater fishes and crustaceans, and patches of broken crab shells or fish scales may be good indications that they were left by a Stripe-necked Mongoose *(above)*.

T IS ALWAYS USEFUL to carry pictorial guides and note down signs of animal presence using a relative scale, such as a pen or a small ruler.

BHASKAR CHOUDHURY/WTI

ALL PHOTOS EXCEPT TOP RIGHT: VIVEK MENON

An easy pointer distinguishing tracks of a small cat *(above left)* with that of a canid *(above right)* is the presence of claw marks on the latter. Cats sheath their claws and don't leave marks.

The tiger's pug marks are deep in loose sand, just an imprint on firm sand, and forms raised pads on wet mud. The outline of the pad, if traced on sand, will form a big square *(adult male forefeet, below middle)*, a big rectangle *(adult male hind feet)* or smaller rectangle *(adult female, below right)*, and a small square *(male cub, left.)* The male's stride is longer than the female's. Space between digits and main pad mean younger animals.

Scats of a mammal are not just undigested food material for the animal but also a way of marking home range and territory. A scat also tells you about an animal that has passed, the food it has eaten and when it has passed through that area. Many mammals use regular 'latrine sites' for depositing their droppings, and large ones like the rhino are unmistakable. Large elephant dung, Nilgiris, *(left)*, are easy to see and, depending on the forest type and climate, make it easy to guess the number of days ago that the animal passed the area.

Visiting a protected area

THERE ARE MORE THAN 600 national parks and sanctuaries in India, of which about half can be visited by the ordinary wildlife tourist. Visitors are expected to follow a code of conduct so that they have the minimum impact on the fragile ecology and species of the area. Whenever you visit wildlife, remember that you are in *their* territory. Here are six simple rules to make their and your life safer and better.

VIVEK MENON

RULE 1: Take permits: Inform the forest officer on duty where you are going. Where you can, take a guide, such as these forest guards and trackers in Gir, Gujarat *(left)*. Follow park rules to a T.

RULE 2: Respect wildlife and be safe: Remember that all the animals you are watching are wild and many of them are dangerous. Many parks do not permit you to walk. Even if permitted, do not go near dangerous animals on foot. Treat wildlife with caution. Watch for signs of their losing their tolerance, such as this tusker raising its foot and spreading its ears in Rajaji NP, Uttarakhand, *(below)*, signs that it will probably charge.

RULE 3: Leave the forest as you found it: Do not break branches, pluck wild flowers, or collect wildlife souvenirs from inside the park. The forest floor is not for plastic bags, cans and other litter. Not only does this dirty the place, but it can also it can prove fatal to wildlife if eaten.

ANIRUDDHA MOOKERJEE/WTI

RULE 4: Keep distance and don't threaten: Animals watch you just as you watch them, just as this herd of Swamp Deer peer in Kaziranga *(left)*. Flight distance is that distance beyond which the animal feels uncomfortable and flees. Don't cross that line.

G.S. BHARDWAJ

RULE 5: Do not harass: Do not hem an animal in, nor pursue it for long distances. This stresses wildlife. Do not do what these tourists are doing in Ranthambore, Rajasthan *(right)*.

RULE 6: Blend with the forest: Don't wear loud colours. Don't make loud noises. The forest is not a picnic spot, so avoid loud conversation when an animal is close. Avoid microphones and music players even at campsites or resorts. Avoid bright lights in wilderness areas. Use eco-friendly modes of transport like coracles *(Nagarhole, Karnataka, below left)*, or licensed park elephants *(Kaziranga, Assam, below)* and, when permitted, go on foot, with a guide *(Manas, Assam, left)*.

ALL PHOTOS ON THIS PAGE: VIVEK MENON

INDIA HAS A LONG HISTORY of conservation from when kings earmarked areas for hunting. Communities like the Bishnois, ideas like 'sacred groves' and later, projects of governments and non-governmental organizations (NGOs) have all contributed to this. These measures are for large, charismatic animals, but more than two-thirds of our mammal are made up of shrews, rodents and bats, which are equally threatened by habitat loss and changes.

ANIL KUMAR CHHANGANI

AJITH KUMAR

Wildlife is part of Indian culture as well as of our land. The grey langur *(top left)* is as much a god, worshipped in the form of Hanuman, as a part of the urban landscape – here, on top of a government vehicle *(above right)*.

Blocked by 1.2 billion Indians, wild mammals appear in the strangest of places. Here, two endangered wild species, framed by the windows of an ancient fort: tiger *(left)*, and Lion-tailed Macaque *(right)*, in Ranthambore NP, Gujarat.

KALYAN VERMA

G.S. BHARDWAJ

Poaching and the illegal wildlife trade in wildlife parts *(tiger skin seizure in New Delhi, right)* as well as the live animal trade that supplies the needs of zoos and private owners, both in India and abroad, are major threats to wild animals. Hunting animals for food adds to this. Poaching may be the main cause for sudden decline in a species' numbers, but loss of habitat has a deep and long-term effect.

Habitats are being lost due to our increasing needs. Huge demands for fuel, timber and fodder mean that more and more forests are being cut and pastures overgrazed. Industry, mines and dams take away important habitats. Encroachment of forests by the landless and shifting cultivation in the North-East *(Jhum clearance of forests in the Garo Hills, Meghalaya, left)* add to extinction pressures.

However, all is not lost. India has 60 per cent of the world's tigers, 65 per cent of the Asian Elephants, 80 per cent of the One-horned Rhinoceroses *(here in Jaldapara, Assam, left)* and 100 per cent of the lions in Asia *(here in Gir, Gujarat, below)*. Two classic stories of mammal conservation in India are of the Asiatic Lion and the One-horned Rhinoceros. In the past century, lion numbers have gone up from a few dozen to a few hundred and there are now nearly 2,000 rhinos.

VIVEK MENON

VIVEK MENON

KALYAN VARMA

31

PRIMATE FEET

Langur feet

Macaque feet

PRIMATE SKULLS

 a

 b

 c

 d

(a) Human (b) Grey
Langur (c) Rhesus
Macaque (d) Loris

Where they live

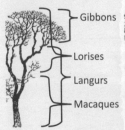

Gibbons

Lorises

Langurs

Macaques

INDIAN
PRIMATES
AT A GLANCE

NUMBER
OF SPECIES **22**

BIGGEST
**HIMALAYAN
GREY
LANGUR**

Primates

Bonnet Macaque eating
Flame of the Forest flowers,
Bandipur NP, Karnataka

VIVEK MENON

SMALLEST	MOST COMMON	MOST ENDANGERED	ACTIVITY
MALABAR GREY SLENDER LORIS	**RHESUS/ BONNET MACAQUE**	**WESTERN HOOLOCK GIBBON**	**LORISES, MACAQUES** 🌙 **LANGURS, GIBBONS** ☀

▶What is a primate?

Ranging from the great apes to the lorises, primates have certain common features. All primates have forward-facing eyes in sockets, an opposable thumb (opposite the fingers) or big toe, nails instead of claws on digits, a flattened muzzle, and the ability to stand upright to varying degrees. Indian primates can be divided into four groups: the small, round-eyed lorises; the stocky, short- to medium-tailed macaques; the long-tailed langurs; and the tailless gibbons.

▶How do primates move?

Among Indian primates, lorises and gibbons have specialized movement. Lorises cannot touch all four fingers with their thumb, but they hold on to thin branches and lock on to them with a firm grip. They do not jump but slowly let go one or two limbs from the perch and 'creep-crawl' forwards.

The gibbons are the most specialized 'movers' among Indian primates, using a swing-arm type of movement along treetops, called *brachiation*. They hang by the arms and swing at a high speed, reaching up to 40 km per hour. Their arms are more than one and a half times the size of their legs! They can also stand up and run along branches. They seldom come to the ground and, if forced to, walk like 'surrendered terrorists' with their hands held high above their heads.

Both macaques and langurs are good at climbing, both in trees and on the ground. Some langurs are high-canopy dwellers (e.g., the Capped Langur), some are mainly middle-of-the-tree dwellers (e.g.,

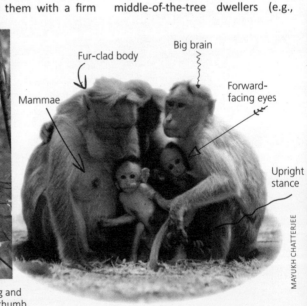

Gibbon brachiating and *(inset)* opposable thumb, Kaziranga NP, Assam

VIVEK MENON

Fur-clad body

Big brain

Mammae

Forward-facing eyes

Upright stance

MAYUKH CHATTERJEE

A social macaque unit, Bandipur NP, Karnataka

Lion-tailed Macaque) and others are mainly ground-dwellers (e.g., the Rhesus Macaque). Both langurs and macaques can walk for short distances on two limbs, though on ground they walk mostly on all fours.

▶ What do they eat?

Insects and bird eggs are the main food of lorises, but they also eat nestlings, frogs, lizards, fruits, leaves and seeds. Gums and resins make up a large part of the food of the Bengal Slow Loris. Lorises have lower incisors and canines that merge to form a 'tooth comb' used for scraping gums and resins. They can eat even some poisonous or blister-causing insects (e.g., the Cantharidin Beetle) because of a large *caecum* (a pouch at the junction of the small and large intestines) with special bacteria that help digestion.

The diurnal macaques are largely omnivorous, the langurs mostly leaf-eating and the gibbons

Threat display: a Golden Langur hoots, Manas NP, Assam

VIVEK MENON

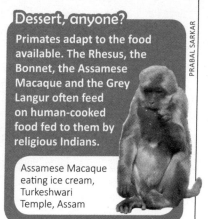

Dessert, anyone?

Primates adapt to the food available. The Rhesus, the Bonnet, the Assamese Macaque and the Grey Langur often feed on human-cooked food fed to them by religious Indians.

Assamese Macaque eating ice cream, Turkeshwari Temple, Assam

mainly fruit-eating. Primates adapt to the food available in their locales, for e.g., the Crab-eating Macaque to a seashore diet that includes crabs, while the Lion-tailed Macaque even eats giant squirrels!

▶ How do they communicate?

Many primates combine calls with touch and facial expressions to communicate. Slender Lorises screech more than Slow Lorises, sounding like a cross between an owl and a monkey. Their varied calls are described as whistle (territorial), chitter (anger), growl (aggression), zic (infant call), kriks (appeasement) and screams (fear).

Gibbon calls are amongst the most complex and loud among Indian primates, and resound at dusk and dawn. Sounding like a loud 'hooko-hooko-hooko', gibbon songs are sung by one family group at a time, the chorus continuing till the sun is high up in the sky.

Macaques and langurs have a range of calls: For e.g., in Rhesus a short bark and grunt are the most

Well-groomed

Primates groom one another when they meet. Grooming is a typical primate social trait.
Here, Bonnet Macaques grooming, Bandipur NP, Karnataka

common; while the Assamese Macaque's call is a loud and quite musical 'pio'.

▶ How do they live?

Elephants and monkeys suffer more than other animals if kept alone in captivity, as they have a complex social organization in the wild. All primates have a distinct family unit (a 'troop'), though of different types. Lorises, for example, are solitary with clearly marked home ranges, but spend time grooming each other when they meet.

Hoolocks are the only primates in India that may have a monogamous bonded social system, in which a male and female are partners for life. Subadults and juveniles are closely bonded to the adults until old enough to leave.

Being mainly fruit-and leaf-eaters, macaques and langurs feed together in the forest and live in large troops. In Rhesus sometimes, these troops come together (fusion), or if they get very large, break into two or more splinter groups (fission). Having larger troops may have drawbacks such as high competition among individuals for food and safe roosts, but a larger troop raises the chances of the early detection of predators, reduces chances of predation and discourages predators.

▶ Young ones

Langurs have a pregnancy period of 190–220 days; macaques have a shorter one, for e.g., the Rhesus has one of 150–180 days.

Males often kill male babies to reduce future competition. The pregnancy period is over 100 days for the lorises, and generally twins though sometimes single infants are also born. Gibbons have a single baby after a pregnancy of nearly seven months.

Western Hoolock Gibbon mother with its infant

▶ Threats and conservation

For many years, primate species like the Rhesus Macaque were exported in large numbers for medical experimentation to the west. Although the Indian Government banned this in the 1970s, illegal pet trade still threatens species like the lorises while the traditional dancing of the Rhesus for entertainment continues. The consumption of primate meat is a threat limited to tribal populations.

Forest loss is a danger mainly for gibbons who need trees to make their way from one forest patch to another. It is also a big threat for endangered forest dwellers such as the Lion-tailed Macaque in southern India. The macaques, on the other hand, are used to raiding crops and for them killings by people are the main problem.

Roadkills and electrocutions are threats, with even the Lion-tailed Macaques (which normally live in high places on trees) dying in road accidents, and lorises and golden

Crop raiding is common among macaques. A troop raids a paddy field, Borajan WLS, Assam

Madaris, traditional 'monkey dancers', represent an old way of life.

langurs often being electrocuted in the North-East. Monkeys around settlements are affected by the cutting of avenue trees.

Monkeys are more the subject of research than conservation. Conservation projects include ones aimed at connecting forest fragments using community-based village reserves in the Garo Hills, Meghalaya, rehabilitating rescued individuals at the Centre for Wildlife Rehabilitation and Conservation (CWRC) in Kaziranga, Assam, and the complete translocation of an isolated population of the Eastern Hoolock in Dello, Arunachal Pradesh.

Hoolock Gibbon

Family: Hylobatidae
Indian Status: Uncommon
Social Unit: Paired couples; small families of 3-6
Size: HBL: 48-54 cm, Wt: 6-8 kg
Best seen At: Borajan WLS, Assam (Western Hoolock Gibbon); Mehao WLS, Arunachal Pradesh (Eastern Hoolock Gibbon)

There are two kinds of Hoolock Gibbons found in India, the Western Hoolock Gibbon and the Eastern Hoolock Gibbon.

The Western Hoolock Gibbon, a tailless ape, is a jungle gymnast known more by its loud calls than by sight. It is the second largest gibbon in the world after the Siamang. Newborns are milky white or yellowish, but turn dark brown in nine months, and black by two years. Males stay black, but between 18–24 months females turn a golden colour with white brows and a white frame to the face. These white brows (also found in males) give this ape its other name of White-browed Gibbon. Long arms, almost double the length of its legs, help in moving on treetops. When standing upright, it is the height of a small human child.

The Eastern Hoolock Gibbon is very similar to the Western in size and looks except that the adult female is paler, with even paler arms compared to its body. Its white eyebrows have a distinct gap and it may have strands of white in the beard.

VIVEK MENON

Close-set white eyebrows

Long limbs

All black coat

Tailless

Western Hoolock Gibbon male, Borajan WLS, Assam

Pale arms

BHASKAR CHOUDHURY/WTI

Eastern Hoolock Gibbon adult female and infant, Roing, Arunachal Pradesh

Bengal Slow Loris

A small, furry, nocturnal primate, this loris has large eyes that dominate its face. Its fur can vary from ash-grey to buff-yellow, with head and shoulders a shade lighter. It is tailless. At night, its eyes shine a bright orange in torchlight. It can hang upside down while feeding on gums and resins, gouging out dozens of holes into soft tree bark. It is found throughout the North-East, in forests south of the River Brahmaputra. It was recently seen in northern West Bengal too.

Family: Lorisidae
Indian Status: Uncommon
Social Unit: Solitary; pairs/mother and young
Size: HBL: 19-33 cm, Wt: 880-2,700 g
Best Seen At: Kaziranga NP, Assam

Dark eye rings

Distinct stripe on back

Stocky build

RATHIN BURMAN/WTI

Bengal Slow Loris, Manas NP, Assam

Grey Slender Loris

This loris is the southern thin cousin of the Slow Loris, with a not very clear stripe on the back. It signposts trees by spraying urine on its palms and leaves scented handprints on the branches. It is found in open jungle as well as in forests south of the River Godavari in the Eastern Ghats and in the Western Ghats south of River Tapti.

Family: Lorisidae
Indian Status: Uncommon
Social Unit: Solitary; pairs; mother and 1-2 young
Size: HBL: 15-22 cm Wt: 180 g
Best Seen At: Aralam WLS, Kerala

Unclear stripe on back

Circular eye rings

Thin and lanky

KALYAN VARMA

Grey Slender Loris, Anamalai WLS, Tamil Nadu

Rhesus Macaque

Family: Cercopithecidae
Indian Status: Abundant
Social Unit: Troops of 2–250
Size: HBL: 47-63 cm (male), Wt: 5-8 kg
Best Seen At: Most northern Indian towns

The most widespread of Indian primates, the Rhesus is the common monkey of northern India, living in close association with humans. It is brown with fur varying from very thick and dark in Kashmir to sandy brown in Rajasthan. The orangish tint to the fur on its back is always there, and separates it from the similar looking Assamese Macaque. It also carries its medium-sized tail erect with a slight bend at the tip.

Males assert their dominance with threat displays, such as shaking tree branches. In cities, this translates into shaking electric lines. It can live in different habitats, such as temple surrounds, urban, rural, village-cum-pond, pond sides, roadsides, canal sides and forests. It is found all over northern India except in the Himalayan cold deserts, the high Himalayas and the hot deserts of the Thar.

Dense brown fur

Medium- sized tail carried bent at tip

Orange loins

VIVEK MENON

Rhesus Macaque male, Borajan WLS, Assam

MIX-UPS

Hybrids between closely related primates are known, especially when two species come into contact with each other in the wild. At times when such interbreeding occurs, the offspring are mistaken in the field for a new species or a subspecies as they show characteristics of both parent species. In southern India, Nilgiri Langurs and the Grey Langurs are known to produce hybrids where they live together and in Assam, Assamese Macaques and Rhesus are known to hybridize.

VIVEK MENON

A Rhesus Macaque and an Assamese Macaque, Borajan WLS, Assam (*Note* the tail carriage)

Bonnet Macaque

Family: Cercopithecidae
Indian Status: Abundant
Social Unit: Troops of 5-40
Size: HBL: 34-60 cm, Wt:3-5 kg
Best Seen At: Periyar, Kerala; southern Indian towns

This is the medium-sized, common monkey of South India. It is distinguished by two clear characteristics: a cap or bonnet of long hair, arranged in a circular way and parted clearly, and a very long tail that is longer than its body. The back, tail and limbs are all dark greyish brown, and change from a shiny brown in winter to scraggy buff-grey in summer.

The face is flesh coloured and turns pink or flushed red during breeding seasons. As among most monkeys, the males are larger and heavier than the females. The monkeys also show the 'fear grimace', which looks like a smile, and 'neck chewing' of subordinate males by dominant males.

Bonnet Macaques are found in urban and rural areas as well as tropical forests all over southern India.

Bonnet Macaque family at one of its northernmost addresses, Hampi, Karnataka

Peaked ear

Cap of parted hair

Grey fur

Pale belly

VIVEK MENON

Family: Cercopithecidae
Indian Status: Locally Common
Social Unit: 5-50
Size: HBL: 44-68 cm, Wt: 4-12 kg
Best Seen At: Siliguri and Darjeeling, West Bengal; Assam

Assamese Macaque

This is a heavy monkey whose fur varies from dark chocolate-brown to much paler. The lower body is darker than the upper. It resembles the Rhesus, but does not have the orange-tinted backkside and has a different tail carriage. Adults have a pronounced beard, long cheek hairs and white eyelids. Like many monkeys, it drops from trees to the ground, if alarmed, and scampers into the bushes. It is found in the forests of Arunachal Pradesh, Assam, Sikkim, northern West Bengal, Nagaland, Manipur, and Mizoram.

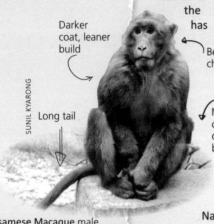

Darker coat, leaner build

Beard and cheek hair

No orange on backside

Long tail

SUNIL KYARONG

Assamese Macaque male, Darjeeling, West Bengal

Arunachal Macaque

Family: Cercopithecidae
Indian Status: Uncommon
Social Unit: 20-25
Size: HBL: 56 cm, Wt: 15 kg
Best Seen At: Tawang, Arunachal Pradesh

Dark patch in hair

Short tail

KRIPALJYOTI MAZUMDAR

Locally called Munzala, this is a dark, large monkey that could be a new species, a subspecies or a colour variation of the Assamese Macaque. The dark brown face has a heavy jaw and is not bearded like the Assamese Macaque. A dark patch of hair on the centre of its head, sometimes surrounded by pale hairs, helps to identify it. It has been seen in the forests of high mountains and human-inhabited areas in western Arunachal Pradesh.

Arunachal Macaque male, Tawang, Assam

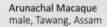

Long-tailed Macaque

Family: Cercopithecidae
Indian Status: Locally Common
Social Unit: 25-56 animals
Size: HBL: 35-45 cm, Wt: 1.5-5 kg
Best Seen At: Great Nicobar Island

Also called the Crab-eating Macaque, this is the common macaque of South-East Asia. It has a long tail (like the Bonnet), short, fat legs and a heavy bottom. Its cheek whiskers are long and prominent. A good swimmer, it is more tree-dwelling in inland forests and more ground-dwelling on coasts. In India, it is found in coastal forests, mangroves and coconut plantations in Great Nicobar, Little Nicobar and Katchal islands of the Nicobar chain.

No bonnet, and whiskered face

Very long tail

VIVEK MENON

Long-tailed Macaque, Great Nicobar Island, Andaman & Nicobar Islands

Northern Pig-tailed Macaque

Family: Cercopithecidae
Indian Status: Rare
Social Unit: Solitary; small troops
Size: HBL: 43-60 cm, Wt: 4-16 kg
Best Seen At: Garampani WLS, Assam

This large forest monkey can be told apart from the Assamese and Rhesus Macaques by its deeply parted, dark cap of short hair and a short, naked straight tail, curled at the tip, which gives it its name. It has olive-brown to golden fur and a white underside. Red streaks of fur are sometimes there between the eye and ear. It is the most arboreal and fruit-eating of the north-eastern macaques. It is found in forests, and sometimes in swamps, south of River Brahmaputra in the North-East.

Dark hairs on head

Long cheek whiskers

NARAYAN SHARMA

Northern Pig-tailed Macque female, Gibbon WLS, Assam

Stump-tailed Macaque

Family: Cercopithecidae
Indian Status: Rare
Social Unit: Troops of 12-65
Size: HBL: 50-70 cm, Wt: 7-10 kg
Best Seen At: Gibbon WLS, Assam

Also known as the Bear Macaque, it is the largest and heaviest macaque species in India. On its head, its hair radiates uniquely from a central whorl and falls sleekly to the back of the head. It also has long cheek hair covering the ears and going down to its throat in a ruff-like beard. The reddish pink face turns darker with age and has prominent cheek pouches. It has the shortest tail among macaques and is very terrestrial. This fearless monkey emits a smell that protects it from predators. It almost always sits on its tail. Like humans, it grows bald with age from forehead backwards, but both males and females get bald. It is found in hills and lowland forests throughout the North-East, south of the River Brahmaputra.

Stump tail

Stocky, paunchy build

Red-blotched face

SANDESH KADUR

Stump-tailed Macaque male, Gibbon WLS, Assam

Phayre's Leaf Langur

Family: Cercopithecidae
Indian Status: Uncommon
Social Unit: Troops of 8-30
Size: HBL: 55-65 cm, Wt: 6-8 kg
Best Seen At: Sepahijala WLS, Tripura

It is also called the Spectacled Monkey because of the white eye patches in its black face. A white lip-guard gives it the look of a modern cricketer with sunblock on. Its body is slate-grey, darkening to black towards the limbs, with a lighter underside. The tail is longer than the body and lightly tasselled. Both males and females have a peaked crest. The male has circular white eye rings while those of females are roughly triangular. It leaps on to branches in a spreadeagled fashion rather than jumping on to a single chosen branch.

It is found in forests, bamboo patches, forest fringes and tea gardens in southern Assam, Tripura and Mizoram.

White 'eye spectacle' marking

Dark grey fur

Pale lips

VIVEK MENON

Phayre's Leaf Langur young, Cachar, Assam

Capped Langur

Family: Cercopithecidae
Indian Status: Locally Common
Social Unit: Troops of 5-16
Size: HBL: 45-70 cm, Wt: 10-12 kg
Best Seen At Kaziranga NP, Assam; Tawang, Arunachal Pradesh; Cachar, Assam; Manas NP, Assam

Dark cap

Pale cream or reddish body and whiskers

VIVEK MENON

Capped Langur male, Manas NP, Assam

This common forest langur of the North-East has a cap of differently coloured hair, a greyish back and a long tail with a darker end. The thighs' insides are light blue, deeper in males. It lives exclusively on trees. It squeals and has a deep bark. It is found in forests and in bamboo patches in Meghalaya, Nagaland, Assam, Tripura and Arunachal Pradesh.

Golden Langur

Family: Cercopithecidae
Indian Status: Locally Common
Social Unit: Small troops of 5-10
Size: HBL: 49-72 cm, Wt: 9-10.9 kg
Best Seen At: Manas NP, Assam; Chakrashila WLS, Assam

Golden cap and whiskers

Golden coat

VIVEK MENON

Golden Langur male, Umanando Temple, Assam

Arguably the most beautiful Indian monkey, the Golden Langur's face, palms and soles are black and it has long, golden cheek whiskers and a golden cap to match. Its tail is long and tasselled. Females are more golden with more orange on the backside. First found in 1956, it has been the flag bearer of Indian langurs since. It is active in the day and chooses tall trees near food sources to sleep at night. It is found in forests between rivers Manas and Sankosh in Assam.

Lion-tailed Macaque

Family: Cercopithecidae
Indian Status: Rare
Social Unit: Troops of 7-40
Size: HBL: 46-60 cm, Wt: 7-10 kg
Best Seen At: Puthuthottam Estate & Silent Valley NP, Tamil Nadu

Ashy grey hair on head

Glossy black coat

Lion-tailed Macaque male, Puthuthottam Estate, Tamil Nadu

VIVEK MENON

This monkey is a medium- to large-sized forest macaque of southern India, with a dark glossy coat. It is told apart from the other black monkey of southern India, the Nilgiri Langur, by its long, grey facial hair and a medium-sized tail with a prominent tuft of longer hair. The females are slightly smaller. The call of this monkey is like a human's and sounds like a 'coyeh' or a 'coo'. Lion-tailed Macaques are found in dense forests along the Western Ghats.

Nilgiri Langur

Family: Cercopithecidae
Indian Status: Locally Common
Social Unit: Small troops of 4–25
Size: HBL: 55-75 cm, Wt: 9-14 kg
Best Seen At: Annamalai WLS, Tamil Nadu

Slim and black, this is the common rainforest monkey of the Western Ghats. It has blond hair on the head (the Lion-tailed Macaque's mane is ashy grey) and a long, glossy black coat. Newborns are pinkish white with reddish hair that turns black in 2-3 months. The most vocal of southern forest monkeys, its 'hoo-hoo' call can be heard at dawn and sometimes at dusk. It is found in forests and plantations in the Western Ghats.

Yellow-buff mane

Coarse black coat

Long tail

VIVEK MENON

Nilgiri Langur male, Nilgiris, Tamil Nadu

Grey Langurs

Family: Cercopithecidae
Indian Status: Locally Common
Social Unit: Troops of 5-16
Size: HBL: 55-76.2 cm, Wt: 9-20.9 kg

These are the common long-tailed monkeys found in India and recently split into six species.

NORTHERN PLAINS LANGUR: The most widespread in India, it is crestless, yellow-brown/pale orange, with a buff chest and forward-looped tail. It is found across north India except in the desert. Best Seen At: Sariska NP & Ranthambore NP, Rajasthan.

SOUTH-WESTERN LANGUR: The backward-looped tail of this average-sized, crestless langur separates it from the South-Eastern Langur. It is found iin Gujarat, Karnataka Maharashtra and Kerala. Best Seen At: Nagarhole NP, Karnataka.

SOUTH-EASTERN LANGUR: The crest of some subspecies looks like the headgear of Priam, King of Troy, giving it its scientific name *Semnopithecus priam*. It is found in Andhra Pradesh and Tamil Nadu. Best Seen At: Mudumalai WLS, Tamil Nadu.

TERAI LANGUR: Crestless, with a greyish brown back and buff-white/pale grey underside, it has a prominent grey moustache on a black face and pale grey hands. It is found in the Terai forests of Uttarakhand, UP, Bihar and West Bengal. Best Seen At: Rajaji NP and Corbett NP, Uttarakhand.

HIMALAYAN LANGUR: It is maned and pale-pawed like the Terai Langur. The underside is whiter. It is found in forests in Himachal Pradesh, Jammu & Kashmir, Sikkim and Uttarakhand. Best Seen At: Shimla, Himachal Pradesh.

KASHMIR/CHAMBA LANGUR: A large hill langur, it is maned with a forward-looping tail, but dark hands and forearms. It has dark silvery fur. It is found in Himachal Pradesh and Jammu & Kashmir. Best Seen At: Chamba Valley, Himachal Pradesh.

When you look out for Slow Lorises in the dark, look for the fact that their shining eyes are closer set than those of Flying Squirrels. If you have one in the hand, watch out for its razor-sharp teeth, it can puncture your hand in seconds. I found this out when I released one in Kaziranga.

ILLUSTRATIONS: VASUNDHARA KANDPAL

My first scientific paper was on captive Rhesus Monkeys in the Delhi zoo in the 1980s and soon thereafter I co-authored a management plan for the Rhesus in Delhi with Dr Iqbal Malik.

The southernmost mammal I have seen in India is the Long-tailed or Crab-eating Macaque on Great Nicobar before the tsunami. The adults were peaceably feeding on coconuts and the

youngsters were playing on the main road, pulling each other's tails.

The Golden Langurs that have been brought to Umanando Temple in Assam by a priest are the easiest to view the species. They lie around in sloppy postures reminding you of youngsters lolling in college corridors.

The only primate I have seen even more comfortable is a Western Hoolock Gibbon male in upper Assam who looked like he was slung in an imaginary hammock.

The Terai Langurs are the only ones that have a very noticeable moustache.

ASIAN ELEPHANT SKULL

ELEPHANT TRUNKS

African two-fingered *(top)* and Asian one-fingered *(bottom)* trunk

ELEPHANT TEETH

Jagged-edged tooth of Asian Elephant *(left)*; lozenge-shaped African Elephant tooth *(right)*

ILLUSTRATIONS: VASUNDHARA KANDPAL

Where they live

Elephants

INDIAN
ELEPHANTS
AT A GLANCE

NUMBER
OF SPECIES **1**

ACTIVITY
✿

Elephants

An Asian Elephant bull wades through a swamp next to Hog Deer, Kaziranga NP, Assam

VIVEK MENON

▶What is a proboscidean?

Proboscideans or 'trunked creatures' are large land mammals with naked, wrinkled grey skin, enlarged incisors that form tusks, an elongated snout that forms a trunk, extra-large ears that aid cooling of the body, column-like legs that support their massive weight, and a medium-sized tail with stiff bristles forming a tuft at the end. Having a long lifespan, they are intelligent animals who live in complex social groups. Currently, there are three species of elephant in Africa and Asia: the Asian Elephant, the African Savannah Elephant and the African Forest Elephant.

▶What do they eat?

Elephants need a large amount of food. They eat almost any kind of plant matter, including twigs, bark, pith, grass, whole plants, fruit and roots of up to 59 kinds of woody plants and 23 species of grasses. Their flexible trunk ensures that they can get to vegetation out of reach of most ungulates (except perhaps the giraffe in Africa).

Elephants move continuously while feeding, allowing the vegetation they leave behind to regenerate in a natural cycle. They also defecate constantly as they feed (about 16–18 times a day) producing about 100 kg of dung in a day!

▶How do they communicate?

The Asian Elephant uses a range of calls, from tummy rumbles (for contact communication) to low chirps (in confusion or alarm), roars and loud trumpets. The latter two are mostly used in aggression or when they are disturbed, and by young calves in play. Elephants are also the first land mammals

Daily meal

JOSE LOUIES/WTI

A full-grown cow elephant may eat up to 240 kg of fresh plant matter over an 18-hour day!

Elephant with browse, Kaziranga NP, Assam

Fan- or Africa-shaped ears

Concave back

Ribbed trunk

Tusks in both males and females

VIVEK MENON

Male African Savannah Elephant

N.A. NASEER

Elephants like to play! Splashing water in Periyar NP, Kerala

to be known to communicate infrasonically, especially when they are separated by thick vegetation or great distance. They also use the foot stomp to communicate long-distance with one another.

▶How do they live?
Elephants are social animals that live in close-knit family groups led by a matriarch or a cow elephant who is the head. Family groups join to form larger herds, which can have females

How to tell the African and Asian elephants apart?

WHAT TO LOOK FOR	AFRICAN ELEPHANT	ASIAN ELEPHANT
Back	A saddle-shaped back that looks fit for a human to ride on!	A convex back, sloping sharply towards its hindquarters.
Trunk	The trunk is heavily ridged with crossways skinfolds, with two fingers at its tip.	A smooth trunk with one finger at the tip.
Tusk	Both males and females normally have tusks.	Only the male Asian has tusks and not all males do.
Ears	Massive ears the rough shape of the African continent.	Wedge-shaped ears.
Toes	Four toes on its forefeet and three on the hind, making 14 toes.	Can have four on all feet, or five on the front and four on the back, or even five on all limbs, making 16–20 toes.

SUMANTA KUNDU/WTI

Hello, there!

Often two elephant families that are not known to be related may show complex greetings when they meet.

Elephants greeting, Corbett NP, Uttarakhand

of varying ages and young immature males. Adult males are usually solitary and join family groups only for mating. Occasionally, two adult males may bond and stay together for a while, and rarely, all-male groups are also seen.

Elephants have a family system where when food gets scarce, they become nuclear (one mother and her calves), and when it is plentiful, they rejoin to form larger herds. When together, the oldest female (the matriarch) makes the decisions, and the herd follows her in direction of movement, in rest, in feeding and in avoiding threats.

When the matriarch is not around, the split groups keep in touch with the main herd by using infrasonic communication. A raised trunk, rumblings, touch and companionship are used to bond with each other within and outside the herd.

▶How intelligent are they?

Very – they are among the most intelligent living beings! They are known to exhibit grief, compassion, humour and concern for the good of others, and some scientists believe they have a language. Even a die-hard scientist like Charles Darwin said: 'The Indian elephant is said sometimes to weep.'

▶Young ones

Elephants may live on the average for 60 to 70 years. Females can give birth by 12 years. Pregnancy lasts 20–22 months and one calf is born

Brains with brawn

With a brain mass of five kilos, elephants come close to cetaceans (whales and dolphins), apes and even human beings in intelligence, so close, in fact, that some scientists refer to them as 'near-persons'.

ELEPHANTS IN INDIAN CULTURE

The most recognizable figure in Indian religion and folklore is that of Ganesha, the elephant-headed god. Although classic Ganesha figures appeared only in the fifth century CE, Hindu mythology says that the elephant was created by Brahma, the Lord of Creation. Out of a broken eggshell that he held in his right hand came eight bull elephants, the first of which was the holy white elephant Airavata. Out of the other half that he held in his left hand came eight cow elephants, and these two sets were the ancestors of all elephants. It's unlikely that the entire elephant race originated from eggshells, but the story supports the divine origin of the elephant race.

AMRIT MENON/WTI

The Vedas (1500–600 BCE), and the epics, the Ramayana and the Mahabharata (1100–700 BCE) all feature elephants, and other ancient Indian texts, such as the *Arthashastra*, mention *Gajavanas* or elephant preserves, the first ever protected-area systems in India or perhaps even the world.

that suckles for more than a year. The female can thus give birth to only one calf every 4–5 years.

▶ Elephants in captivity

Elephants have been captive in India at least for 4,000 years. The earliest authentic records of such elephants go back to 2500 BCE as Mohenjo-daro seals show elephants with a cloth on their back, a sure sign of a captive beast. The *Gajasastram* in the fifth or sixth century BCE records the keeping of elephants and instructs people in this art. They were mighty war machines in the heroic battles fought by Porus and Alexander in northern India in 326 BCE, and in Mughal times.

Today between 3,400 and 3,600 elephants are held captive in India, from the ones used in religious ceremonies and private elephants used for illegal logging in the North-East, to the ones in forest camps for patrolling or tourism, and the few living in cities such as Delhi and Jaipur. A Central Government Elephant Task Force has recommended, in the long term, to phase out elephants in commercial use.

▶ Threats and conservation

Four words that define an elephant are big, social, intelligent and nomadic. Because they are big (mega-herbivores) they need to eat large amounts of forage and move, for if they do not, they eat themselves out of a habitat. Asian Elephants may use over 300–1,000 sq. km annually. As they do this,

Solitary tusker, Mudumalai WLS, Tamil Nadu

as millets, sugar cane and bananas, leading to crop raiding.

While man–elephant conflict is the biggest threat to the elephant in India, poaching for the tusks of male elephants for the illegal ivory trade continues. India used to lose well over a hundred elephants a year to poaching for tusks. This has come down drastically, but there is an ever-present demand for ivory from the Far East for use as *hankos* or 'name seals'.

The Government of India conserves our National Heritage Animal mainly through Project Elephant in the Ministry of Environment and Forests. Leading elephant conservation organizations in India include the Wildlife Trust of India (WTI), the Asian Nature Conservation Foundation (ANCF), WWF-India and local NGOs. WTI's work has included putting elephants back into the wild and securing safe corridors for them to move.

they may come into conflict with humans on the edges of protected forests. Worse still, in some areas, their habitat itself is disturbed by houses, roads and railways, mining, and use of forest resources, and elephants come into daily conflict with their neighbours. Elephants go for nutrient-rich crops they like, such

Elephants can lose their cool when young men and boys pelt stones at them in crop fields, as shown here in Assam

Asian Elephant

Family: Elephantidae
Indian Status: Common
Social Unit: Family; herd; solitary adult male
Size: HAS: 245-275 cm, Wt: 3,000-5,400 kg
Best Seen At: Nagarahole NP, Karnataka; Kaziranga NP, Assam

The largest land mammal in India, the Asian Elephant's wrinkled skin, long trunk and sail-like ears make it easy to recognize. Only male Asian Elephants have large tusks, while females have very small dental knobs called tushes. Some males, called 'makhnas', are tusk-less.

Elephants move over long distances for food and water, or for security, using the same forest corridors for hundreds of years. If these are blocked, they enter human settlements, sometimes attracted by crops, or by local alcohol-making units they can smell from miles away.

Living in forests, scrub, floodplains and grasslands, elephants are found in four parts of India: (1) in the south, in the Western Ghats and adjoining hills of the Eastern Ghats in Karnataka, Kerala, Tamil Nadu and Andhra Pradesh; (2) in east–central or south–east India, in Odisha and Jharkhand, moving seasonally into southern West Bengal and Chhattisgarh; (3) in north India in Uttar Pradesh and Uttarakhand; and (4) in the North-East in Assam, Arunachal Pradesh, Nagaland and Meghalaya.

Ears start folding over

Forehead and cheeks start hollowing (old adult)

Ears still unfolded (young adult)

Twin-fingered smooth trunk

VIVEK MENON

Younger *(front)* and older *(back)* female Asian Elephant, Anamalai WLS, Tamil Nadu

FIELD NOTES: Trunk Calls

In 1997, I toured the forests of Kollegal and Sathyamangalam in Tamil Nadu, the haunt of the legendary forest brigand Veerappan, for two weeks in a coracle, with a local fisherman and a friend. My task: to count the number of elephants poached in an area that even forest officials could not enter. My tally in 15 days: 15 carcasses!

In the mid-90s, I was actively tracking the poaching of elephants and the illegal smuggling of their ivory to the Far East. In Japan my main contact was a trader who had nine tonnes of ivory in his garage!

Tolerance is India's biggest wildlife conservation asset, but it is running thin. In Assam, where even elephants killed accidentally by a train are worshipped traditionally with bananas and incense, 11

animals were poisoned in 2003 in a crop field. On one carcass was written in chalk: 'Paddy Thief, Bin Laden'!

Putting orphan elephants back into the wild has been the most satisfying experience for me in many ways. As the first herd took tentative steps into Manas National Park in Assam, I knew WTI-IFAW and the Assam Forest Department had reversed a centuries old belief that elephants never go back to the wild.

RHINOCEROS SPECIES OF THE WORLD

Black Rhinoceros

White Rhinoceros

Sumatran Rhinoceros

Javan Rhinoceros

Greater One-horned Rhinoceros

VASUNDHARA KANDPAL

Where they live

Rhinoceroses, Equids

VIVEK MENON

INDIAN ODD-TOED UNGULATES **AT A GLANCE**

NUMBER OF SPECIES **3**

LARGEST **RHINO**

Odd-toed Ungulates

A Greater One-horned Rhinoceros calf follows on the heels of the mother in burnt grass, Kaziranga NP, Assam

VIVEK MENON

SMALLEST	MOST COMMON	MOST ENDANGERED	ACTIVITY	
KHUR	**KIANG**	**RHINO**	**RHINO** ☼ **EQUIDS** ☼	

▶What is an ungulate?

Easy... an ungulate is a hoofed mammal. Its hoof is actually a modified nail! Ungulates are grouped into two orders – Artiodactyl and Perissodactyl – based on if they have an even number of toes (even-toed) or an odd number (odd-toed). 'Artio' means 'even' in Greek and 'Perisso' means 'uneven'. Wild Artiodactyls in India include mountain goats and sheep, wild cattle, deer and mouse deer, antelopes and wild pigs.

▶What is an equid?

Equids are grazers such as horses, zebras and asses. India has both the Tibetan Wild Ass or Kiang, and the Indian Wild Ass or Khur. Though closely related, the domestic horse, the wild horse, the domestic donkey, the wild ass and the zebra are all a bit different from one another. Wild asses are larger than the domestic donkey but smaller than horses. Their ears are longer than those of donkeys and horses. Wild asses are plain coloured except for the stripe near their tail, while domestic asses have horizontal stripes on the shoulder and sometimes on the legs. Zebras can be told apart from donkeys by their stripes.

What is a perissodactyl?

Eighteen species of ungulates (equids, rhinos and tapirs), all of which have an odd number of toes and most of which are endangered, are known as Perissodactyls. Of those found in India, equids have a single toe and rhinos have three. Of the five species of rhinoceros in the world, two are African and three Asian.

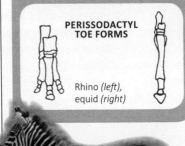

PERISSODACTYL TOE FORMS

Rhino *(left)*, equid *(right)*

Przewalski's Horse

ALL PHOTOS: VIVEK MENON

Burchell's Zebra (not from India)

Domestic pony and donkey

►How do they move?

Both Indian equids are very swift runners, touching 60 km an hour and maintaining 45–50 km an hour for over 5 km. A horny cushion covering the heel acts as a shock absorber in the hoof. The rhino normally ambles, but when aggressive or under threat, it can clock up to 55 km an hour over shorter distances.

►What do they eat?

Equids are mainly grazers and can survive on coarse food, such as a variety of grasses and some flowering plants. Khur are mostly grazers when grass is available and turn browsers in drier times. Browsers eat leaves, bark and green stems from plants, while grazers clip grasses at or near ground level.

More recently, they have turned to raiding crops, wheat and green cotton pods. Rhinos both graze and browse, though they prefer to graze on grass. They browse on land and on aquatic vegetation.

►How do they communicate?

Rhinos have at least ten different forms of calls, but the snort before they charge is what most people hear. They also honk (in face-to-face encounters between rhinos, normally the subordinate – the younger or weaker rhino – honks), bleat (submission), roar (intense aggression), squeak-pant (courtship chases) and moo-grunt (mothers calling young ones). They also communicate with scents from foot glands and dung toilets.

Wild asses are mostly silent, though a loud bray during breeding or when fighting over territory is known. Dominant males make deeper calls than subordinates, who squeal.

►How do they live?

Equids are more social than the naturally solitary rhinos. Horses and zebras form permanent herds, but the size of the group of wild asses changes, often breaking up into smaller subgroups. The Kiang, for example, form groups with six or seven animals but rarely herd permanently. Temporary groups are mother-and-foal based, or of young bachelor males. Older males are mostly solitary and very territorial.

The Khur have a well-structured group of females, family and bachelors. The rhino is a loner except when young males join up, or when the female is with her calf for nearly four years.

►Young ones

The Kiang breeds from June to September. The females have a pregnancy period of 355 days. Foals are seen by July and suckle up to a year. The Khur breeds around June to August, which is monsoon in the Rann. Pregnancy in the Khur lasts about 320–330 days. A single foal is born, and suckles for eight to 10 months. The female rhino has a pregnancy period of over 15 months, producing one young that suckles for four years.

55 million years ago (mya) is when equids originated in North America. They spread in Asia 1.8 mya.

▶ Threats and conservation

Rhinos are poached mainly for their prized horns, which find their way into Far Eastern markets for use in Traditional Oriental Medicine.

Rhinos are good swimmers, even breasting River Brahmaputra, Assam, in the floods.

VIVEK MENON

lost most of its rhinos in the 1990s. Four more rhinos have since been moved. Three of these seven have given birth here, in the wild, making this effort a success.

Because they follow the same trails, poachers find it easy to target them! Efforts to conserve rhinos, especially through protection and creating suitable habitats — fresh grasses or water wallows — are on. In 2006, the WTI and Assam Forest Department moved three hand-raised orphaned calves back to Manas NP that had

Domestic livestock are the most serious threat to wild equids. More than 200,000 livestock share the Kiang pastures in Ladakh, Jammu & Kashmir, and 2,500 yaks and sheep compete for drinking water in the small habitat in Sikkim. Livestock also carry diseases that can infect and destroy wild equid populations.

SUMANTA KUNDU/WTI

A rhino female with twins, a very rare occurrence, Jaldapara WLS, West Bengal

VIVEK MENON

Orphan rhino calf being bottle-fed at IFAW-WTI's Centre for Wildlife Rehabilitation and Conservation, Kaziranga, Assam

Rhino with horn cut off by poachers, outside Kaziranga NP, Assam

Greater One-horned Rhinoceros

Family: Rhinocerotidae
Indian Status: Locally Common
Social Unit: Solitary, in pairs during breeding, and loosely associated feeding groups of females and subadult males at good grasslands
Size: HBL: 335-346 cm, Wt:1,500-2,000 kg
Best Seen At: Kaziranga NP, Assam

The second largest mammal in India after the elephant, the Greater One-horned Rhinoceros is identified by its large bulk and single horn (a compacted mass of a hair-like substance called keratin). Two large folds of skin across its flanks give it an armour-plated look, separating it from the other rhino species. Its colour is a deep slate-grey, but looks ashy when covered with mud, or ink-black when wet. Horns weigh around 750 g; they are 25 cm long in males, 24 cm in females.

Its newborns are pinkish-grey, turning fully grey in a few months. The horn starts to grow by a year and a half. It does not use its horn to gore victims (as you might think!), but rather its sharp teeth to bite off chunks of flesh, as it does while fighting with other rhinos. It follows the same paths or *dandis* every day when foraging and the same spot to defecate, forming large 'toilets'.

It is found in nine populations in northern India, and in the Brahmaputra River basin in the North-East – mainly in Kaziranga NP and in Manas NP. in Assam. It lives in tall alluvial grasslands and riverine forest–grassland areas with swampy patches in the Gangetic and Brahmaputra river systems in the Himalayan foothills.

Large grey, armour-plated body

Single horn

Greater One-horned Rhinoceros in a swamp near a grassland, Kaziranga NP, Assam

Asiatic Wild Ass

Family: Equidae
Indian Status: Locally Common
Social Unit: Five distinct groupings: dominant stallion leads breeding band of adult females; females and young (foals, yearlings and subadult males); territorial solitary stallions; all male groups of young males; and groups of old or ostracized males
Size: HBL: 200-250 cm, Wt: 200-240 kg
Best Seen At: Wild Ass WLS, Gujarat

Also known as Khur, this is medium-sized, and fawn or chestnut with a dark chocolate fringe of hair on its neck. Where this ends, a broad chocolate stripe edged with white takes over, going to the end of the tail, which is short and tipped with a tuft of black hairs. The coat length is the same year-round, but its colour varies from reddish grey to greyish fawn in summer to pale chestnut in winter. Ears are long with dark brown tips. Hooves are black. Stallions or males are a bit larger and darker than mares. They fight viciously in the breeding season, with the victorious male gaining breeding and territorial rights.

It tends to eat at night, raiding wheat, millet and cotton fields. It was limited to the Little Rann of Kutch in Gujarat originally, but now has spread along the southern and eastern edges of the Greater Rann and eastern Rajasthan. It is found in open salt mudflats, scrublands, grasslands, *bets* or small clumps of grasslands in the Rann, and the edges of the Rann mixed with cropland.

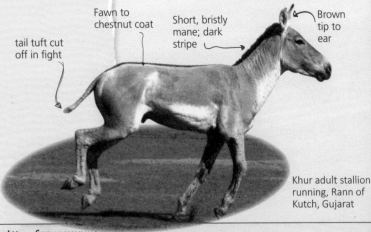

Fawn to chestnut coat

Short, bristly mane; dark stripe

Brown tip to ear

tail tuft cut off in fight

Khur adult stallion running, Rann of Kutch, Gujarat

Feral horses are free-ranging domestic horses, descendants of domestic breeds that escaped into the wild long ago. In India, two main populations are known from protected areas: in Dibru–Saikhowa WLS, Assam (80 animals) and in Point Calimere WLS, Tamil Nadu (150 animals). They do not have many wild genes, but they are wild in behaviour and do not allow close access.

Tibetan Wild Ass

Family: Equidae
Indian Status: Locally Common
Social Unit: In herds; average group of 6–7 animals; female–foal groups more common; stallions mostly solitary; young male bachelor herds also known
Size: HBL: 182-214 cm, Wt: 250-400 kg
Best Seen At: Chang Chenmo Valley and Hanle Basin, Ladakh, Jammu & Kashmir

Also known as the Kiang, it is bigger and ruddier than the Khur. It has a longer and thicker muzzle, and the head is proportionately larger. The body is darker chestnut-brown (paler in winters) with white venters (belly or underside). The mane and the tail is longer than in the Khur and the stripe on the back is dark but narrow, going all the way from neck to tail.

The Kiang is known to scrape on soft mud as a territorial marking. It coexists with other ungulates and is even tolerant of wolves, but flees if a Snow Leopard or humans come into view. It is found in eastern plateaus of Ladakh in Jammu & Kashmir, and Sikkim and Himalayan cold deserts. It has been recently reported from across the Himalayas in Uttarakhand. It is found from valley bottoms to higher grasslands in summer and only in valley bottoms in winter.

Ruddy colour, thin stripe on the back up to tail

Larger head and muzzle, longer mane

Tibetan Wild Ass mares and six- to seven-month-old foals, Ladakh, Jammu & Kashmir

Having been a part of capture and translocation operations of both the Black Rhinoceros in Kenya and the Greater One-horned Rhinoceros in India, I have learnt one important behavioural difference between the two. The African rhinos butt with their horn, and ours bite with their powerful incisors!

Rhinos are one of the most dangerous animals in India to come across on foot. Beware, especially if a mother that you have been careful to avoid is separated from its calf, which you have not seen, in the tall elephant grass of rhino habitat. Rhinos

can clock 55 km an hour when they chase you.

The Changthang, Tibet's northern and western plateau, extending into south-eastern Ladakh, is the Indian Serengeti and the Kiang is our equivalent of the zebra. Grazing in large herds amidst mountain goat and sheep, watching this high-altitude equid run through grass is an unparalleled delight.

I have had the good luck of seeing 60 per cent of Perissodactyls in the wild: Three of the world's five rhinoceros species, all three zebras, two of the three wild asses and one of four tapirs. The most memorable was the Brazilian Tapir that I helped radio-collar in the Pantanal Conservation Complex in South America. For my humble part in the operations, the team named the individual after me, a most confused 'Tapirus vivek'!

The horn of the rhinoceros is a densely packed bunch of hair loosely attached to its nasal bone. Keeping it on the rhinoceros and outside the illegal rhino-horn trade has taken up as many as two decades of my anti-poaching and anti-smuggling work.

EVEN-TOED UNGULATES ANTLERS AND HORNS

Antler

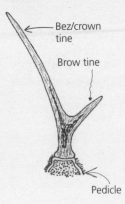

Bez/crown tine

Brow tine

Pedicle

Cross-section of Horn

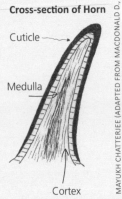

Cuticle

Medulla

Cortex

MAYUKH CHATTERJEE (ADAPTED FROM MACDONALD D., 2001)

Where they live

Ungulates

INDIAN EVEN-TOED UNGULATES **AT A GLANCE**

NUMBER OF SPECIES **35-38**

BIGGEST **BULL GAUR/ BULL YAK**

Even-toed Ungulates

A Nilgiri Tahr stands on a rocky outpost amidst Strobilanthes (blue) and other flowers, Eravikulam NP, Kerala

VIVEK MENON

SMALLEST	MOST COMMON	MOST ENDANGERED	ACTIVITY
PYGMY HOG/ MOUSE DEER	**CHITAL/ WILD BOAR**	**PYGMY HOG**	**ALL EVEN-TOED UNGULATES (EXCEPT PIGS)** ☼ **PIGS** ☾☼

▶What are Artiodactyls?

Artiodactyls are even-toed hoofed mammals that include mouse deer, musk deer, deer, antelope, cattle, sheep, goats, camels, pigs, peccaries, hippopotamus, giraffes and pronghorns.

▶What are deer, antelope, cattle, sheep, goats and pigs?

The Cervidae or deer family are ruminants. Male deer have solid, branched appendages on the head, called antlers. Musk deer are antlerless; they have a musk gland in the abdomen (no other deer has this). Mouse deer are small ruminants, with slender limbs and a two-toed hoof, and no antlers or horns.

Ninety-one species of ungulates of the family Bovidae, either sheep, cattle, goat or antelope, are called bovids. The most visible difference from deer is their bony, unbranched horns that last for life, while the deer's branched ones shed every year.

Cattle are large-sized ungulates. Both males and females have big horns (male horns are bigger) that are not shed. Pigs are barrel-shaped Artiodactyls with a small neck, large head, spindly legs and a snout.

▶What do they eat?

All ungulates, except pigs, are herbivores and are either grazers or browsers or both. Pigs are omnivores, with fruits, seeds, roots and tubers forming about 90 per cent of their diet. They also eat snakes, insects, offal and carrion.

Mouse deer forage on the forest floor for fruit, roots, leaves and herbs. Musk deer graze on grass, moss and lichen, and browse on shrubs, eating different food in different seasons. Muntjacs eat fallen fruit and nibble on shoots and leaves. Most deer are browsers, but Swamp Deer are mainly grazers. Sambar are mostly browsers. Antelope like the Blackbuck are mainly grazers, but dry-zone antelopes such as the Chinkara are browsers. The cold-desert Tibetan Antelope and the Gazelle do a bit of both. Common peninsular antelope like the Blackbuck and Nilgai also raid crops.

Goats and goat–antelopes are mainly browsers who graze too. They can reach up to trees and even climb them (e.g., Markhor) to feed. Bharal and sheep like the Argali are primarily grazers but browse too.

▶How do they move?

Bovids are fast movers, some of them are among the fastest ungulates in the world. Horned bovids living in open country run fast while those that live in dense cover have

A Nilgiri Tahr browses, Eravikulam NP, Kerala

VIVEK MENON

What are ruminants?

Ruminants get nutrients from plants by fermenting it through microbial action in a specialized stomach before digestion.

shorter limbs and scurry. Cattle living in swampy areas, like the Water Buffalo, develop splayed hooves, and those that live on hard ground, like the Gaur, have compact ones. Small cattle and antelope tend to crosswalk, while large ones amble or walk with both the legs on one side moving together.

Deer are generally fast runners, leap easily and stand on their hind legs to browse. Most bovids and cervids are also strong swimmers. Musk deer leap long distances, with their pointed fore hooves pencil-pointing their landings. The lateral hooves are splayed, giving them surer footing on uneven ground. Mouse deer tend to freeze or scurry away, when threatened. Pigs move at a trot or crosswalk, but can gallop or leap when alarmed.

N.A. NASEER

Bull Gaur drinks from a pool, Chinnar WLS, Kerala

Cattle such as the Gaur, Yak and Buffalo are classic bulk food eaters.

▶How do they live?
Broadly speaking, forest-dwelling ungulates are solitary, and those living in open grasslands, plains and mountains have more complex social groupings. The Indian Chevrotain and musk deer are largely solitary except in the breeding season or in mother-young groups. Musk deer, like mouse deer, use their canines to fight rival males, but unlike the mouse deer, also to defend territory.

The social organization of deer varies greatly, with the Barking Deer being largely solitary while larger deer are found up to 100 individuals at times. Chital congregate in the hundreds while Hog Deer rarely congregate in such large numbers.

Solitary bovids are rare; Other than the Goral and Serow, most goats are social animals with herds of up to 50-100 animals. Even these two come together in small groups of 4-5 (with male, female and young). All other goat and sheep have all-male and all-female groups for most of the year and mixed herds during the breeding season.

Pigs are non-territorial social animals that live in groups called sounders, comprising the female or sow and her offspring, subadults (not fully adult), related females, and sometimes an adult male or two.

▶How do they communicate?
Mouse deer communicate more by scent than calls. Soft bleats and squeals are reported between mother-and-young, and high-pitched chatters and screams in male-male interactions.

In musk deer, generally a silent species, a loud hiss or peep is the normal call, with a shorter chirp

Adult boars fight for mates, slashing at rivals' flanks and shoulders.

Wild Boar leaps across a ditch, Nagarhole NP, Karnataka

VIVEK MENON

or a double peep indicating alarm. The major communication is done through 'latrines', regularly used and having special smells investigated by other deer. The muntjac, on the other hand, is an extremely vocal animal, with a sharp bark indicating alarm and a longer, shriller version used commonly.

Different deer species have different calls: in the Sangai, a sharp grunt indicates alarm. The Sambar alarm call is a loud 'dhonk'. Chital have a sharp 'ack ack' call and a loud 'wow' alarm call. Takin have a hoarse cough, serow have a piercing shriek. Goral hiss and cough, and the Tahrs have a piercing whistle. Markhor grunt loud and long, and cough, Ibex have a birdlike chirp and snort, and Bharal have a squirrel-like 'chirrt'.

Pigs are strong callers: grunting, growling, squealing, and gnashing tusks and molars. They make exaggerated gestures like bristling the crest, strutting, pawing the air and charging in aggression.

▶Territoriality and display

Mouse deer do not defend territory though they seem to have defined home ranges. However, during the breeding or 'rutting' season, male deer battle each other, complete with loud calls and sparring, and decorating their headgear with vegetation and wallowing in mud. Male goats too compete by rearing

up on their hind legs and battering opponents with their horns. Among wild sheep, who have specialized skulls for batterings, rival males run at each other and fight with a loud thud of the horns. Goat–antelopes wrestle–spar, horn-butting the abdomen and sides of rivals. Male Blackbuck jump around, with their corkscrew horns laid flat against their backs to impress females. Gaur male bellow loudly but rarely have dramatic fights.

▶Young ones

Mouse deer young are born after six to nine months of pregnancy and twins are very common; the young leave off mother's milk in another six months. In musk deer, after a pregnancy of 5-6 months, a single young is normal. It depends on the mother for nine months to a year and lies hidden most of this time. In muntjac, pregnancy is 210 days and the one young born is weaned in only 70 days. Swamp Deer normally have one young after about eight months of pregnancy. Pigs bear a litter of up to a dozen. The litter size of the Pygmy Hog is only four to six; the female is pregnant for 120 days, and for 115 days in the case of the Wild Pig.

▶Threats and conservation

Hunting for eating and for trade, habitat loss, disease and competition from domestic livestock for food are the main threats. The money-making illegal trade in musk pods, used in cosmetics and medicines, endangers all four musk deer species. Deer antlers are also traded illegally for velvet used in Traditional Oriental Medicine, as antler ash used in the Unani and Ayurvedic schools, and into Europe for cutlery handles and pistol butts. The Pygmy Hog is the world's most endangered pig because of habitat loss due to the burning of grasslands in its breeding season.

Major conservation efforts include the relocation of Gaur to Bandhavgarh in Madhya Pradesh, the collaring of Eastern Swamp Deer to Manas in Assam, a recovery plan for the Indian Wild Buffalo in Udanti WLS in Chhattisgarh and the Hangul deer in Dachigam NP, Jammu & Kashmir.

Mouse Deer

India's smallest deer, also called Indian Chevrotain, has a speckled olive-brown coat with white stripes and spots. The undersides are creamish beige, the head and face dark brown. It has no antlers. This shy and well camouflaged deer usually makes its den in a tree hollow and does not call often. It is found in tall grasslands, plantation and forests all over south India, and north up to Jharkhand and Rajasthan.

Family: Tragulidae
Indian Status: Uncommon
Social Unit: Solitary; females with young
Size: HBL: 55-59 cm, Wt: 2-4 kg
Best Seen At: Mudumalai WLS, Tamil Nadu; Bandipur NP, Karnataka

White spots on olive brown coat

Shoulder stripe

Indian Chevrotain, Craigmore, Nilgiris, Tamil Nadu

RAMITH M./ WTI CAMERA TRAP

ANTLERS

Most male deer, except the mouse deer and musk deer, can be known by their antlers, which differ from the horns of goats, sheep, antelope and cattle in three ways. They are solid, usually branched (perhaps to allow fighting among males) and are shed yearly. Among the most rapidly growing tissues in the animal world, new antlers come up within a month or so of the deer shedding its full-grown bony antlers.

Musk Deer

Family: Cervidae
Indian Status: Locally Common to Uncommon
Social Unit: Solitary, except when with young
Size: HBL: 40-100 cm, Wt: 10-18 kg

Pale rump, but dark legs

S. SATHYAKUMAR

Himalayan Musk Deer male, Kedarnath WLS, Uttarakhand

Spots visible in summer

INTESAR SUHAIL

Kashmir Musk Deer female, summer coat

MOHIT AGGARWAL

Brownish grey face

White chest and stockings

Alpine Musk Deer, male, captive

WII CAMERA TRAP/ COURTESY S. SATHYAKUMAR

Dark brown body, grey head

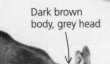

Black Musk Deer, Khangchendzonga NP, Sikkim

The **Himalayan Musk Deer** is a shy, brownish yellow, dog-sized deer told apart from the Alpine Musk Deer with its dark legs and stripeless chest. It is called White-bellied Musk Deer due to its paler underparts. The thick, bristly coat seems speckled with white. It is found in oak, rhododendron, coniferous and thick bamboo forests in the Himalayas from central Kashmir through Himachal Pradesh up to Sikkim. **Best seen at:** Kedarnath WLS, Uttarakhand

The **Kashmir Musk Deer** is medium-sized to large, grey-brown and recognized by the spots on the back being more prominent, a pale grey instead of creamy throat, underside and legs, and a noticeable copper-red saddle on the grey-brown back. It is found in oak and conifer and scrub in Jammu & Kashmir. **Best seen at:** Kazinag NP, Jammu & Kashmir

The **Alpine Musk Deer**, a very large, reddish grey musk deer, differs from the Himalayan Musk Deer in that it has white stockinged legs, and a broad creamy throat and chest. It is found in mountain scrub and meadows across central and eastern Himalayas, in Arunachal Pradesh and Sikkim. **Best seen at:** Kedarnath WLS, Uttarakhand

The **Black Musk Deer** can be recognized by its short face and uniform dark brown or blackish brown coat with no throat stripe, and dark legs and underparts. It is found in rhododendron, oak and coniferous forests in the north-eastern Himalayas, from Sikkim through Arunachal Pradesh. **Best Seen At:** Khangchendzonga NP, Sikkim

Red Muntjac

The more common of the two small Indian forest ruminants (the Mouse Deer being the other), the Barking Deer or Indian Muntjac has a glossy, reddish brown coat and greyish or white underparts. Males have small antlers on long bony bases, and two black lines mark these down the face. Antlers curve inwards. Females have no antlers. Although not territorial, males do have home ranges of 6-7 sq. km that they scent mark regularly. It is found in hilly and moist areas, forests, and forest fringes near crops and plantations through most of peninsular India and the Terai, north-eastern India and the low Himalayas. Not present in Kutch, Saurashtra and dry parts of north-western India.

Family: Cervidae
Indian Status: Locally Common
Social Unit: Solitary; in pairs during breeding season; mother and young; occasionally at water or food source, up to 4-5 animals
Size: HBL: 90-120 cm, Wt: 20-28 kg (male)
Best Seen At: Corbett NP, Uttarakhand

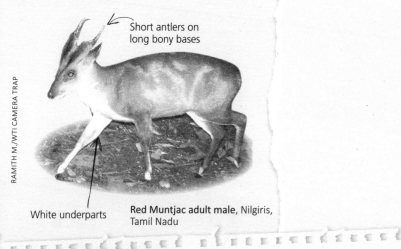

RAMITH M./WTI CAMERA TRAP

Short antlers on long bony bases

White underparts

Red Muntjac adult male, Nilgiris, Tamil Nadu

NORTH-EASTERN MUNTJACS

Recently, skulls and jaws of two muntjac species have been found in Arunachal Pradesh for the first time. They have not been seen in the wild, but information from old hunters and genetic testing of the material collected shows that the Leaf Muntjac – a small reddish brown muntjac half the size of the Indian Muntjac – and the Gongshan/Black Muntjac may be present in east Arunachal Pradesh. Both species are found in Myanmar and this could be a range extension.

Sambar

Family: Cervidae
Indian Status: Common
Social Unit: Solitary males; small subadult male groups; female and young (fawns and female yearlings); in wet areas large congregations of up to 100 known
Size: HBL: 160-210 cm, Wt: 130-270 kg
Best Seen At: Sariska and Ranthambore NPs, Rajasthan; Satpura and Melghat NP, Maharashtra; Periyar NP, Kerala

A typical forest deer with a shaggy, dark brown coat, and large spreading antlers, the Sambar is India's largest deer. The antlers have three branches, with a long main branch that divides into an end fork. Yearlings have a single spiked antler. Subadults over two years of age grow a main beam and a brow tine, thus having a two-branched antler. Adults four years of age grow a three-branched antler. Ears and tail are relatively large.

Coats are redder in summer, and darker brown in winter. Females are lighter and less shaggy. The adult males are largest in the Terai, but the antlers are largest in central India. They often feed in shallow water and when chased by predators such as Dholes, take to water, splashing loudly with their hooves to confuse the attacker. Stamping of feet or raising of hoof as if to stamp is a sign of alarm. They move through forests very silently for their exceptionally large size.

It is found in forests and grasslands near rivers and streams all over India except the high Himalayas, the Kutch desert and the coasts.

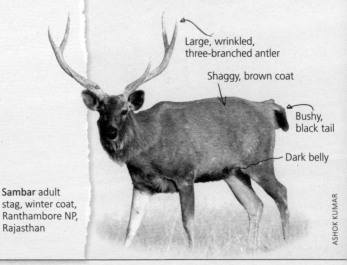

Large, wrinkled, three-branched antler

Shaggy, brown coat

Bushy, black tail

Dark belly

Sambar adult stag, winter coat, Ranthambore NP, Rajasthan

ASHOK KUMAR

Kashmir Red Deer

Family: Cervidae
Indian Status: Rare
Social Unit: Large family groups
Size: HBL: 180-205 cm, Wt: 110-240 kg
Best Seen At: Dachigam National Park, Jammu & Kashmir

The Hangul is a large, dark brown animal with a small orange-white rump patch bordered by a broad black band, and a short black tail. In winter, the coat is dark brown (liver coloured) with lighter sides and limbs. The belly, lips, chin and inner ears are white. In summer, the coat lightens and may be spotted. The five-branched antlers are large. Stags migrate above the snow line in summer, and come down to join the females in October. It is found in forests and mountain meadows in Jammu & Kashmir.

Five- to six-branched antlers

Liver-coloured coat

Circular antlers

Long, splayed hooves

M.K. RANJITSINH

Brow-antlered Deer, Keibul Lamjao NP, Manipur

VIVEK SINHA

Kashmir Red Deer stag, Dachigam NP, Jammu & Kashmir

Brow-antlered Deer

Family: Cervidae
Indian Status: Rare
Social Unit: Solitary males and females with fawns; multi-male–multi-female groups (average six, up to 70)
Size: HBL: 140-170 cm, Wt: 60-125 kg
Best Seen At: Keibul Lamjao NP, Manipur

A large deer with a spectacular circular antlers in stags, this deer, also called Sangai has a dark reddish brown winter coat, which turns paler in summer. The female is fawn all year round. The young are spotted. This deer walks on the hind surface of its hooves with short hops over floating vegetation, and is also called the Dancing Deer. It is found on open flat grasslands and *phumdis* or floating vegetation in marshes only on the Loktak Lake of Manipur.

Swamp Deer

Family: Cervidae
Indian Status: Locally Common
Social Unit: Scattered family groups
Size: HBL: 180-190 cm, Wt: 140-200 kg
Best Seen At: Kanha NP, Madhya Pradesh; Kishanpur WLS, Uttar Pradesh; Kaziranga NP, Assam

A large deer with a spectacular 5-6-branched antler in males, the Barasingha is reddish brown in winter and greyish brown in summer, with whitish underparts. It has a dark brown stripe on the back, a relatively short tail and rounded ears. The full antler development takes up to three years. Females are only a third of the male in size but still much larger than Spotted Deer does, from who they can be told apart by the white instead of pink hair in their ears.

Swamp Deer are creatures of habit and tend to use the same tracks to and from meadows. They don't have vigilant sentries in their herds, often grazing with their heads down simultaneously. If disturbed, they seek tall grass and not woodland.

They are found in five separate populations in three regions: flooded tall grasslands (northern India), tall alluvial grasslands interspersed with swamps (north-east India), and dry grassland bordered by sal forests (central India).

Five- to six-branched antler

Palmate antler shape

White hair in ear

Light coat

Uniform, unspotted brown coat

VIVEK MENON

Barasingha adult female and male in hard antlers, Kaziranga NP, Assam

Spotted Deer

Family: Cervidae
Status: Abundant
Social Unit: Basic unit is of females, fawns and yearlings; small herds in temporary feeding groups; herds of a few hundreds common in large grasslands with plenty of water
Size: HBL: 140-155 cm, Wt: 45-85 kg
Best Seen At: Corbett NP, Uttarakhand; Bandipur NP, Karnataka; Kanha NP, Madhya Pradesh

Popularly known as Chital, this is India's most common, most visible and perhaps most beautiful deer. It is the only mainly spotted deer in the country, with spots present in both males and females in all seasons and through life. Older males are darker and fawns are lighter. Males and females are almost identical except for size (males are about 50 per cent heavier than females) and the presence of antlers in the male. The antlers are largest proportional to body size and the body is longer proportional to height among all other deer in the world. The tail is relatively long, and the ears are medium-sized and narrow compared with the Sambar. It is also one of the few deer that does not wallow.

The Spotted Deer is found in grassland–forest overlaps, swampy meadows, plantations, mangroves and scrublands across peninsular India till Gujarat and in the North-East till Manas.

N.A. NASEER

Long three-branched antlers

White throat patch

White spots on brown coat

Spotted Deer adult stag (hard antlers) and young doe, Mudumalai WLS, Tamil Nadu

Hog Deer

Family: Cervidae porcinus
Indian Status: Least Locally Common
Social Unit: Solitary; small family groups of female, fawn and yearling; temporary feeding herds of up to 100 animals
Size: 130-150 cm, Wt: 30-55 kg
Best Seen At: Kaziranga NP, Assam; Dudhwa NP, Uttar Pradesh

A medium-sized grassland deer, the Hog Deer is fatter and has shorter legs than the Chital, and is larger and more rounded in form than the Barking Deer. The coat is darker and glossier in winter and has a yellow appearance with pale brown or white spots appearing in summers. The antlers are shorter than the other large deer but considerably longer than its own head and fairly thickset. It has a brown tail with a white flashing underside like the Chital and the Barking Deer.

When alarmed, it erects its tail, calls in a low bark like the Chital and scurries into the grass with its neck lowered and stretched out. It is also known to make a whistling sound and a bleating call.

It is found in wet, tall grasslands near forests, swamp or riverine areas, from Punjab to Assam and Arunachal Pradesh.

Short three-branched antlers

Higher hindquarters

VIVEK MENON

Hog Deer adult male in velvet, Kaziranga NP, Assam

Gaur

The largest wild cattle in peninsular India, the Gaur is mistakenly called the Indian Bison; it is not related to the North American Bison. It is a large, dark bovine with white stockings from hoof to hock. Both sexes have a massive head, deep chest and a muscular shoulder ridge that forms a step midway along the back. They both bear short horns that rise from a hairy and pale forehead, and curve outwards, and then inwards and slightly backwards. Adult males have short, glossy, black fur, while the young and females are coffee-brown.

Bulls inhabiting dry sal forests are less dark than those inhabiting teak forests. The newborn calf changes colour from golden yellow to fawn, light brown, and then red-brown. The young develops white stockings at around three or four months.

A very calm creature for its size, the Gaur rarely attacks unless tormented, and in most parts of south India will allow humans to approach very close. It has an acute sense of smell. If a herd is taken by surprise, it might start a stampede with calves getting run over in the process.

It is found in bamboo and teak forests, but favours open grasslands the most as well as evergreen forests in southern, central and north-east India.

Family: Bovidae
Indian Status: Locally Common
Social Unit: Old bulls can be solitary or in company of a younger bull; groups of 5-12 (20-100 also known); female and young
Size: HBL: 250-330 cm, Wt: 650-1,000 kg
Best Seen At: Nagarhole NP, Karnataka; Mudumalai WLS, Tamil Nadu; Wayanad WLS, Kerala

Massive ridge on back

Curved, hooked horns

Grey temporal boss

Big dewlap

JOSE LOUIES

Gaur bull, Bandipur NP, Karnataka

Wild Buffalo

Family: Bovidae
Subfamily
Indian Status: Locally
Common (Assam),
Rare (Central India)
Social Unit: Herds led
by adult females and a
mature bull (average 10
animals); occasionally
more are also known to
congregate; young males
have bachelor herds of
up to 10 animals; old
adult bulls are solitary
Size: HBL: 240-300 cm,
Wt: 250-1,200 kg
Best Seen At: Kaziranga
NP, Assam; Udanti WLS,
Chhattisgarh

Large, black and strong with flat sweeping horns, the Wild Buffalo is considered to be one of the most dangerous animals to encounter in India. It is a sleeker, heavier version of the domestic buffalo and has the largest horns of any animal in the world.

There are two horn types: in one, the horns curve upwards in a semicircle and almost meet at the tips; in the other, they grow in a parallel way upwards and then inwards. The body is dark grey, usually wet and black (because of their frequent mud wallows) and largely hairless. The tail is long, with a slender, bushy tip almost reaching the ankle. Wild Buffaloes have dirty white stockings not as white as that of the Gaur. The female is smaller with thinner and less crescent-like horns. Calves are hairy and fawn in colour, and at six months, horns appear and the coat reddens.

The Wild Buffalo can be differentiated from domestic buffaloes and their hybrids by a number of characteristics including a straight back, larger and more spread-out horns, pinkish instead of white hairs in the insides of the ears, and large hooves leaving big telltale footprints. The buffalo snorts, stomps its feet and shakes its head as it prepares to charge. It forms a tight herd around the young calves when threatened by predators.

It is found in low-lying grasslands near rivers, forests and woodlands in small isolated pockets in north-east India and central India.

Massive horns

Large size

R.P. MISHRA

Wild Buffalo male, Udanti WLS, Chhattisgarh

Wild Yak

Thickset and shaggy mountain cattle, yaks have been domesticated across most of their range. Compared to its domestic cousins, the Dzo, the Wild Yak is a massive animal with dark blackish brown fur that in males falls from the chest and sides like a woollen skirt over its legs. The ears are small, and the tail is thick, long and as shaggy as the coat. Both males and females have grey-black horns, but those of males are thicker and sweep outwards and forwards while females have narrower, straighter ones. The female is slightly greyer but is one-third the size of an adult male. Its young are dark brown. It grunts hoarsely and grinds its teeth, a habit unique to the yak. It has few sweat glands and needs to constantly cool off. It is often seen standing in icy rivers in winter! It is found in mountain grasslands in cold deserts only in Ladakh in a few small populations.

Family: Bovidae
Indian Status: Rare
Social Unit: Variable with solitary males; bachelor males of up to a dozen animals; herds of females, young, yearlings and a few adult males; and mixed herds of 200 and even 400
Size: HBL: 137-380 cm, Wt: 300-1000 kg
Best Seen At: Chang Chen Mo Valley, Ladakh, Jammu & Kashmir

Thick, sweeping horns

Shaggy, black fur extending to ankles

GEORGE SCHALLER

Wild Yak male, Tibetan Plateau

VIVEK MENON

Two-humped Bactrian Camel

VIVEK MENON

Mithun, Mehao WLS. Arunachal Pradesh

FERAL UNGULATES

A hybrid of Gaur and domestic cattle, the Mithun is the state animal of Arunachal Pradesh. It has pinkish patches on its dark or two-coloured body. The number of Mithun a man owns signifies his wealth. Male yaks are also interbred with domestic cows to produce the Dzos, used as a beast of burden at lower heights. Feral Two-humped Camels are also known in Ladakh.

Nilgai

Family: Bovidae
Indian Status: Abundant
Social Unit: Variable with solitary males; bachelor males of two or a dozen animals; herds of females, young, yearlings and a few adult males; and mixed female herds of 3-6 common in non-breeding season
Size: HBL: 170-210 cm, Wt: 120-288 kg
Best Seen At: Sariska NP, Rajasthan; Gir NP, Gujarat

India's largest antelope, the Nilgai resembles a horse more than a bull because of its height. Adult males are iron-blue to lighter grey, while females and calves are sandy brown. Both males and females have white and blue markings, two white spots on each cheek, white near the lips, and white on the inside of the tails and belly. Males and females have pretty white bands above and below a black band on the legs, giving the animals a 'low-socked' appearance. The male has a long, wispy beard (much less in females) and short, smooth, conical black horns.

It defecates at regular 'latrine sites', forming large clumps of saucer-shaped droppings. It is a very swift runner in open country, despite its large size. It can go for long periods without water.

It is found, along with its closest relative, the Chousingha, from the Himalayan foothills and Punjab plains through western and central India to the Odisha coast and south to Nilgiris in dry grasslands, open scrub and crop land.

Thinner horns indicating younger age

Brownish grey coat

White neck patch

Black beard

VIVEK MENON

Nilgai subadult male, Gajner, Rajasthan

Four-horned Antelope

Family: Bovidae
Indian Status: Uncommon
Social Unit: Unlike other antelopes, it is found singly, in pairs, or small groups (5-6)
Size: HBL: 90-110 cm, Wt: 15-25 kg
Best Seen At: Mudumalai NP, Tamil Nadu; Gir NP, Gujarat

A small, light brown antelope, the Chousingha is only slightly darker than the Indian Gazelle, the female of which it resembles superficially. However, it is much smaller (the smallest bovid in Asia), and can be told apart instantly by the horns in case of the male and the face-markings of the Chinkara doe. The horns are mere spikes, not ringed as in most antelopes. The fur is uniformly light brown, sometimes washed with red (especially in young animals), fawn or grey. Older males are yellowish. Despite its resemblance to the Chinkara, it is most closely related to the Nilgai. Horns develop only around a year of age (10-14 months).

It often lives near water, on which it is very dependent. It uses the same 'latrine sites' regularly for defecation and lays droppings in piles like the Nilgai; this probably serves as a means of communication.

It is found from the Terai through central and peninsular India, north of the Nilgiris. Also present in Gir NP, Gujarat. It is found in dry deciduous forest and scrub.

Four horns

Warm brown colour

KALYAN VARMA

Chousingha male, Kanha NP, Madhya Pradesh

Indian Gazelle

Family: Bovidae
Indian Status: Common
Social Unit: Usually small groups of 5-6 to a dozen animals
Size: HBL: 90-110 cm, Wt:15-23 kg
Best Seen At: Village boundaries all over Rajasthan and parts of Gujarat, especially close to Bishnoi communities

Arguably the most elegant ungulate in India, the Chinkara is a sandy or brown, medium-sized antelope with long neck, ears and legs. The underparts are white and the tail is dark brown, set in the middle of two white streaks. White and dark rufous streaks down the face, a dark nose-bridge and a white fleck on the forehead are characteristic. Both males and females have thin, curved horns. The female's horn is smaller (half the size of the male's), straighter and thinner. The horns are relatively straight and curve slightly outward only at the tip.

The Chinkara is uniquely adapted to go for long periods without drinking water and to obtain moisture from its food, along with which it eats soil.

It is found in open scrub, thorn forest, dry forest, dry and semi-dry habitats and sand dunes in parts of western and central India from Punjab and Rajasthan, eastward through the Gangetic valley and southward to the Deccan Plateau.

Curved, ringed horn

Sandy brown upperparts

Dark tail

White underparts

VIVEK MENON

Chinkara adult male winter coat, Gajner, Rajasthan

Blackbuck

A native antelope found only on the Indian subcontinent, the beauty of the Blackbuck is glorified in many cultures. Adult males are dark brown to velvet black with white undersides, buttocks, legs, eye rings, nose and lower muzzle. Females and young are light brown above and white below, with white eye rings. By the end of the third year, young males males attain a dark colouration and the trademark spiralled horns with one to four spirals. When alarmed, the Blackbuck leaps up as if on a spring (a movement known as 'pronking').

It lives in short grassland, open salt pans, open scrub as well as in dry forest fringes, riverbanks and dry areas, but avoids hills. It is found in northern India, from Rajasthan to Punjab and down to Tamil Nadu in the south and Odisha in the east.

Family: Bovidae
Indian Status: Locally Common
Social Unit: Solitary and bachelor herds of males; males with multiple females and young; females and offspring; solitary females
Size: HBL: 120-150 cm, Wt: 31-45 kg
Best Seen At: Velavadar NP, Gujarat; Calimere Sanctuary, Tamil Nadu

Corkscrew horns

Jet black underparts

White ankles

M.K. RANJITSINH

Blackbuck adult male, Jodhpur, Rajasthan

Tibetan Antelope

Family: Bovidae
Indian Status: Rare
Social Unit: Solitary males; mixed herds; mother and young
Size: HBL: 100-140 cm, Wt: 22-42 kg
Best Seen At: Chang Chenmo Valley, Ladakh, Jammu & Kashmir

The Chiru is a large-bodied, antelope-like animal instantly known by the long, slender black horns of the males. Slightly flattened, they rise almost vertically except for a slight curve back in the middle. It has a luxuriant, woolly, tan and grey winter coat (white undercoat) and a reddish fawn summer coat. Females do not have horns and are rust-fawn. Their bellies, the tip of their noses and eye rings are white, and the rest of the muzzle and the front of the legs are grey. Young males, coloured like the females, start growing horns when they are a year old. They live in Himalayan grasslands and cold desert lands in two populations in Ladakh, Jammu & Kashmir.

GEORGE SCHALLER

Long, black horns

Black face

Dark leg markings

White underside

Tibetan Antelope male in winter, Tibetan plateau

Tibetan Gazelle

Family: Bovidae
Indian Status Rare
Social Unit: Females and young; temporary groups
Size: HBL: 90-105 cm, Wt: 13-15 kg
Best Seen At: Kalak Tatar, Ladakh, Jammu & Kashmir

A small antelope, it has short, greyish fawn fur in summer and thick, pale fawn fur in winter. It is easily identified by a large, heart-shaped patch on the backside, flashing white in both males and females. Undersides are white, legs paler than the body and tail black-tipped. Females are hornless, and the slender male horns rise up, curve sharply back and rise up again, black and ridged almost all the way. The Tibetan Gazelle is found in mountain grasslands and valleys in Ladakh, Jammu & Kashmir and northern Sikkim.

Small, curved horns

Short, dark fawn coat

White patch on backside

PRANAV CHANCHANI

Tibetan Gazelle male, Tso Lhamo plateau, Sikkim

Asiatic Ibex

A large mountain goat with close relatives in Central Asia and Europe, the Himalayan Ibex male is easily recognizable by his horn and beard. Females are grey-brown, have thin parallel horns and dark markings on legs. Both males and females have a dark stripe down their back, and short, dark, furry tails. The male's dense coat is brownish in summer. From autumn to spring, males are dark brown or black with a dull white saddle on the back.

The male has thick, scimitar-shaped horns that diverge and curve backwards. The front face of the horn is flattened and has thick horizontal ridges. Yearlings are like females, with a small beard and short, spike-like horns.

The Ibex does not always migrate to lower heights in winter and often stays at fairly high altitudes. It digs craters through snow to get to eat in winter. It lives in steep crags above the treeline in the Himalayas in Ladakh in Jammu & Kashmir and Himachal Pradesh. It grazes on mountain pastures and wet meadows but always close to rocky cliff faces.

Family: Bovidae
Indian Status: Uncommon
Social Unit: Large feeding groups of up to 100 animals in spring; average herd size is 10-15 animals
Size: HBL: 85-132 cm, Wt: 30-130 kg
Best Seen At: Pin Valley NP, Himachal Pradesh; Kanji WLS, Jammu & Kashmir

Scimitar-shaped horns, deeply ridged

Shaggy brown fur

Short, bushy tail

Asiatic Ibex males, Pin Valley NP, Himachal Pradesh

YASH VEER BHATNAGAR

Markhor

Family: Bovidae
Indian Status: Rare
Social Unit: Females, yearlings and juvenile males in herds of 8-9; larger herds also known
Size: HBL: 155-170 cm, Wt: 30-108 kg
Best Seen At: Limber and Lachipora nullahs of Kazinag NP, Jammu & Kashmir

The largest mountain goat in the world, the Markhor has long fur like the Himalayan Tahr, a flowing beard, and corkscrew horns. Males vary from iron-grey to off-white in winter with hints of red-brown in summer. Females are light brown and are only about half the size of an adult male. Yearlings resemble females but are smaller in size with slightly larger and broader horns. Females are also slightly lighter than yearlings. It can climb trees like goats do and the steepest of terrain.

It is found in three populations in Kazinag in Jammu & Kashmir in dense pine and fir forests, open barren slopes and grassy meadows, all near steep rocky cliffs with often more than 60° slope.

Thicker head and neck, and darker brown fur of young male compared with the female's

RIYAZ AHMED

Markhor adult female *(background)*, yearling male *(foreground)* and kid *(right)*, Kazinag NP, Jammu & Kashmir

Greater Blue Sheep

Family: Bovidae
Indian Status: Locally Common
Social Unit: Solitary; medium-sized herds of 10-15 animals
Size: HBL:120-140 cm, Wt: 35-75 kg
Best Seen At Kibber WLS, Himachal Pradesh; Hemis NP, Jammu & Kashmir; Gangotri NP, Uttarakhand

Adult male Bharal have a slate-blue coat. In winter, this colour becomes more pronounced, while in summer the coat turns red-brown especially in females and young, serving as better camouflage. The adult males across the Himalayas have a light, almost cream, colouration while in the Himalayas, the colour is much darker. Adult males in both areas have dark brown to black markings on the neck, chest and legs, and a flank stripe that merges with the colour of the legs. Male horns curve outward, backward and then downward in a crescent formation. The tips of the horn once again point upwards at the very end in prime males over eight years of age.

Females are one-third the size of the males, have much shorter and thinner horns that diverge out, are dull grey in colour and have dark grey instead of black markings on their body. They use areas with crags and cliffs but largely as retreats from danger.

Greater Blue Sheep are found above the treeline, in open grassy or boulder-strewn ground and high cliffs in the Greater Himalayan meadows and Himalayan regions from Jammu & Kashmir to Arunachal Pradesh.

White backside

Sweeping, smooth, crescent-shaped horns

Greater Blue Sheep adult male, Gangotri NP, Uttarakhand

M.K. RANJITSINH

Himalayan Tahr

Family: Bovidae
Indian Status: Uncommon
Social Unit: Mixed herds of up to 75 animals
Size: HBL: 90-170 cm, Wt: 55-124 kg
Best Seen At: Kedarnath WLS, Uttarakhand

The Himalayan Tahr male is a deep copper-brown mountain goat, while females and younger males are light brown. The male Tahr has a coarse, tangled mane (straw-coloured in summer) over its neck and chest, and a coat that covers the sides down to its thighs. The horns on both males and females are short, compressed and wrinkled with a sharp outer edge. They both curve backwards, but female horns are marginally shorter and do not curve as much downwards as male ones do.

Adult males live in all-male herds in spring and rejoin females in the autumn.

It is found in western and central Himalayas from Jammu & Kashmir to Sikkim on forested terrain with grass cover and slopes with oak and bamboo in the Greater Himalayas. They prefer higher altitudes.

Short, ridged horns

Black face

Straw-coloured ruff

Dark mane

SOM B. ALE

Himalayan Tahr male

Nilgiri Tahr

Family: Bovidae
Indian Status: Locally Common
Social Unit: Large mixed groups of 2-140 and all-male groups (non-breeding season) of 2-20 animals; old saddlebacks are solitary
Size: HBL: 110-150 cm, Wt: 50-100 kg
Best Seen At: Eravikulam NP, Kerala

A handsome goat, the male Nilgiri Tahr looks like a shorn version of the male Himalayan Tahr, without the flowing mane and hair. The females have a short, greyish brown coat, whitish underparts and a buff patch around the eyes and the muzzle. The legs are darker than the body with a conspicuous dark spot above the knees

Adult males are blue-black grizzled with white hair, a short bristly mane from neck to mid-back and just after that a clear whitish or pale saddle-shaped patch, giving it the popular regional name of 'saddleback'. The male has two clear, dark patches on the bridge of the nose and on the face below the eyes, separated by a streak of pale fur. The legs are darker in the front as in females, but exactly where the females have dark spots above the knees, the males have a pair of white spots.

Both males and females share a dark band along the back. They have medium-sized horns that are parallel, heavily ridged and curved backwards. Yearlings are grey and have shorter horns. While the herd rests in the hot afternoon hours, a very conspicuous sentinel, which could be a female or a subadult male, stands guard. The Nilgiri Tahr is found in mountain grasslands and rocky crags of the Nilgiris, in Kerala and Tamil Nadu along the Western Ghats.

Nilgiri Tahr saddleback and adult female, Eravikulam NP, Kerala

Curved, ridged horn and darker brown colour

Silver saddle in old males

N.A. NASEER

Urial

Family: Bovidae
Indian Status: Uncommon
Social Unit: All male herds; female with young; mixed herds in breeding season
Size: HBL: 68-116 cm, Wt: 35-90 kg
Best Seen At: Nimdum WLS and Rong Nallah, Ladakh, Jammu & Kashmir

Previously also called the Red Sheep, the Urial resembles the Argali, but is smaller with shorter, thinner horns. Adult males in winter are reddish grey (some being clearly chestnut). The saddle patch is black in front and white at the back. A dark stripe on the sides, separating the upper parts and the underparts, and dark hair above and below the knee are present in both males and females.

The face, bib, undersides and lower legs are white. The backside is a much smaller white patch than in the Argali but looks conspicuous. Females do not have the saddle patch or bib and are lighter, while the young are greyer and smaller. Females have short horns and the lateral stripe is limited to a black spot under the forelegs.

Urial rams have large, semicircular horns that in large males form three-fourths of a circle. Most Ladakh Urial have horns that point inwards towards the back of their necks. Some males may have sickle-shaped deeply ridged horns. Yearlings are smaller and greyer than adult females. The horns are marginally bigger than the those of the females.

It is found on mountain grasslands, rolling hills and open dry land in Ladakh, Jammu & Kashmir, and usually avoids steep slopes.

M.K. RANJITSINH

Large, semicircular horns

White saddle patch

Copper-red colour

White stockings

Black lateral stripe

Urial adult male spring coat, Hemis—Shukpachen, Ladakh, Jammu & Kashmir

Argali

The Argali is largest among India's wild sheep. Both males and females sport a light grey-brown coat in summer, darker along the back, with white face, undersides and a white backside. The dark upper sides are separated from the light undersides by a dark lateral line. In winter, the red in the coat gives way to darker grey.

Males (rams) are about three times the size of the female (ewes) The rams have massive curled horns with their tips pointing outwards from the spiral and sometimes upwards as well. The tail is short and black-tipped. As both ends of the male are white and the back dark, it looks very much like a light sheep wearing a dark dinner-jacket! Ewes are smaller than males as in most sheep, have smaller horns that are less ribbed and rump patches are not as distinct as the rams'. Argali young are dark grey and, as yearlings, start assuming adult colour.

It does not seek cover even when running from predators such as a wolf, tending to outrun them. Females commonly give birth to twins. It lives in high rolling hillsides, cliffs, rugged regions and areas with more than 20 cm of snow in eastern Ladakh, Jammu & Kashmir. It is rare in Lahaul and Spiti in Himachal Pradesh.

Family: Bovidae
Indian Status: Rare
Social Unit: Mixed herds; all-male herds; all-female and young herds
Size: HBL: 167-148 cm, Wt: 68-105 kg
Best Seen At: Gya Miru and Tsokar Basin, Ladakh, Jammu & Kashmir

Reddish brown dinner-jackets

PRANAV CHANCHANI

Argali adult male, summer coat, Tso Lhamo, Sikkim

Takin

Family; Bovidae
Indian Status: Rare
Social Unit: Mixed herds with males, females and young; usually herds have 4-5 individuals, an average of 20-30 animals and occasionally even 100
Size: HBL: 170-220 cm, Wt: 150-350 kg
Best Seen At: Mehao WLS, Arunachal Pradesh

The Mishmi Takin is a bulky animal, clothed in brownish grey shaggy fur with dark facial markings and a dark stripe that runs from head to tail on the back. The tail is dark and short, but bushy. The horns are short cones with a knob at the base, curving up, out and then back. The tips of the horn always point out. Males have a darker face and limbs (almost blue-grey) and a very short beard. The fur is long and hangs under the chin and neck in a fringe. In an adult male, the rest of the body is pale brown with a lighter saddle on the back.

The females are much smaller, with smaller horns, and more uniformly grey with less black on the face. The Bhutanese believe it to be a mixture of a sheep, a yak and a cow! Overall, the Mishmi Takin is a darker animal with more grey in it. The Bhutanese Takin is a lighter animal with more brown, and black only on the legs and the face.

The Takin is attracted to hot sulphur springs and salt licks, where it gathers in large numbers. It is more crepuscular (active in twilight) than most ungulates, but it does venture out in daylight too. It is found in bamboo and rhododendron thickets, forests and steep slopes with dense vegetation in Arunachal Pradesh and in northern Sikkim.

Dorsal stripe

Shaggy, grey-brown coat

Bulky legs

VIVEK MENON

Takin young male, Mehao WLS, Arunachal Pradesh

Himalayan Brown Goral

Family: Bovidae
Indian Status: Locally Common to rare
Social Unit: Adult males are solitary but can join with female groups especially for feeding
Size: HBL: 82-120 cm, Wt: 35-42 kg (male)
Best Seen At: Mehao WLS and Namdapha NP, Arunachal Pradesh; Majhatal WLS, Himachal Pradesh

The Brown Goral is a small, brown goat–antelope; shaggy, brownish grey in winter to a sleeker greyish brown in summer. Its horns are short, ridged and backward pointing, and thinner in the females. If alarmed, it stands its ground, sneezing and hissing, and then bounds away in a zigzag course into scrub cover. It lives in steep but grassy mountain slopes (more than 30°) with low tree cover and moderate shrubs interspersed with cliffs.

The Himalayan Grey Goral is a predominantly grey-furred animal with a creamy white lower lip, chin, throat and belly. It has an indistinct black band on its back. It lives among tall vegetation on steep, south-facing slopes.

The Red Goral is a small fox-red goral, it has a dark back, paler undersides and a bright chestnut front. It prefers sunny slopes when feeding. It likes steep, rocky woodland and scrub, and higher, moister forests than other goral species. Gorals are found in northern India, along the Himalayas to Arunachal Pradesh, north of River Brahmaputra.

Brown fur

Brown Goral young male, Khangchendzonga NP, Sikkim

WII CAMERA TRAP/COURTESY S. SATHYAKUMAR

Himalayan Serow

Family: Bovidae
Indian Status: Occasional
Social Unit: Solitary; groups of less than10
Size: HBL: 140-170 cm; Wt: 85-140 kg
Best Seen At: Himalayan form: Kedarnath WLS, Uttarakhand; Red form: Mehao WLS, Arunachal Pradesh

Long, oval, donkey-like ears and a habit of standing with forelegs apart make the Serow an ungainly goat—antelope. Its coarse coat varies from black to red. Male and female both have a rough, dark, sometimes salt-and-pepper mane and a dark stripe on the back, more visible in some. The ears have creamy white hairs inside, fringed black. The tail is dark. The hooves are black. Relatively short, conical, wrinkled horns are thicker in the male and thicker at the base in older animals.

When alarmed, the Serow bounds away with a hissing snort or a whistling scream. It is found in thickly forested valleys and scrub with dense cover and boulder-strewn hills in Jammu & Kashmir to Arunachal Pradesh, Meghalaya, Manipur, Mizoram, Tripura and Nagaland.

DUSHYANT PARASHER

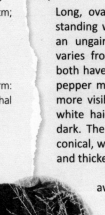

Long, 'ass-like' ears

Black body

Rust-coloured thighs

White stockings

Serow, Sattal, Uttarakhand

Indian Wild Pig

Family: Suidae
Indian Status: Abundant
Social Unit: Groups of 6–20 animals, sow and piglets; solitary old adult males; subadult groups
Size: HBL: 90-200 cm Wt: 45-320 kg
Best Seen At: Almost all Indian forests

The Indian Wild Pig is one of the most widely distributed of all ungulates in the world. It has a short muzzle, with a round disc at the end of its nose. It has large ears. The fur is brown, with black and grey hairs. The female (sow) is much smaller than the male. The piglets have

Pygmy Hog

Family: Suidae
Indian Status: Rare
Social Unit: Males are normally solitary; females and a few young (4-5) form a basic unit
Size: HBL: 55-70 cm, Wt: 6-9.7 kg
Best Seen At: Manas NP, Assam

The rarest and most endangered of all wild pigs globally, the Pygmy Hog was feared to be extinct until rediscovered in 1971. It has a bullet-shaped body and at first sight, looks like a miniaturized wild pig with a much shorter snout and tail. The animal appears tailless. The young are lighter with very faint stripes that are visible for a few weeks.

Pygmy Hogs are known to groom each other often and make soft grunting sounds as they eat, both of which help form and keep groups together. They are unique in building grass nests for resting and sleeping.

They live in tall Terai grassland undisturbed by human activity in north-western Assam to the north of River Brahmaputra.

Bullet-shaped body with very small tail

White moustachial stripe

Shortened snout

VIVEK MENON

Pygmy Hog adult male, captive, Assam

longitudinal stripes for the first six months or so. Extremely pugnacious, an angry Wild Pig can cause more damage than larger beasts, as it rarely abandons a charge. It wallows in shallow mud pools. It is found in grasslands, forests and agricultural fields along forest fringes throughout India, except the deserts of Rajasthan and Gujarat, and the high Himalayas.

Large grey-brown body

Long hog bristles

R.P. MISHRA/WTI CAMERA TRAP

Indian Wild Pig adult boar, Achanak TR, Chhattisgarh

Antlers and Horns

DEER

Red Muntjac

Hog Deer

Spotted Deer

Sambar

Brow-antlered Deer

Kashmir Red Deer

Swamp Deer

ANTELOPE

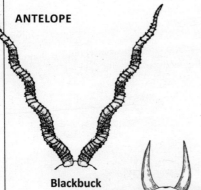

Blackbuck

Tibetan Antelope

Tibetan Gazelle

Four-horned Antelope

Nilgai

Indian Gazelle male

Indian Gazelle female

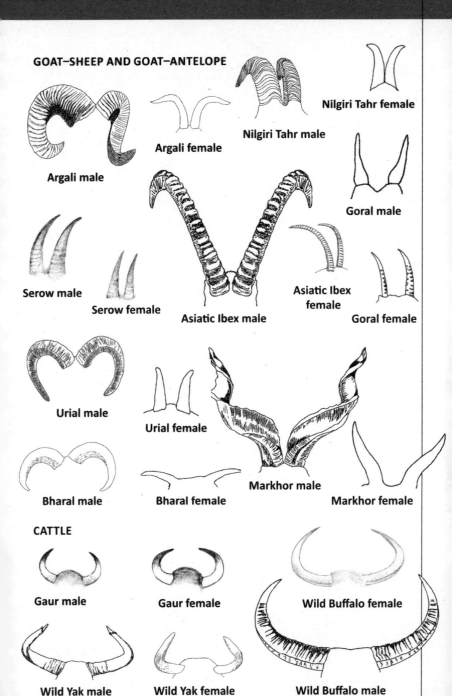

GOAT–SHEEP AND GOAT–ANTELOPE

Argali male

Argali female

Nilgiri Tahr male

Nilgiri Tahr female

Goral male

Serow male

Serow female

Asiatic Ibex male

Asiatic Ibex female

Goral female

Urial male

Urial female

Markhor male

Bharal male

Bharal female

Markhor female

CATTLE

Gaur male

Gaur female

Wild Buffalo female

Wild Yak male

Wild Yak female

Wild Buffalo male

FIELD NOTES: From Tip to Toe

The first ever wildlife photographs that I took were those of a Wild Boar. I used to walk the Pandanus fringed beaches of Point Calimere WLS in Tamil Nadu where I researched the Brahminy Kite every

evening. Nearly every day I used to go past an adult Wild Boar coming the other way. The photos were black and white, and not world beaters in class, but they still remain my favourite in terms of memory.

The state animal of Chhattisgarh is the 'Van' Bhainsa or wild buffalo. However, it is fast becoming the 'one' Bhainsa! There is only one female left amongst seven males in Udanti WLS. WTI along with the Chhattisgarh forest department is trying a conservation project outside their natural habitat to bring the central Indian population back from the brink. The one female is called Asha or 'hope'!

The only place you can see an endangered mountain goat without getting out of your car is at Rajamalai in Eravikulam National Park. Drive on the road

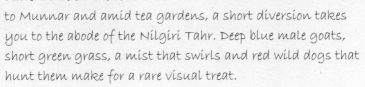

to Munnar and amid tea gardens, a short diversion takes you to the abode of the Nilgiri Tahr. Deep blue male goats, short green grass, a mist that swirls and red wild dogs that hunt them make for a rare visual treat.

In the Changtang in Ladakh, with a WTI team surveying the Tibetan antelope, the jeep ahead of us came face to face with a magnificent Argali ram. Just then a wolf came from another cliff-face and, on a mountain road with nowhere to go, decided on a bold lunge to grab the sheep by its scruff. The impressive ram stood its ground and with a toss of its muscled neck threw the wolf clean off the cliff-side! So much for the feared predator.

The strangest looking ungulate in India is the Takin, which the Bhutanese believe is the handiwork of a playful monk who joined a goat's head to a cow's body. I saw my wild Mishmi Takin on cliffs that promised to drop you down a thousand feet if you took a wrong step in Mehao WLS in Arunachal Pradesh.

CARNIVORE SKULLS

Clouded Leopard

Striped Hyaena

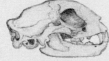

Wildcat

Otter

Dhole

Mongoose

Wolf

Brown Bear

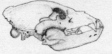

Binturong

Sloth Bear

RADHIKA BHAGAT (ADAPTED FROM MACDONALD D, 2001)

Where they live

Cats, Civets, Pandas

Linsangs

Bears, Badgers, Weasels, Martens

Dogs, Wolves, Foxes, Mongooses, Hyaenas, Otters

INDIAN CARNIVORES **AT A GLANCE**

NUMBER OF SPECIES **57**

BIGGEST **HIMALAYAN BROWN BEAR**

Carnivores

A tiger sees you a hundred times for each time you see it; a young male in Corbett NP, Uttarakhand

VIVEK MENON

SMALLEST
SMALL INDIAN MONGOOSE

MOST COMMON
JACKAL, JUNGLE CAT & GREY MONGOOSE

MOST ENDANGERED
MALABAR CIVET

ACTIVITY

▶ What are carnivores?

Carnivores are animals adapted to eating flesh. Many carnivorous species are not mammals; however, all carnivorous mammals share common features such as well-developed teeth with cutting edges, and feet with four or more sharp and strong claws.

The 40 cat species or 'felids' found globally vary greatly in size and colour, but all have slender, graceful bodies, round heads, shortened muzzles and erect ears. Most cats hunt by stealth, aided by pads on their soles and their sharp claws can be retracted into sheaths. While traditionally the tiger, lion, leopard, Snow Leopard, and Clouded Leopard are called Big Cats, there are 10 species called smaller cats. All cats have strongly patterned coats, except four or five, in which the adults lose the coat markings present in juveniles.

Canids in India are of two groups: the wolf-like canids including jackals, wolves and wild dogs; and foxes, three species of which are found in India. Their tail is long and bushy, and the ears long and pointed. Hyaenas are doglike carnivores with large heads, strong jaws and muscular front legs. Civets can be distinguished by their unique civet gland, a modified skin gland. Their ears are large, they are omnivorous and nocturnal while in contrast mongoose ears are short, they are carnivorous and insectivorous, and most are diurnal. Linsangs are slender animals, with a spotted coat and a long neck and tail. Mustelids include badgers, otters, weasels and martens. Though classified as carnivores, bears are omnivorous. All bears (except the Polar Bear) are dark and mainly vegetarian.

▶ What do they eat?

While most carnivores are meat-eaters, a few are specialized, like otters and Fishing Cats, which are piscivores or fish-eaters. Most Palm Civets eat large amounts of fruit besides small prey. Mongooses eat insects besides other small prey. However, the Red Panda is nearly completely a vegetarian.

At the other end, cats are nearly completely hypercarnivores. Tigers eat Sambar, Wild Pigs and other prey mostly more than 30 kg in weight. Lions eat a lot of Chital in the Gir and

Canid alert!

The world's 35 canid species are successful predators, many of which hunt on the run, using their long bodies and limbs, and digitigrade feet (standing/walking on toes) with non-retractile claws.

Two endangered species stand together: the Indian Grey Wolf and the Great Indian Bustard), Nannaj WLS, Maharashtra

DHRITIMAN MUKHERJEE

also livestock. Leopards prefer prey of 10-50 kg, and deer, langur, porcupines, hares and small birds are a large part of their diet. Small cats mostly eat rodents and small birds, along with insects and other invertebrates. For Jungle Cats and Caracals, rodents form 50-70 per cent of their diet. Rodents, hares, pikas, marmots and birds add to the Snow Leopards' diet of antelope, sheep, goat and livestock.

Small but strong!

Weasels and martens are powerful predators, killing with a bite to the neck and head of small prey.

A Mountain Weasel with a dead pika in its jaws, Ladakh, Jammu & Kashmir

Bears spend hours foraging for berries, fruits and nuts, and adding on insects. The Black Bear is mainly a frugivore or fruit-eater. Brown Bears, too, are largely plant-eaters, though marmots provide meat protein. Sloth Bears are largely omnivorous.

Hyaenas eat plants and insects, and predate on animals. Large canids such as Dholes and wolves catch medium-to-large-sized prey, mostly as a social hunting unit. Medium-sized canids like jackals hunt in packs or alone, and scavenge and predate. Small-sized canids like foxes hunt alone, by stealth and in a leaping-and-grabbing way. Weasels and martens take rodents and hares. Martens eat fruit, and hunt on land and in trees. Badgers dig for invertebrates. Linsangs take rodents, birds, reptiles and insects.

▶ How do they move?

Carnivores move in different ways to forage or hunt for food, to escape predators and for other needs. Most cats and dogs have lean limbs, and a digitigrade mode of motion, meaning that they walk or run on their toes, giving them speed and flexibility. All cats and some civets can sheath their claws, allowing stealth and speed. Many carnivores are arboreal, some more so, like fruit-eating civets, and others less so, such as cats. Many carnivores are strong swimmers, but otters have paddle-like tails and webbing on feet for swimming. Some carnivores such as bears walk with a bow-legged shuffle and often rear up on their hind legs to peer at objects with their weak eyes. Mustelids' body shape allows them to 'weasel' into burrows, swim well and bound on land, but large badgers shuffle.

▶ How do they live?

Most felids are solitary except when breeding or when the mother is with her cubs. An exception is the lion, which lives in large groups or prides. However, Asiatic Lion males join the pride only for a large kill or to mate.

Bears are usually solitary, but sometimes group to feed together.

Mustelids, linsangs and civets are usually solitary, except otters, which live in groups called pods.

Generally, small canids such as foxes live in small groups. Medium-sized canids like jackals, Dhole and wolves live in packs.

▶How do they communicate?

Felids are the most vocal of carnivores and use calls with facial gestures, tail carriage and fur posture to communicate at a close distance. For medium- to long-range, calls are used with spraying of chemical scents. The roars of tigers and lions are well known, but less known is that lions end every roar with a unique short burst of grunts. Leopards have shorter calls called 'sawing' (like the sawing of logs). Clouded Leopards, Caracals and Desert Cats mew like domestic cats. Fishing Cats utter short, two-toned 'barks'. Besides their normal call, leopards and lions also use a short sneeze (puffing), tigers, Clouded Leopards and Snow Leopards use a snort (a prusten) and all others have a gurgle-purr too. Snow Leopards cough, snarl, hiss, spit, growl and yeowl. Contact calls of mothers and

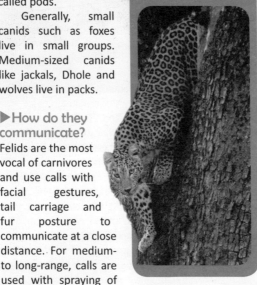

Cat in a tree

Leopards are adept at climbing trees. Here, one climbs down a tree at Biligiri Rangaswamy Temple WLS, Karnataka

KALYAN VARMA

cubs are unique, like the loud 'aaahoonh' of a tigress calling her cubs.

The hyaena's wailing cackle is often heard at night. Its many calls include growls, lowing, whining and a short, sharp yelp. The jackal has a well-known howl, and also yelps and barks. Dholes are the only canids to use a low-pitched whistle while hunting, a contact call when the pack attacks.

Pandas deposit chemical signals in excreta. Their seven recorded calls include a 'whee', a 'wheet', a 'whuff' and an 'uuh'.

Mustelids, civets and linsangs mark their territory by mixing scent from glands with their excreta, and 'pasting' plants in the area. Otters are social and use calls, touch and scents left in their 'spraints' (dung).

▶Young ones

In lions, the young are born after a pregnancy period of 100-114 days; litter sizes range from 1-6, the average being three. In Snow Leopards pregnancy lasts 90-103 days and the 2-3 cubs stay with the mother for up to two years. Tigers have a pregnancy of 102-108 days and the 2-5 cubs start hunting with the mother within the year. In leopards pregnancy is for 98-105 days and average litter size is 1-3 (two is common). They become independent in a year.

Mustelids give birth to a single litter every year, in hidden burrows or dens. The young remain with the mother for a few months.

The larger canids have larger litters. Smaller canids, such as foxes, hyaenas and wolves, have smaller ones. Pregnancy is around two months and cubs live in a den for 2-3 weeks. Packs or mothers provide food, and guard dens.

In mongooses, several litters are born yearly and pregnancy varies from 42-80 days. Litter size is up to six; the young are born in a burrow or den and are looked after for 3-6 months.

Among bears, pregnancy is generally two months. In Himalayan Brown Bears, it is 120 days and the cubs stay with the mother for 2-3 years. The Sloth Bears' average litter size is two and the mother stays in the den for up to 10 weeks, living off fat reserves. In Black Bears, two cubs are born and weaned at 3.5 months.

▶ Threats and conservation

In India, carnivore conservation focuses on the tiger, with some spotlight on other charismatic carnivores such as the lion, the bears, the Snow Leopard, the wolf, the leopard and the Dhole. Lesser

Carrying pups

MAYUKH CHATTERJEE

Otter with pup

Lioness with pup

cats, certain civets and mongooses, foxes, pandas and otters have had some research and conservation actions. But the only large carnivore conservation project sponsored by the central government is the National Tiger Conservation Authority and the only major State-sponsored conservation activity is that for the lion in Gujarat. Lesser known carnivores or even large ones such as the Honey Badger or Clouded Leopard have had little research and conservation attention.

Forest degradation affects large carnivores as does poaching for their parts, such as tiger skin and bones, bear bile, leopard pelt, otter skin and mongoose hair. Another key threat is the loss of their prey base by poaching or habitat loss. Besides, there is the ever growing man–animal conflict, in which sometimes large carnivores turn livestock lifters, man-attackers and man-eaters. Small carnivores suffer from forest loss, insecticides and pesticides, and an indifference to their existence.

ANJAN SANGMA/WTI

Walking the bears during rehabilitation in the wild, Manas NP, Assam

Tiger

Family: Felidae
Indian Status: Uncommon
Social Unit: Solitary
Size: HBL: 240-310 cm, Wt: 100-260 kg
Best Seen At: Ranthambore NP, Rajasthan; Kanha, Pench and Bandhavgarh NPs, Madhya Pradesh

Undoubtedly the most charismatic animal of India, the majestic tiger has a tawny orange coat patterned with broad black stripes. The stripe patterns on the body are unique in each individual.

The underparts of the tiger are pure white as are patches around its eyes and on its cheeks. The back of each ear is black with a winking white spot on it. The eyes are large, round and forward-facing, which helps the animal in the forest catch its prey- and captivates the world instantly. The whiskers are long and important for sensing. The head is set almost on to the body with a short muscled neck that combines with its long canines to bite long and deep into the prey and make it the top carnivore of the Indian forests.

Tigers vary a lot in coat colour. Melanistic (black form) and white tigers are the best-known coat variations in the tiger in India. The White Tiger, which originated around Rewa in Madhya Pradesh, was caused by a gene that inhibits yellow and red pigments while allowing black pigments to be exhibited. In nature, it does not survive but its popularity in captivity has led people to think that this is a separate species. Similarly, tigers around Odisha tend to have a rare colour variation known as 'pseudo-melanism': the black stripes appear very thick and the tawny colour is not seen as much through the black pattern.

The tiger prefers to hunt large deer, which in India mean the Sambar. However, it can

PRAVEEN MOHANDAS

White face-markings

Orange coat striped black

Long, striped tail

Tigress, Bandhavgarh NP, Madhya Pradesh

survive on smaller prey such as Wild Pig, Spotted Deer or even fish in the mangroves. Large animals such as rhinos, elephant calves and even bull Gaur are also taken. Tigers hunt at night, but in certain sanctuaries have turned diurnal, being used to tourists. They stalk their prey through high grass cover or undergrowth and, with a sudden onrush, take them down with a swipe at the neck, followed by a swift bite to the jugular.

Tigers tend to eat the prey from the backside up as opposed to leopards, which eat belly up; this can be a useful clue to identifying the predator responsible for killing prey. Tigers may attack humans if prey is unavailable, or if the tiger is old or injured. This behaviour has earned it the fearsome title of man-eater, although other mammals such as the leopard, the bear or the elephant take far more human lives in India.

Tiger, white form, marks a tree with its claws

Today, shrinking tiger numbers and habitat are major conservation issues globally and in India. It is estimated that there are only 2,200-odd tigers left in India- about 65 per cent of the world's population. Tigers are found in tropical deciduous forests (a key habitat), evergreen forests and riverine forests. In India, the tiger is distributed along the Terai foothills of the Himalayas, in north-east India, in central India the Eastern Ghats and the Western Ghats. The states of Madhya Pradesh, Maharashtra, Odisha, Bihar, West Bengal, Arunachal Pradesh and Andhra Pradesh have large tiger habitats left while those in Assam, Karnataka, Uttarakhand and Rajasthan support tigers in protected areas. In the Sunderbans, it is adapted to a mangrove habitat and in Sikkim and Arunachal Pradesh, it inhabits coniferous, oak and rhododendron forests.

Tiger, black form, Simlipal NP, Odisha

Asiatic Lion

Family: Felidae
Indian Status: Uncommon
Social Unit: Prides of 2-15
Size: HBL: 158-250 cm, Wt: 110-190 kg
Best Seen At: Gir NP, Gujarat

A large, brown cat with an unpatterned body and a long naked tail with a tuft at the tip, the lion is an unmistakable feline. It is also the only cat in which the male possesses a mane, which is one of the easiest-to-see differences between the African and Asian subspecies. The male African lion has a full mane around its head and neck while the male Asiatic Lion's mane is thinner than the African Lion's, with the ears more clearly visible. The mane is usually around the cheek and chin, leaving the head slightly bald. Manes can vary in colour from pale blonde to jet black, both as a sign of age or as just a variation.

Lionesses are coloured similar to males, but are slightly smaller and do not have a mane. Cubs have a faint spotted pattern that fades as they mature.

The Asiatic Lion is less social than the African Lion although both are the only cats that live in groups called prides. These prides have 2-5 females and their young. Males join in only to eat and mate. Cattle contribute significantly to the lion's diet in Gir in Gujarat. This has changed somewhat from being mostly livestock In the early 1970s, and mostly ungulates in the late 1980s.

The Asiatic Lion had a close brush with extinction as its numbers plummeted to around 20 about 100 years ago. Like the One-horned Rhinoceros, the lion has staged an amazing return. Today, there are around 400 lions only in a single, tiny pocket in Gujarat and their number is increasing. They inhabit dry teak forests and scrub jungle and are found in the Greater Gir area of Gujarat.

Bald head

Mane around cheeks and chin

VIVEK MENON

Asiatic Lion male, Gir NP, Gujarat

Golden tawny coat

Asiatic Lion female looks up, Gir NP, Gujarat

VIVEK MENON

Common Leopard

Family: Felidae
Indian Status: Occasional
Social Unit: Solitary
Size: HBL: 180-243 cm, Wt: 30-77 kg
Best Seen At: Gir NP, Gujarat; Sanjay Gandhi NP, Borivili (Mumbai), Maharashtra

The leopard has a clear gold to tawny coat marked with black rosettes or 'flower patterns'. The rosettes are unique to each leopard. More like large solid spots on the limbs and face, on the body they become rosettes with a darker tawny centre than the coat.

It has a small, spotted head, powerful jaws and a long tail, and a white underside. It uses its hearing and smell, rather than its vision, in survival. 'Melanistic' or 'black form' leopards have dark rosettes against a dark brown or black background. Even in the black ones, the rosettes can be seen from up close. These animals are popularly called 'black panthers', but they are no different from leopards.

The Common Leopard is good at hunting langurs up in trees, and also at feeding on hares, rodents and even birds like peafowl and junglefowl. It hunts both in the day and at night. As they are often seen near rural habitations (where they prey upon cattle, dogs and even children), they are mistakenly thought to be not under threat. Leopards live in forests, scrub jungle, open country and near human habitation throughout India except in dry parts of Kutch and Rajasthan, and the high Himalayas.

VIVEK MENON

Cheetah

CHEETAH

One of the fastest predators of the Indian plains, the Cheetah (whose name means that which bears 'chith' or spots) became extinct in India in the 20th century. The Cheetah is taller than a leopard and has a longer tail, but its head is smaller. Its yellow body is stippled with black spots (not rosettes) and a black 'tearline' runs from the eye to the upper lip. It resorts to a short, fast burst of speed to capture prey (and not stealth like the leopard), thus making it the fastest mammal in the world. There is an ongoing project to reintroduce Cheetahs to India.

MANOJ DHOLAKIA

Long, white-tipped tail

Black rosettes on tawny coat

Common Leopard male with Chital kill, Gir NP, Gujarat

Snow Leopard

Family: Felidae
Indian Status: Uncommon
Social Unit: Solitary, although overlap of home ranges of males with other males and with females have both been recorded
Size: HBL: 86-125 cm, Wt: 35-55 kg
Best Seen At: Hemis NP, Ladakh, Jammu & Kashmir

One of the most aptly named animals, the Snow Leopard is adapted completely to live in snow-covered areas. It is a little smaller than the Common Leopard, with a more luxuriant coat. It has black spots on its limbs and face, and its pale smoky grey coat, with ghostly, dark grey rosettes, makes for excellent camouflage. The centres of the rosettes are darker and the pattern of rosettes of each animal is different. The pale back of the ears have black edges.

Its limbs are long and muscular, and the paws are massive compared to its body, all of which help to fell the larger prey that it often needs to hunt. An enlarged nasal cavity, which warms the air that it breathes, and dense, long fur especially on its undersides (up to 12 cm on the belly) and under the tail help this cat to live where the temperatures can dip to -40°C. The tail is long (75-90 per cent of head and body), well furred and thick and often used as a muffler by it!

It cannot roar, but can growl, cough, snarl and yeowl. Despite being a large carnivore, the harsh terrain and climate it lives in forces it to have a varied diet, including rodents, birds and wild goats. It kills every 10-15 days and possibly feeds on 20-30 adult wild goats annually. During the lean season, it goes for marmots, pikas and hare.

It inhabits mountain grasslands and scrub above the treeline. It favours lightly forested and steep, rocky terrain with cliffs through the high Himalayas from Jammu & Kashmir to Arunachal Pradesh and the trans-Himalayas of Ladakh, Lahaul–Spiti, Gangotri and Tso Lhamo. Its range overlaps the range of its large prey, the Bharal and the Ibex.

Long and furry tail

Black rosettes on smoky grey body

DHRITIMAN MUKHERJEE

Snow Leopard, Ladakh, Jammu & Kashmir

Indo-Chinese Clouded Leopard

Family: Felidae
Indian Status: Rare
Social Unit: Solitary
Size: HBL: 68.5-106 cm
(adult males are larger
than adult females),
Wt:11-23 kg
Best Seen At:
Nowhere commonly
seen

The Clouded Leopard is the smallest of the big cats in India and can reach the size of a small Common Leopard. It has a warm yellow-brown coat with grey elliptical clouds, edged with black, floating on it. These cloud marks turn into black oval spots on its legs and into blurred rings on its very long tail, which is marked with spots. Its head is spotted, with two broad bars on its neck and stripes on its cheek. The back of each ear is black with a grey spot in the middle. The Clouded Leopard's short legs give it a heavy appearance, but it is one of the most lithe of the big cats. It can hang from tree branches by its hind legs and tail, and clamber down tree trunks head first. It has broad pale feet. Among felids, it has the longest canine teeth in proportion to its skull size, reaching up to 4 cm in the upper jaw.

A very secretive cat, it is rarely seen in the wild. Unlike other leopards, it does not leave telltale scats and scrapes along its trails. Very arboreal, it ambushes prey from trees and drags the kill up to eat. Monkeys are an important part of the diet. It also shelters its young in tree hollows. It lives in tropical forests in north-eastern India though the exact distribution is not known.

Indo-Chinese Clouded Leopard, Ripu-Chirang, Greater Manas, Assam

Black cheek stripes

Cloud-like markings edged black on tawny coat

SASHANKA BARBARUAH/WTI

Asian Golden Cat

Family: Felidae
Indian Status: Rare
Social Unit: Solitary
Size: HBL: 66-105 cm,
Wt: 8-15.7 kg
Best Seen At: Nowhere
commonly seen

Normal golden brown
coat colour

Asian Golden Cat, Pakke TR,
Arunachal Pradesh

This medium-sized cat, mostly with an unpatterned golden coat, looks like a miniature North American Puma in general appearance. The golden colour is broken only by a broad white moustache-like stripe, two white stripes lining the inner rims of the eyes, and a white line on the end of the tail. The tail tip is black on the top.

It is a terrestrial species by habit but can climb well. It takes down large prey, sometimes including domestic sheep, goats and buffalo calves. It is found in tropical forests in southern Himalayan north-east India.

Marbled Cat

Family: Felidae
Indian Status: Rare
Social Unit: Solitary
Size: HBL: 45-60 cm,
Wt: 2-5 kg
Best Seen At: Nowhere
commonly seen

Pale-edged
cloud marks

Long tail, shorter
than Clouded
Leopard's

Marbled Cat, Namdapha NP,
Arunachal Pradesh

A miniature version of the Clouded Leopard, the Marbled Cat is one-third the size of the former. It has a shorter, rounder skull and a long tail equal to the length of its own body (the Clouded Leopard has a tail longer than its own body). The fur colour is variable in its grey or reddish colour but has a brownish yellow background. Blotches or patches are found all along the body. These patches have pale borders unlike the black-edged pattern of the Clouded Leopard. There are black spots on its legs and tail.

It has a typical arched-back stance when it freezes or is resting. Due to its arboreal nature, birds as well as rodents and smaller mammals are part of its diet. It is found in tropical forests of north-east India.

Caracal

Family: Felidae
Indian Status: Rare
Social Unit: Solitary
Size: HBL: 60-105 cm,
Wt: average 6 kg
Best Seen At:
Ranthambore and
Sariska NPs, Rajasthan

Tall and slender, the brick-coloured Caracal is one of two cats with a plain coat, the other being the Golden Cat. Its short fur is pinkish brown on the back, and buff on the undersides and limbs. It has two black bars above its eyes and at the corners of its mouth, and white around the eyes and nose. Its most striking feature is its long, narrow, black-tufted ears up to 5 cm long.

It can be confused from a distance with a large Jungle Cat, but the Caracal is taller, with longer legs and unique ears. This open-country cat relies largely on speed and agility rather than stealth, to capture prey. It is found in scrub and broken, rocky areas in dry parts of Punjab, Haryana, Rajasthan, Gujarat and Madhya Pradesh.

Long tufted ears, black at back

Buff-pink coat may be faintly spotted

G.S. BHARDWAJ

Caracal, Ranthambore NP, Rajasthan

Asiatic Wildcat

Family: Felidae
Indian Status: Uncommon
Social Unit: Solitary
Size: HBL: 47-60 cm,
Wt: 3-4 kg
Best Seen At: Desert NP, Rajasthan

The closest relative of the domestic cat, the Asiatic Wildcat is small and spotted, unlike its striped European counterpart. It has a pale sandy fur colour with black spots all over its body. The underparts are whitish. There are two clear, black markings on its cheeks and the inner side of its forelimbs. The long, black-tipped tail has spots near the base and rings near its tip. On the whole, the cat is long-legged, long-tailed and long-bodied compared with domestic cats. It is the only cat that lives in a burrow system like foxes. It is found in scrub forest, semi-dry and desert areas, and cultivated areas in dry parts of Rajasthan and Gujarat.

Short ears, small tuft

Black-ringed tail

JUGAL KISHOR TIWARI

Asiatic Wildcat, Kutch, Gujarat

Eurasian Lynx

Family: Felidae
Indian Status: Rare
Social Unit: Solitary
Size: HBL: 80-110 cm,
Wt:15-29 kg
Best Seen At: Nubra
River Valley, Ladakh,
Jammu & Kashmir

India forms the southern edge of the range of the Eurasian Lynx. It has a buff or sandy grey coat that is spotted profusely. Forms with unpatterned or larger-spotted coats or with rosettes are known, but they are not common in India. The Lynx can be told apart from other mountain cats by its long, black ear tufts (up to 6 cm). The roundish face has sideburns. The body is thick with long hind legs and slightly shorter forelegs. The tail is short, only reaching its knees. It shelters in willow and reed patches. It lives in cold desert, scrub woodland and barren rocks above the treeline in Ladakh, Jammu & Kashmir, and Sikkim.

Long, tufted ears

Sideburns

Spotted body on sandy grey coat

GEORGE SCHALLER

Eurasian Lynx

Pallas's Cat

Family: Felidae
Indian Status: Rare
Social Unit: Solitary
Size: HBL: 45-65 cm,
Wt: 2.5-4.5 kg
Best Seen At: Nowhere commonly seen

Also known by its German and Russian name of Manul, this is a greyish cat with white tips to its hairs, giving it a frosted look. Like the Snow Leopard, it has very long fur on its undersides and tail to keep it warm in its frozen habitat. Its flat head with small, rounded ears set wide apart (almost at its cheeks), gives it a low profile that helps it hunt stealthily in open mountainous areas. It has two stripes on its cheeks up to the eyes, and spots on the head and forehead. The thick black-tipped tail has broad rings. The legs are short and stout. It is known to use the dens of foxes or marmots, and also rock crevices or caves for shelter. It is found in open rock-strewn mountain grasslands in Ladakh and Sikkim.

PRANAV CHANCHANI

Black-tipped, long, ringed tail

Flat head, small ears

Pallas's Cat, Tso Lhamo, Sikkim

Jungle Cat

Family: Felidae
Indian Status: Locally Common
Social Unit: Solitary and pairs
Size: HBL: 60-85 cm, Wt: 2-12 kg; average weight in India: 4 kg
Best Seen At: Ranthambore NP, Rajasthan; Kaziranga NP, Assam

The most common wild cat in India, the Jungle Cat is buff or grey-brown and unmarked except for faint red stripes running across the forehead and on the outer side of the legs. The fur has black tips, giving it a grizzled look. The face is slim and the muzzle has some white on it. Its eyes are ringed with white, with a dark tear stripe running down each cheek. The medium-sized perked-up ears, shorter than the Caracal's, have a reddish back and short black tufts of hair on the tip. It has two black stripes on its lanky forelegs, and its black-tipped tail, which is shorter than that of a domestic cat, has black rings towards the end.

Kittens are marked all over the body for the first few months and their ears are dark reddish brown in colour.

The Jungle Cat can hunt animals much larger than itself, such as porcupines or Chital fawn. However, it can also live on very small prey such as lizards, small snakes, mice, rats and frogs.

It prefers grassland, scrub, dry forests as well as semi-urban areas and villages throughout India, except deserts.

G.S. BHARDWAJ

Small black tufts on long ears (shorter than the Caracal's)

Dark marks on legs

The **Jungle Cat**, Kanha NP, Madhya Pradesh

Family: Felidae
Indian Status:
Uncommon
Social Unit: Solitary
Size: HBL: 45-75 cm,
Wt: 3-4 kg
Best Seen At: Corbett
NP, Uttarakhand

Leopard Cat

In India, the Leopard Cat is the most common small cat after the Jungle Cat from which it can be instantly told apart by its spotted body. The coat is brownish buff to ochre and the muzzle has some white in it. There are two black streaks between the eyes and ears, and two white ones between the nose and eyes. At a glance, it looks like a miniature leopard. Unlike leopards, however, it does not have rosettes on its buff coat. Instead, it has solid black spots or patches throughout the body, which merge into two broad streaks at the shoulders. Its limbs, longer than those of other cats, give it a graceful look. The tail is ringed and tipped black at the end.

An extremely versatile cat, it is arboreal by nature and is also comfortable in water. It is found in grassland, scrub and forests, even close to human habitation, in the Himalayas and Terai, the North-East and southwards to the Western Ghats.

NCF CAMERA TRAP/
COURTESY APARAJITA DATTA

Spotted and
ringed tail

Leopard Cat (Himalayan and north-eastern form) Namdapha NP, Arunachal Pradesh

Fully spotted body

White spot on
back of ears

RAMITH M./WTI CAMERA TRAP

Leopard Cat (peninsular form), Craigmore, Nilgiris, Tamil Nadu

Fishing Cat

Family: Felidae
Indian Status: Rare
Social Unit: Solitary
Size: HBL: 57-115 cm,
Wt: 5-16 kg
Best Seen At: Keoladeo
Ghana NP, Rajasthan

Easily recognized by its olive-grey coat (other spotted cats are tawny), it has short legs set on a stocky body. Black elongated spots run in parallel lines over its back, merging into longitudinal stripes on its neck. Its pale cheeks have two darker stripes. This cat is larger than the Leopard Cat and Desert Cat (with which it could be confused easily) by at least a foot and has a shorter, more muscular tail ringed with black. The feet are partially webbed.

The most adept Indian cat in water, it preys on fish and waterfowl, and also hunts small prey on land. It dens in tree trunks and ground near water. It is found in wetlands, marshes, tidal creeks, mangroves, dense jungle and scrub in the Terai, Rajasthan (Bharatpur), southern Western Ghats, West Bengal (Sunderbans), the North-East and Odisha (Chilika Lake).

Olive-grey coat

Large size

ANSAR KHAN

Fishing Cat, Keoladeo Ghana NP, Rajasthan

Rusty Spotted Cat

Family: Felidae
Indian Status: Uncommon
Social Unit: Solitary
Size: HBL: 35-48 cm,
Wt:1.1-1.6 kg
Best Seen At:
Mundanthurai NP, Tamil
Nadu; Gir NP, Gujarat

The smallest cat in the world (half to three-quarters the size of a domestic cat), it has a fawn coat with rusty brown spots in neat lines on its back, head and sides. Its forehead has two longitudinal, black-edged, white stripes. Its eyes are ringed with white, and its lips, chin and undersides are white too, but may be spotted. The tail is faintly ringed with rusty bands. It is very tolerant of human habitation and even gives birth to kittens on rooftops. It is found in rocky areas, scrub, dry forests, and near human habitation throughout southern and central India, and in the west in Gujarat and Rajasthan.

Rusty, spotted coat

RAMAKRISHNAN A.

Rusty Spotted Cat, Bandhavgarh NP, Madhya Pradesh

Family: Paradoxurinae
Indian Status:
Common to Rare
Social Unit: Solitary
Size: HBL: 31-96 cm
Wt: 0.6-14 kg

Civets

Probably the most common civet in India, the **PALM CIVET**'s body colour varies from a rich cream to brownish black or jet-black. Dark brown or black spots merge into stripes on the sides and the base of the tail. It has three long stripes down its back to the tail. The face is greyish with a dark mask with varying amounts of white. A nocturnal omnivore, it has a sweet tooth for the fruit of palms, and honey. It is mainly arboreal and is found often on palm trees and so also called the 'toddy cat'. It is found in forests, wooded countryside and plantations, and in human habitations (attics and rooftops!) throughout most of non-Himalayan India except the dry west. **Best Seen At:** Nowhere commonly seen

A.M.A. NIXON/WTI CAMERA TRAP

Dark coat

Three longitudinal stripes on back

Black tail

Palm Civet, Nilgiris, Tamil Nadu

The **HIMALAYAN** or **MASKED PALM CIVET** is a dark brown to black, large hill civet with greyish buff underparts. It has a thick, black, unpatterned tail, and a black chin and throat. The face has a dark mask split by a greyish white line down the forehead, white splotches around the eye and nose and markings from the ear to the cheek. The tail is long and thick. Skunk-like, it ejects a foul-smelling liquid when disturbed. It is found in mountain forests and near human habitation in the Himalayas from Jammu & Kashmir to Arunachal Pradesh, north-eastern hills and the Andaman Islands. **Best Seen At:** Himalayan forests

WII CAMERA TRAP/COURTESY
S. SATHYAKUMAR

Pale face with black mask

Black chin and throat

Himalayan Civet,
Khangchendzonga NP, Sikkim

The largest of the civets in India, the BINTURONG'S all-black, grizzled coat is set off by long white whiskers and a white edge to its ears. It was earlier thought to be a small bear, earning it the name Bearcat. The head is speckled with grey, more so in juveniles. Females are larger than males. Mainly arboreal, it uses its muscular tail (almost as long as its head and body) to climb trees. It is strictly a dense-forest resident found in north-east India, from Sikkim to Arunachal Pradesh. Best Seen At: Nowhere commonly seen

Black, bushy and prehensile tail (capable of grasping)

Black, coarsely furred, large body

White ear edges

GOPINATHAN MAHESWARAN

Binturong, Pakke TR, Arunachal Pradesh

At first glance, the BROWN PALM CIVET looks like the Palm Civet without the markings on the face and body, but is more uniformly chocolate-brown. Its head, tail and limbs are darker, the shoulders more buff, and the sides greyer. The tail is longer. Its neck hair grows in the opposite direction to the rest of its fur – an adaptation to deter predators. Omnivorous, but mostly frugivorous, it depends on rainforest fruits. It is found in wet evergreen forests and coffee plantations in the Western Ghats south of Goa. Best Seen At Kalakkad–Mundanthurai NP, Tamil Nadu

Head, tail and limbs darker than body

SIDDHARTH RAO/ WTI CAMERA TRAP

Brown Palm Civet, Someshwar WLS, Karnataka

Brown unpatterned body

This SMALL INDIAN CIVET is buff to grey with dark spots all over its sides, which meet to form three to five lines on its back. The black-and-white ringed tail has 6-10 dark bands and a pale tip. It lacks a spinal crest and has a cream throat with two thin, dark bands across it. Its small, rounded ears are set close on top of the head, like a cat's. The young are entirely looked

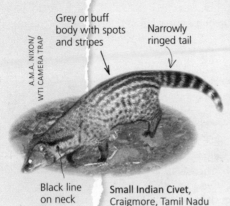

Grey or buff body with spots and stripes

Narrowly ringed tail

Black line on neck

Small Indian Civet, Craigmore, Tamil Nadu

after by the female civet and housed in a small burrow at the bottom of trees or a drainpipe near human habitation. The civet is easily tamed and, historically, was kept in many southern Indian homes as a pet and for yielding 'civet'. A stake was put next to the animal on a string. The civet rubbed its anal glands on to the stake and the resulting waxy secretion was collected by the houseowners, for use in medicines and perfumes. It is found in forests, open land, plantations and riverine habitats except wet evergreen forests and mountains throughout India, from the Himalayan foothills to Kanyakumari. **Best Seen At:** Nowhere commonly seen

The most endangered civet and possibly the most endangered mammal in India, the MALABAR CIVET was last reported from Kerala in 1990. It has a dark, standing crest of hair down its spine. Unlike the Large Indian Civet, the dark band runs to the tip of the tail. The underside of the tail has five black and white bands. The black spots on the grey coat are splotchy. This civet is most closely related to the Large Spotted Civet of South-East Asia. In the past it was found in lowland coastal forests and cashew plantations in Kerala and Karnataka. **Best Seen At:** Not sighted since 1990

Body with spots and bars

Black upright crest up to tail tip

Broadly banded tail

Dark limbs

Malabar Civet

SIMILAR SPECIES are the Spotted Linsang (Family Prionodontidae) (north-east India); Small-toothed Palm Civet (north-east India) and the Large Indian Civet (northern West Bengal and north-east India).

Striped Hyaena

Family: Hyaenidae
Indian Status: Uncommon
Social Unit: Solitary; pairs; colonies of 5-15
Size: HBL: 66-115 cm, Wt: 26-41 kg
Best Seen At: Kumbalgarh WLS, Rajasthan; Velavadar NP, Gujarat

The Striped Hyaena is a large, shaggy, buff-coloured animal. It has a thick body balanced on spindly legs. The forelegs are longer than the hind ones, giving it an ungainly slouched look.

Similar to the other three bone-cracking hyaenas in the world, it has a thick neck, large head, massive jaws and unique premolar teeth. The buff body has 5-9 black stripes on the sides, two cheek stripes, and horizontal stripes on the legs. It has coarse, long fur from the shoulder to the hindquarters and the back has a dark crest that it can raise as a threat to make itself look a third larger than normal. The fur can vary from a very light buff to grey to pale cream. The muzzle and throat are black. The tail is long and shaggy. There are four toes on each feet with non-retractable claws. The young are pale white, maneless, but with stripes.

The hyaena is known to paste white and black glandular secretions on vegetation; This is its primary means of communication. It is known for the long, laughing call that ends in a cackle, heard at nights in its habitat. Its denning sites could be caves in rocky terrain, burrows dug by it, or even those by porcupines. It lives in open scrub and dry thorn forests, often near human habitation in peninsular India, south of the Himalayas, in dry areas, except dense forests, deserts and coasts.

Long, bushy tail

Striped body and legs

Crest limp when subordinate or relaxed

ARPIT DEOMURARI

Hyaena adult female, Velavadar NP, Gujarat

Mongooses

Family: Herpestidae
Indian Status: Locally Common to Rare
Social Unit: Solitary; pairs; groups of up to 4; females with young
Size: HBL: 22-50 cm, Wt: 0.5-3.2 kg

The common **Indian Grey Mongoose** is the famed animal traditionally used in snake and mongoose shows and immortalized as Rikki-Tikki-Tavi in Rudyard Kipling's story. Its tawny grey fur is much more grizzled and coarse than that of other mongooses and each hair has 10 alternate dark and light bands. It is known for tackling venomous snakes adeptly; however, the animal is a general omnivore. All mongooses have excellent colour vision. It is found in scrub, cultivated land, rocky patches, dry forests and forest edges throughout India except the high Himalayas. **Best Seen At:** Throughout India in villages and edges of towns

Grey salt-and-pepper fur

Straight tail with pale tip

JUGAL KISHOR TIWARI

Indian Grey Mongoose, Kutch, Gujarat

The **Small Indian Mongoose** is a small, olive-brown or dark brown mongoose with golden speckles. It is slender with short legs, and its fur is short and silken. Northern and wetter habitat forms are dark brown with paler paws, while desert forms can have a pale, or even whitish, underside. The small eyes have a brown iris. Males are larger than females and have a broader head. It marks actively with its anal pad and has a variety of calls including a weep, squawk, honk, pant, spit, bark, chuck, scream and growl. It inhabits open scrub, hedges, farms, human habitation and even deserts. The **Marsh Mongoose** is found in swampy marshlands in the northern plains, extending to Kolkata, West Bengal, in the east. **Best Seen At:** Keoladeo Ghana NP, Rajasthan; Kolkata, West Bengal

Speckled coat

ANSAR KHAN

Small Indian Mongoose, Bharatpur, Rajasthan

A stocky mongoose with an iron-grey head and varying reddish tints to its body, the **Stripe-necked Mongoose** is the largest mongoose in Asia. It always has a black stripe, thinly bordered with white, from ear to shoulder on both sides of the neck. The reddish colouration increases southwards and, for e.g., in the Anamalais, it is almost a reddish creature. The tail has a black tip that, like the Ruddy Mongoose, it carries with the tip pointing upwards. It feeds on animals as small as a crab and as large as a mouse deer. It is found in forests, plantations and scrub, and likes hilly country and swampy areas or those close to water throughout the Western Ghats.
Best Seen At: Nagarhole NP, Karnataka

Iron-grey head

Black neck stripe

Grey coat

Black-tipped tail

VIVEK MENON

Stripe-necked Mongoose, Nagarhole NP, Karnataka

A large, stocky, secretive forest mongoose of the southern Indian hills, the **Brown Mongoose** is dark brown with speckled yellowish brown fur less coarse than that of the Grey Mongoose. The feet are black. The tail is very bushy and tapers to a conical point- a key feature to help identify it. It lives in forests, and nearby areas, such as coffee plantations in the Western Ghats. **Best Seen At:** Anamalais, Tamil Nadu

Yellowish speckling on brown body

KAMOLIKA ROY CHOWDHURY

Brown Mongoose, Valparai, Anamalai WLS, Tamil Nadu

SIMILAR SPECIES are the **Ruddy Mongoose** (centre, western and peninsular India) and **Crab-eating Mongoose** (West Bengal to north-east India).

Grey Wolf

Family: Canidae
Indian Status: Uncommon
Social Unit: Packs of 5-12
Size: 87-130 cm, Wt: 16-60 kg
Best Seen At: Velavadar NP, Gujarat

At first sight, it looks like a slim Alsatian with a big head, long limbs, a slightly curved tail and shorter ears. Its fur has tones of red and grey fur mixed with black. The undersides are buff or creamish. One of the largest canids of the Indian Subcontinent, it is smaller than Grey Wolves in Europe and America. The subspecies on the peninsula has less underfur and whiter lower limbs, while the Tibetan Wolf has much more underfur, a heavier build, longer muzzle, longer crest of black hair on its back, and in certain cases is black. Wolf packs communicate by howling and gestures with ears, tail, and facial muscles. They live in cold deserts of the Himalayas, dry open country, scrubland and dry grasslands in the peninsula.

Thick fur with red undertones

Bushy, black-tipped tail

VIVEK MENON

Grey Wolf, Ladakh, Jammu & Kashmir

Golden Jackal

Family: Canidae
Indian Status: Locally Common
Social Unit: Solitary; pairs; small groups of 3-5 with females and young
Size: HBL: 74-84 cm, Wt: 6.5-9.8 kg
Best Seen At: Most of India

Its scraggy, buff-grey coat is not as smooth as the fox's, nor as dense as the wolf's, and is mixed with black hair especially on the back. The head and sides of the legs are tawny red. The underside, throat and the area around the eyes and lips are white. Fur colour can vary seasonally from pale cream to tawny. The jackal is one and a half times the size of the Indian Fox and a bit more than half the size of the wolf. Though thought to be scavenger, it is a successful hunter, especially of rodents. Its eerie howls echo in the countryside and jungle. It is found in grasslands, forests, mangroves, urban and semi-urban areas throughout India except the high Himalayas.

Short muzzle

Buff coat

PRAVEEN MOHANDAS

Golden Jackal, Great Rann of Kutch, Gujarat

Wild Dog

Family: Canidae
Indian Status: Locally Common
Social Unit: Packs
Size: HBL: 88-135 cm, Wt: 10-20 kg
Best Seen At: Bandipur and Nagarhole NPs, Karnataka

A uniquely Asian reddish brown forest dog, it has shorter legs, a bushier tail, and a shorter, thicker muzzle than the wolf and the jackal. Also called the Asiatic Wild Dog, the fur on its back is rusty red, though in India it varies from sandstone in the west to brownish yellow in the north and rust-red in the south. Undersides, chest, inner legs and lips have white or cream fur. The tail, russet only at its base, is black, as is the nose. Pups are sooty brown, turning russet in three months.

Dholes hunt in packs whose numbers vary in a given area over time and are efficient predators surrounding their prey, disembowelling it within minutes of the first catch and eating it almost on the hoof, cleaning it to the bones within a few hours. Their contact call during hunting is an infrasonic whistle, which can be heard very faintly.

The Dhole is found in open woodland interspersed with grassy meadows patchily in the central Indian highlands, the Himalayas and trans-Himalayas, the North-East and southern highlands. They are not found in deserts, coasts, hilly terrain, the Terai and mangroves.

Note ear size

NIRAV BHATT

VIVEK MENON

MAYUKH CHATTERJEE

S. SATHYAKUMAR

PRANAV CHANCHANI

Note muzzle length

VIVEK SINHA

VIVEK MENON

Bushy tail with large black tip

Short red-brick coat

Long legs

Wild Dog, Bandipur NP, Karnataka

Facial proportions and coat differences among (*top* to *bottom*) Grey Wolf, Golden Jackal, Dhole, Red Fox, Tibetan Sand Fox and Indian Fox

Indian Fox

Family: Canidae
Indian Status: Occasional
Social Unit: Solitary; pairs
Size: HBL: 39-57 cm, Wt:1-3 kg
Best Seen At: Rollapadu WLS, Andhra Pradesh

The common peninsular fox, the Indian or Bengal Fox is more daintily built than the Red Fox and is told apart by its bushy, black-tipped tail. Its legs look darker than the body. The long ears are brown. There are small black hair patches, like dark smudges on the nose. The tail, which normally trails, is held parallel to the ground when the animal is in flight and raised upwards when it makes a sudden turn. It uses three types of dens: simple dens with two openings, dens under rock ledges or crevices, and complex dens with many openings. It is found in open rocky country, desert, and near human habitation and crop fields from the Himalayan foothills throughout India, except the coasts and the Western Ghats.

Greyish brown fur

Slender legs

Black smudge on muzzle

VIVEK SINHA

Black-tipped tail

Indian Fox, Rollapadu, Andhra Pradesh

Tibetan Sand Fox

Family: Canidae
Indian Status: Rare
Social Unit: Mostly solitary or pairs
Size: HBL: 49-65 cm, Wt:3-4.6 kg
Best Seen At: Sikkim trans-Himalayas

The Iron-Grey Sided Fox is another name for this high-altitude, short, squat fox. It has a unique round-faced look because of its pronounced cheek ruffs, a flattened head and very short ears. The tail is bushy and mostly grey with some upper parts being tan, and a white tip. In winter, the fur is lighter and furrier with the greys fading and the tan turning cream. A clear line separating the tan from the grey on the sides in summer is a clear difference between it and the Red Fox. It feeds on pikas, rodents and small animals. It lives in mountain grasslands, cold deserts, and uplands above the treeline in Ladakh in Jammu and Kashmir, and the Sikkim trans-Himalayas.

Flat head

Very short ears

Cheek ruffs

PRANAV CHANCHANI

Tibetan Sand Fox, winter fur, Tso Lhamo, Sikkim

Red Fox

The most widely distributed carnivore in the world, this fox varies in body colour and size. Its three subspecies found in India can be told apart from the Indian Fox and the Golden Jackal by their long and bushy, white-tipped tail and dark patches behind the ears. They have five toes on their forefeet and four on the hind feet, with long, non-rectractile claws.

The Himalayan or Hill Fox is the common fox of the Himalayas, east of Ladakh. It is fox-like-red overall and the chest, belly, muzzle and cheek have white fur mixed with the red. It develops thick underfur during the winters. The Kashmir or Afghan Fox is slightly smaller and has a rust-orange coat with dark grey fur on the throat, chest and outer part of the legs. The Desert or White-footed Fox is the smallest and lightest of the three, with short, greyish fur mixed with rust-brown hairs. They all give off a characteristic odour often referred to as 'foxy'.

It is found in varied habitats, including dry areas, mountain forests and close to human habitation in the Himalayas from Jammu & Kashmir to Sikkim, and in the dry areas of Rajasthan and Kutch, Gujarat.

Family: Canidae
Indian Status: Occasional
Social Unit: Pairs; solitary; groups up to 6
Size: HBL: 45-90 cm, Wt: 3-14 kg
Best Seen At: Himalayan hill stations, Jammu & Kashmir, Gujarat

VIVEK SINHA
VIVEK MENON
VIVEK MENON
AISHWARYA MAHESHWARI
PRANAV CHANCHANI
VIVEK SINHA

Fox-like red colour

Thick coat

White tail tip

WII CAMERA TRAP/ COURTESY S. SATHYAKUMAR

Red Fox, Khangchendzonga NP, Sikkim

Tail differences among Indian canids (*top* to *bottom*) Grey Wolf, Golden Jackal, Dhole, Red Fox, Tibetan Sand Fox and Indian Fox

Asiatic Black Bear

Family: Ursidae
Indian Status: Uncommon
Social Unit: Solitary; mother with cubs
Size: HBL:110-190 cm, Wt: 35-250 kg
Best Seen At: Dachigam NP, Jammu & Kashmir

A large forest-dwelling bear of the Himalayas, this bear is also called the Moon Bear due to the crescent-shaped creamy or white mark on its glossy black chest. Its black fur is much shorter than that of the other black bear of India, the Sloth Bear. Its muzzle is shorter and tan-brown, the brown colour stopping short below the eyes, and its chest marking is crescent shaped instead of 'V' shaped and extends all the way to its armpits.

It has longer hairs in the neck region, probably an evolutionary adaptation to escape the bites of predators such as tigers. It has noticeable powder-puff ears and a very short tail. The feet are large with black pads and make the largest tracks among Indian bears. The claws on its digits are pronouncedly curved but shorter than those of the Brown and Sloth Bears. The Asiatic Black Bear is much more arboreal than Brown or Sloth Bears, climbing trees to feed on fruit or honey or escape intrusion, though it does not sleep on trees like the Sun Bear.

It prefers heavily forested broadleaved and coniferous forests and uses orchards, agricultural fields and human habitation to move between forest patches. It is found throughout the Himalayas from Jammu & Kashmir to Arunachal Pradesh and in hilly regions of other north-eastern States (Assam, Meghalaya, Mizoram, Nagaland and Tripura).

VIVEK SINHA

Powder-puff ears

Black glossy coat

Buff snout

Thin white crescent mark

Asiatic Black Bear adult male, Dachigam NP, Jammu & Kashmir

Sloth Bear

Family: Ursidae
Indian Status: Locally common
Social Unit: Solitary
Size: HBL: 140-190 cm, Wt: 45-95 kg
Best Seen At: Mudumalai WLS, Tamil Nadu; Daroji WLS, Karnataka

This widespread peninsular bear was unfortunately familiar to most Indians as the performing bear in the streets, a practice which has now been stopped. A forest bear with a long snout and long, shaggy hair, the Sloth Bear is so named because of its lumbering gait. The hair is black, long and matted, and the all-black look is broken only at four places; its cream to dirty yellow long muzzle, its white, V-shaped chest marking, off-white patches at the ends of the limbs, and the ivory-coloured claws. The hair is particularly long over the head and shoulders, giving it a maned appearance. The front legs are bowed. The tail is slightly longer than that of other Indian bears.

This bear uses its long claws to tear up termite mounds, and sucks up termites and ants through the gap in its arrangement of teeth due to its missing front incisors. It can be lethal if confronted as it is dim-sighted and rears up on its hind legs and bites or claws when alarmed.

It inhabits a wide variety of habitats including forest, scrubland and grassland in peninsular India, south of the Himalayas up to Assam in the North-East in a patchy fashion. It is absent in the high Himalayas, the western desert, and some areas of southern and central India.

Long, tan muzzle

Long, black, shaggy coat

Bowed limbs

SUSHOVAN ROY/WTI

Sloth Bear

Himalayan Brown Bear

Family: Ursidae
Indian Status: Rare
Social Unit: Solitary
Size: HBL:150-280 cm, Wt: 80-550 kg
Best Seen At: Great Himalayan NP, Himachal Pradesh

Pronounced hump

Reddish brown coat

Very large size

India's largest terrestrial carnivore, this bear is much smaller than its more famed relatives, the Grizzly and the Kodiak Bears. It has a thick, reddish brown coat with no clear chest markings. The coat is shorter in summer and longer in winter, with hair as long as eight inches. Its claws are white unlike the black of the Himalayan Black Bear. It is the least arboreal bear and is mostly terrestrial. It hibernates in winter. Not a forest animal, it inhabits mountain scrub and meadows above the treeline in Jammu & Kashmir, Himachal Pradesh and Uttarakhand.

VIVEK MENON

Himalayan Brown Bear female

Sun Bear

Family: Ursidae
Indian Status: Rare
Social Unit: Solitary
Size: HBL: 100-150 cm, Wt: 30-80 kg
Best Seen At: Nowhere commonly seen

Yellow, U-shaped mark

Pale face mask

A small forest bear of South-East Asia, it is identified by its small size, short black coat, U-shaped chest mark, protruding lips and bowed legs. The muzzle is grey to cream and the colour extends onto the face above the eyes, making it look like a mask. It is also called the Dog Bear as it looks like a large dog. It uses its very long tongue (25 cm) to lick out grubs from tree holes and honey from hives.

The most arboreal of Indian bears, it makes nests of bent branches in trees to sleep in. It uses its long claws for digging and tearing up bark, and thrusts its arms into termite mounds to lick the insects off its paws. It lives in forests and is known from patchy sightings and camera-trap photos in Arunachal Pradesh, Assam, Mizoram, Nagaland and Manipur.

BRIJ KISHOR GUPTA

Sun Bear

Red Panda

The Red Panda is one of the most striking creatures of India's north-eastern forests. Its chestnut-coloured body is contrasted by the white snout, inner ears and cheek patches. The cheek mask has chestnut 'teardrop stains,' which along with its large, liquid brown eyes, give it a special appeal. Its tail is ringed with six light and dark chestnut and buff bands. The chest, underparts and legs are black.

It is unique in India in having white furred soles. It has strong, inwardly curved paws and semi-retractile claws. This and a false thumb (like the Giant Panda's), and the ability to rotate its ankle more than other tree-living carnivores, help it to climb trees and come down headlong. Newborns have thick buff fur and turn to adult colouration in around two months.

It scent-marks its territory with urine, droppings and secretions. Communication is through a wide range of squeaks, snorts and whistles. It feeds only on fresh bamboo leaves at the stalk base and does not eat the stalk itself as the Giant Panda of China does. It lives in dense forests with thick bamboo and rhododendron undergrowth in Sikkim, northern West Bengal, Meghalaya and Arunachal Pradesh.

Family: Ursidae
Indian Status: Rare
Social Unit: Solitary; groups of 3-5 related individuals
Size: HBL: 50-73 cm, Wt: 3-6 kg
Best Seen At: Singalila NP, West Bengal

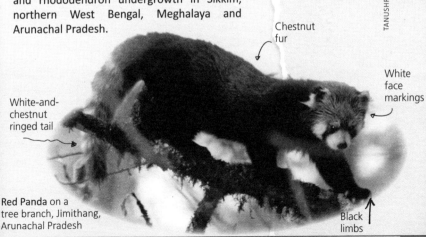

TANUSHREE SRIVASTAVA

Chestnut fur

White face markings

White-and-chestnut ringed tail

Red Panda on a tree branch, Jimithang, Arunachal Pradesh

Black limbs

Badgers

Family: Mustelidae
Indian Status: Uncommon to Rare
Social Unit: Solitary
Size: HBL: 33-77 cm, Wt: 1-14 kg
Best Seen At: Kaziranga NP, Assam; Melghat NP, Maharashtra

Probably the commonest badger of the North-East, the Hog Badger looks like an odd cross between a Wild Boar and a small bear. Its coat is a uniform grizzled grey in contrast to the Honey Badger's (its closest relative) double colouration. The snout is longer, giving it a pig-like look. The whitish face has two dark stripes through its eyes. Its throat is pale and it has a black streak on the cheek. It has prominent white ears and its legs and head are darker than the rest of its body. The tail and claws are white unlike the Honey Badger's black ones. It relies more on smell than sight and runs awkwardly like a bear when running. Besides using its teeth and claws in defence if cornered, it releases a pungent odour. It is found in well-wooded countryside and forests in north-east India. **Best Seen At:** Kaziranga NP, Assam.

DHRITIMAN MUKHERJEE

White tail

Hog Badger, Kaziranga NP, Assam

A large, pied badger, the Honey Badger or Ratel has a broad streak of unwashed silver-grey from the crown to the base of the tail, with the underparts being deep brown or black. The fur is short and coarse yet glossy. The head is broad, the snout small and the ears are flattened flaps, giving it a boxer's face. The forefeet are adapted for digging. The Ratel is said to dig up graves- a local belief that is based on its scavenging habits. It is also a predator that feeds largely on flesh, supplemented by a vegetarian diet. It is found in hilly, stony, dry country, and forests from the Himalayan foothills to southern India. **Best Seen At:** Melghat NP, Maharashtra.

MAYUKH CHATTERJEE

Broad silver streak

Honey Badger

SIMILAR SPECIES are the **Small-toothed/Chinese Ferret Badger** (northern West Bengal and the North-East) and **Large-toothed Ferret Badger** (the North-East).

Martens

Family: Mustelidae
Indian Status: Rare to Locally Common
Social Unit: Solitary; pairs, trios; up to five
Size: HBL: 40-70 cm, Wt: 1-3 kg

Only slightly bigger than a giant squirrel, the Beech or Stone Marten is long and weasel-shaped, and lighter in colour than the other Indian martens, varying from liver-brown to drab tawny brown. The neck is white or pale yellow, split into two or patterned by the body colour spreading into the white. It creeps like a cat due to its short legs and often raids hen coops. It is found in mountain forests, open stony ground above the treeline and near habitation in the western and central Himalayas. **Best Seen At:** Ladakh, Jammu & Kashmir

Prominent white throat and chest patch

Short, stalky tail

MAYUKH CHATTERJEE

Stone Marten

The common forest marten of India, the Yellow-throated Marten is colourful, and easily told apart by its long tail and colouration. It has a black face, crown, tail and legs. The rest of the body is made up of shades of yellow. The throat is the brightest part of the yellow on the marten. Bold and agile, this marten hunts with equal ease on trees as well as on the ground. It is found in forests in hilly areas of the Himalayas. **Best Seen At:** Kedarnath WLS, Uttarakhand

Yellow throat, chest, shoulders and back

MAYUKH CHATTERJEE

Yellow-throated Marten

The largest and rarest Indian marten, the Nilgiri Marten is a dark brown to black animal with a pale yellow to bright yellowish orange neck and a flat skull, with a depression on its forehead. The yellow is limited to the underside of the neck and chest, down to the upper front legs. it is found often at tree canopy level but is equally terrestrial. A native of the Western Ghats, it is found in mountain and evergreen forests. **Best Seen At:** Eravikulam NP, Kerala

Black face

N.A. NASEER

Canary yellow neck and chest

Nilgiri Marten, Pambadum, Shola NP, Kerala

Otters

Family:
Mustelidae
Indian Status:
Near Uncommon
to Locally
Common
Social Unit:
Solitary; mother
and offspring;
paired couples;
small groups of
4-11; a pair and
several litters
could form
each pod
Size:
HBL: 36-80 cm,
Wt: 2-12 kg

The most common otter of India, the Smooth-coated Otter is easily identified by its grey-brown coat with a clear line separating it from a lighter (normally grey) underside. The lips, cheek, throat and chest are of this lighter colour. Its paws are brown but lighter than the body. The tracks of the Smooth-coated Otter are bigger than other Indian otters. Spraint or toilet sites may smell of rotten fish.

Essentially a creature of the plains, it inhabits lakes, rivers, dams, irrigation canals and swamps throughout India, with the exception of the high Himalayas and the dry parts of north-west India and the Deccan. They are as much at home in deep dam sites as in shallow, flooded rice paddies and mangroves but may prefer less fast-flowing waters than the Eurasian Otter. They also prefer sloping banks with vegetation. Best Seen At: Chambal WLS, Uttar Pradesh; Periyar NP, Kerala

The Eurasian Otter is a large otter with a coarse, dusky brown coat that looks shaggy when dry and bedraggled when wet, but never as smooth as the Smooth-coated Otter's. The tail is long, over half the head and body length, and is conical and not flattened as in the Smooth-coated Otter. The five toes have strong claws and webbing, and it is known to underwater with its forepaws and hind paws propelling it forwards. This otter is found in rapidly flowing headwaters and upstream habitats along

Grey-brown upper side

Paddle-like, flattened tail

Almost fully webbed feet

Smooth-coated Otter, Periyar NP, Kerala

VIVEK MENON

rivers, hill creeks and streams that have adequate cover in Jammu & Kashmir, Uttarakhand, Sikkim and Assam, and in southern India. **Best Seen At:** Corbett NP, Uttarakhand

Strongly webbed feet

Large size; grizzled fur

Eurasian Otter

NICOLE DUPLAIX

The smallest otter in the world, the **Small-clawed Otter** has short, spiky claws. The fur on its back is short, velvety and dark brown with a grey sheen, and its underside is light brown to yellow. The sides of its lip, chin and throat are almost white. The eyes are larger, proportional to the head, than other otters, giving it a babyish look.

The incomplete webbing on its feet makes it more dextrous in handling crustaceans. The tail is about a third of total body length and is long, thick and muscular.

Largely a crab and shellfish eater, it is not as dependent on fish for its diet and catches its prey with its paws and not mouth like other otters. It is found in rivers, streams, coastal wetlands, mangroves, marshes and flooded paddy fields in the Himalayan foothills (Himachal Pradesh), eastern (Sunderbans) and north-eastern (Assam and Arunachal Pradesh) India, and in the hills of southern India (Karnataka, Tamil Nadu and Kerala). **Best Seen At:** Periyar NP, Kerala

Cream underparts; splotches on muzzle

Small-clawed Otter, Sunderbans, West Bengal

DHRITIMAN MUKHERJEE

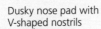

Dusky nose pad with V-shaped nostrils

Pinkish, trapezium-shaped nose pad

W-shaped nostrils

VIVEK MENON

DHRITIMAN MUKHERJEE

NICOLE DUPLAIX

Nostrils *(left* to *right):* Smooth-coated, Asian Small-clawed and Eurasian Otters

Weasels

Family: Mustelidae
Indian Status: Uncommon
Social Unit: Solitary
Size: HBL: 9-34 cm, Wt: 122 g-2 kg
Best Seen At: Nowhere commonly seen

The Mountain or Pale or **Altai Weasel** is perhaps the commonest weasel of India. Like most mustelids, it has a flat, narrow skull, a long cylindrical body, short close-set ears and short legs. It has two colour phases; brownish above and creamy yellow below in the winter, and slightly more grey in the fur on its back in the summer. Its paws are conspicuously white. Its long, spindly tail, which is 40 per cent of the head and body, is the same colour as its back. This easily distinguishes it from the other white-pawed weasels, the Stoat, which has a black tip to its tail. It winters in deep holes in the ground. It is found in mountain meadows and forests in the Himalayas from Jammu & Kashmir to Sikkim. **Best Seen At:** Ladakh, Jammu & Kashmir

Golden brown coat

BISWAPRIYA RAHUT

Mountain Weasel, north Sikkim

Pale paws

A small, chestnut-brown weasel, the **Himalayan Stoat** or **Ermine** is the smallest weasel in India. It is flecked with white, with a white chin, throat, belly and paws. Many individuals change colour dramatically to become pure white in the winter months from October to December. The tail is very short, much shorter than other weasels, giving it the other name of Short-tailed Weasel. The tail tip, however, remains black all year round, distinguishing it from all other mustelids. This weasel is active by day. It is found in pine and temperate forests; prefers banks of rivers and open rock-strewn plains near lakes in the Himalayas from Jammu & Kashmir to Sikkim. **Best Seen At:** Nowhere commonly seen

MANSOOR NABI SOFI/WTI

Chestnut-brown coat

White chest

An orange-brown animal, the **Siberian Weasel** is the largest Indian weasel and the only one with a uniformly coloured body. Its face has white flecks, and a

Pale paws

Himalayan Stoat, Wadavan Valley, Kishtwar, Jammu & Kashmir

black or dark chocolate patch from its snout to the eyes. Its throat varies from white to pale brown. A very efficient carnivore, it is found from Ladakh in Jammu & Kashmir to Uttarakhand and in the eastern Himalayas from Sikkim to Nagaland. **Best Seen At:** Nowhere commonly seen

Foxy orange coat

White muzzle and brown face mask

Pale chest

RIYAZ AHMED

Siberian Weasel, Poonch, Jammu & Kashmir

A chocolate-brown weasel, the **Back-striped Weasel** is identified by a pale silver line running along its back from head to tail, and a corresponding yellow stripe from chin to abdomen. It has a shorter and bushier tail than other weasels. Active at night, it lives in the forests of northern West Bengal, Sikkim, Assam, Arunachal Pradesh and Nagaland). **Best Seen At:** Nowhere commonly seen

Silver line on the back

ULRIKE STREICHER

Back-striped Weasel

A chocolate-brown, medium-sized weasel with a sulphur-yellow belly, the **Yellow-bellied Weasel** is one of the least-known weasels. Its upper lip, chin and upper throat are whitish, and its long tail is the same colour as its back. In Nepal, this nocturnal weasel is tamed by villagers to catch rats. It is found in forests from Uttarakhand to the eastern Himalayas and North-East India. **Best Seen At:** Nowhere commonly seen

Yellow-bellied Weasel with a rodent prey, Mishmi Hills, Arunachal Pradesh

Yellow chest and belly

Chocolate coat and tail

Brown paws

SACHIN RAI

Carnivore Paws

Tiger (Male)

Asiatic Lion

Leopard

Snow Leopard

Clouded Leopard

Jungle Cat

Leopard Cat

Fishing Cat

Caracal

Golden Cat

Pallas's Cat

Rusty Spotted Cat

Indian Fox

Yellow-throated Marten

Grey or Ruddy Mongoose

Large Indian Civet

Beech or Stone Marten

Small Indian Mongoose

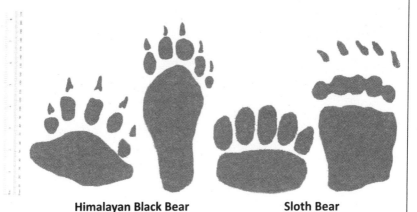

Himalayan Black Bear　　　　**Sloth Bear**

Honey Badger　　**Large Domestic Dog (Boxer)**　　**Asiatic Wild Dog (Dhole)**

Indian Wolf　　**Striped Hyaena**　　**Golden Jackal**

FIELD NOTES: Cat-walking

Which tiger do I remember the most? My first one or the closest one? The biggest one or the most aggressive? It is a difficult choice. But I do remember, on elephant back in Pakke, crossing a small nullah and suddenly from the tall grass a tiger charging across (not at the elephant, just 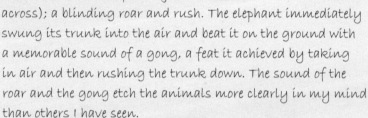 across); a blinding roar and rush. The elephant immediately swung its trunk into the air and beat it on the ground with a memorable sound of a gong, a feat it achieved by taking in air and then rushing the trunk down. The sound of the roar and the gong etch the animals more clearly in my mind than others I have seen.

Before I saw the Clouded Leopard cubs that WTI restocked into Manas National Park, I saw the beautiful beast in a cage in a damp room... four of them on the way to Myanmar, being smuggled from the North-East. This was after tailing a trader for two months, when he took me Clouded Leopard hunting. After placing the snare he set the bait of fish (not meat, which will bring the Common Leopard, he said) and then cleverly a slippery bamboo pole just shy of the trap - a speedbreaker for the cat to put its paw over and into the snare!

My closest brush with a bear was in my teenage years, trekking to Rohtang. En route were the apple orchards of the Kulu Valley. We went into one of them, wanting a bit of stolen

fruit. A Himalayan Black Bear was already there, eating fruit, and we were chased half a kilometre by it. The bear is shortsighted and what probably saved us was that we were running upwind and once he lost sight of us around a turn, we could shake off the charge. Downwind, he would have smelt us out in no time.

On a speedboat with the head of the park in Periyar we came across a pod of Smooth-coated Otters. I was just explaining the difference between the three species to the officer and that the European Otter was probably a misidentification as being found in the park. V-shaped versus W-shaped nostrils and flattened versus conical tail...the otters leapt all around us, swimming alongside the boat, gambolling on the banks and hiding beneath overhanging rocks. No place better to show ID than just there.

The only captive civet I saw was in Bali. It was kept not for farming 'civet', but for ingesting coffee seeds and defecating them. The resultant seeds were ground into a brew that was one of the most expensive coffees in the world - civet coffee. I had a cup.

HARE SKULL

MAYUKH CHATTERJEE

PIKA SKULL

HARE TRACKS

VASUNDHARA KANDPAL

Where they live

⌐ Hares,
  Pikas

**Royle's Pika, Kedarnath,
Uttarakhand**

INDIAN
LAGOMORPHS
AT A GLANCE

NUMBER
OF SPECIES **11**

BIGGEST
INDIAN HARE

Hares and Pikas

DHRITIMAN MUKHERJEE

SMALLEST
NUBRA PIKA

MOST COMMON
INDIAN HARE

MOST ENDANGERED
HISPID HARE

ACTIVITY
HARES 🌙
PIKAS ☀

What is a Lagomorph?

Hares, rabbits and pikas are small- to medium-sized herbivores, forming the order Lagomorpha. In India, what people call rabbits are actually hares. All lagomorphs have small peg-like teeth behind the incisors in their upper jaw, which are not found in any other animal. Hares, like rabbits, have 28 teeth.

Hares and rabbits are known for a peculiar type of digestion and two types of pellets that they excrete: soft pellets rich in proteins; and hard pellets of large, undigested particles of vegetation. Hares and rabbits eat soft pellets immediately after excretion. Pikas either eat them instantly, or store them after drying, to be eaten later. Hares have long limbs built for fast running and jumping, and large ears and eyes help in quick detection of predators.

Pikas or 'mouse hares' are small, brownish grey in colour, and look like guinea-pigs. Unlike hares, they have short round ears, and their hind legs are about the same size as their forelegs. They have 26 teeth.

Pikas live in large family groups in burrows, or under rock piles (smaller family). Very inquisitive, they often sit beside their burrows or on rocks, and are thus easily seen. India has seven pika species that can be told apart by their fur colour (especially behind the ears), skull shape, ear size, geographical distribution, and burrowing or non-burrowing habits.

A vole? Or a pika?

The rounded ears and short legs of pikas make them look very much like voles. But pikas are lagomorphs; voles are rodents. Pikas have small tails, unlike voles. Unlike voles, pikas eat directly with their mouths, not with their paws.

How do they move?

Pikas that live under rocks such as the Royle's Pika, run and leap. Their whiskers, longer than those of burrowing pikas, help them find their way in the dark. Meadow or burrowing pikas, like the Plateau Pika, shovel dirt with their forelimbs and burrow in the ground, and do

How do you tell a hare from a rabbit?

HARES	RABBITS
Longer ears.	Shorter ears.
Do not build nests. They scrape out 'forms' or shallow depressions in the ground.	They build nests.
Their young (called leverets) are born furred with open eyes.	Young (called kittens or kits) are born naked and blind, and need to be cared for by the mother for over 2-3 weeks.
Generally larger than rabbits.	Generally smaller than hares.

Face-off between Woolly Hares, Ladakh, Jammu & Kashmir

not leap or jump much. Hares run fast over long distances and also leap a lot, especially when fleeing predators or disturbances. They can lie camouflaged with their bodies crouched and ears laid flat on their backs when disturbed, can freeze motionless in headlights, and can run zigzag, away from danger.

▶ What do they eat?

The Indian Hare is a herbivore and feeds on grasses, vegetables from gardens and crops, including peas and groundnuts. It may travel up to half a kilometre to reach vegetation. Pikas are generally herbivores and many store food piles of flowers, grasses, pine needles and pine cones during summer, to use in winter.

▶ How do they communicate?

Pikas have shrill calls. Only the Plateau Pika and the Ladakh Pika have loud, long-distance calls among Indian pikas. The Plateau Pika is known to have a continuous, long call or song of 'tsi-tsi, tsi'. Juveniles are extremely vocal: they make a range of trills, whines, muffles and squeaks. The Ladakh Pika makes a repetitive 'piei-piei' call, the Nubra Pika has a single syllable high-pitched call and a higher-pitched alarm call, and the Royle's Pika has a repetitive, shrill whistle and a sharp alarm call. The Large Indian Pika is the most silent, although a sharp whistle and a 3-4 syllable alarm call is known. Hares are less vocal than pikas, although they also have a shrill scream in distress.

▶ How do they live?

Pikas are grouped into two broad types: the meadow-dwelling ones dig burrows in shrub and forests and meadows, are highly social animals, short-lived, with wide fluctuations in numbers over time; the rock-living type live in stony areas or those with boulders, do not burrow and are not social, living in ones and twos. They show less variation in populations.

▶ Young ones

The Indian Hare has 1-4 young. The Woolly Hare has a pregnancy period of about 42 days. One to four leverets are born with their eyes open. They are weaned (leave off mother's milk) after three weeks and are independent in a month. The Desert Hare also has 3-10 leverets. The Hispid Hare has a single young. They have a long pregnancy (37-43 days) and build shallow nests. Pikas, have a pregnancy period of 30 days. They have one or two litters yearly of 2-5 young, born naked, with eyes shut, and are weaned in 30 days.

▶ Threats and conservation

The Indian Hare is hunted for its meat throughout India by locals who use dogs, traps and snares. Habitat destruction, especially by forest fires, is another threat. Livestock grazing and thatch collection are other threats to their habitat.

Family: Leporidae
Indian Status: Locally Common
Social Unit: Solitary or pairs
Size: HBL: 33-53 cm, Wt: 1.8-3.6 kg
Best Seen At: All peninsular forests

Indian Hare

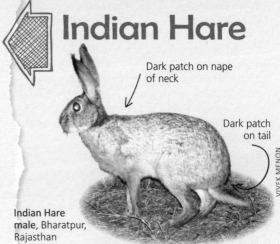

Dark patch on nape of neck

Dark patch on tail

VIVEK MENON

Indian Hare male, Bharatpur, Rajasthan

Large, erect ears

Rufous body colouration

N.A NASEER

Indian Hare male, Chinnar WLS, Kerala

This typical hare of the Indian Subcontinent is reddish brown with black hair mixed throughout its face and back. It has long, oval ears, with clear veins showing against the ears' thin skin. Its legs are long, and the hind legs longer than the forelegs. Females are larger than males. A very territorial hare, it defends up to 100,000 sq. m of land against rival males.

It uses many shelters daily. This shy hare is active mainly during twilight to night.

It is found in open scrub, grass patches and forest land except in high altitudes and mangroves in the Himalayan foothills in peninsular and north-east India.

Desert Hare

Family: Leporidae
Indian Status: Uncommon
Social Unit: Unknown
Size: HBL: 40.1–48 cm
Best Seen At: Ladakh, Jammu & Kashmir

This slim brown hare takes over from the Indian Hare at high altitudes. It has straight hair, unlike the Woolly Hare, and is more uniformly brown with little grey in the fur. It is a slighter, longer-limbed and long-eared animal without the pale grey rump of the Woolly Hare. It is basically crepuscular (active before dawn and after dusk) but can be seen in the day. It is found in mountain shrub, open rocky areas and deserts in Jammu & Kashmir.

No dark patch on neck

Black tail top; dark rump

Woolly fur

White eye ring

MARK BIBBY

VIVEK MENON

White tail

Woolly Hare, Ladakh, Jammu & Kashmir

Desert Hare leaps away, outside India

Woolly Hare

Family: Leporidae
Social Unit: Solitary; pairs
Size: HBL: 40-58 cm, Wt: 2.5-3 kg
Best Seen At: Ladakh, Jammu & Kashmir

A plump, moderately large, grey-faced hare with thick, curly fur, reddish brown limbs and chest, and a back grizzled with brownish grey fur. Its tail is brown above and dirty white below. The ears are long and grey with black patches at the tip. It has white eye rings. It takes cover in marmot burrows. It is found in mountain meadows and plateaus in Ladakh and Sikkim; it prefers open, rocky terrain in the valleys of Jammu & Kashmir.

Hispid Hare

Family: Leporidae
Indian Status: Rare
Social Unit: Solitary; pairs
Size: HBL: 40-50 cm,
Wt: 1-3 kg
Best Seen At: Nowhere
commonly seen

Brown, large and endangered, it has a white belly and a sprinkling of dark hairs, making the back look dark and grizzled. It has shorter, rounded ears and smaller hind legs than the Indian Hare. It does not have the flashing white underside to the tail, and is slower-moving, with rounded droppings, unlike the slightly tapered pellets of the former. Being small-limbed, it has a smaller home range than other hares. Its pellets are normally seen near grass cuttings. The only endemic hare of the Indian Subcontinent, it is found in scattered protected areas of the Terai grasslands in the Himalayan foothills from UP through Bihar and north Bengal to Assam and Arunachal Pradesh.

Large, dumpy brown body with bristly fur

Short ears

VIVEK SINHA

Hispid Hare,
Manas NP, Assam

Indian or Royle's Pika

Family: Ochotonidae
Indian Status: Locally Common
Social Unit: Pairs with offspring
Size: HBL: 15.5–20.4 cm,
Wt: 100-150 g
Best Seen At: High-altitude villages of Uttarakhand

The most common pika of the Himalayas, it is moderately large and richly coloured. It has a reddish-brown–grey body, a chestnut head, shoulders and upper back, reddish purple throat and greyish white to dark grey underparts. The reddish colouration fades in winter. It has moderately sized ears with sparse hair. It does not burrow but moves through existing burrow systems in rocky and scree slopes. It constructs hay piles, hoards food for winter and it is active mainly during twilight. It is found in rocky or broken ground, pine or rhododendron forests, and rock walls in human habitation in southern Ladakh and other regions of Jammu & Kashmir, Himachal Pradesh, Uttarakhand, northern West Bengal and Sikkim.

Rich russet summer coat

Greyish winter coat

SURESH ELAMON

Royle's Pika, Valley of Flowers, Uttarakhand

Large-eared Pika

Family: Ochotonidae
Indian Status: Locally Common
Social Unit: Pairs with offspring
Size: HBL: 15–24 cm, Wt: 120 g
Best Seen At: Lower Hundar, Nubra, Ladakh, Jammu & Kashmir

Often confused with the more common Royle's Pika, this is pale brownish grey with an ochre tinge. In winter, the fur turns a straw-grey. Underparts are dirty white. The ears are broader with long hairs inside. It is found in high mountain areas in the Himalayas: Ladakh to Arunachal Pradesh (higher than Royle's).

Large ears with long hair in them

Black lip and nose (in many individuals)

Grey-brown, with some russet in coat

Deep sandy brown coat

SUNITA KHATIWARA

GEORGE SCHALLER

Large-eared Pika, Kyongnosla Alpine Sanctuary, Sikkim

Plateau Pika

Plateau Pika

Family: Ochotonidae
Indian Status: Occasionally seen
Social Unit: 3-4 animals in a family unit
Size: HBL: 14-19.2 cm, Wt: Unknown
Best Seen At: Tso Lhamo, Sikkim

This is small and sandy brown with paler, yellowish brown underparts. It has distinctive facial markings, with a rust patch behind each ear, a black-tipped nose with a buff patch above the nose, and black lips (giving it the name Black-lipped Pika). A very social animal, it lives in a family unit in burrows. It is found in open grasslands and cold desert areas in north Sikkim, and eastern and northern Ladakh in Jammu & Kashmir.

SIMILAR SPECIES are **Ladakh Pika** and **Nubra Pika** (Ladkah, Jammu & Kashmir), **Forrest's Pika** (Sikkim, Arunachal Pradesh Himalayas) and **Moupin's Pika** (Sikkim, northern West Bengal).

PANGOLIN CLAWS AND TRACKS

Grasping and Digging Claws

Front   Hind

Tracks

Front Hind

MAYUKH CHATTERJEE (ADAPTED FROM WWW.ANIMALDIVERSITY.UMMZ.UMICH.EDU & FROM PIERCE.WESLEYANCOLLEGE.EDU

Where they live

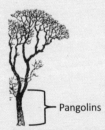

Pangolins

INDIAN
PANGOLINS
AT A GLANCE

NUMBER
OF SPECIES **2**

BIGGEST
**INDIAN
PANGOLIN**

Pangolins

Indian Pangolin, Pratapgarh, Rajasthan

G.S. BHARDWAJ

SMALLEST	MOST COMMON	MOST ENDANGERED	ACTIVITY
CHINESE PANGOLIN	**INDIAN PANGOLIN**	**CHINESE PANGOLIN**	☾

▶ What is a Pholidot?

Pangolins or Scaly Anteaters are long, armour-plated insectivores. They retreat into burrows, sealing them with soil to stay safe. They have overlapping bony scales, a long toothless snout, a protruding, sticky tongue and powerful forefeet with long claws.

▶ What do they eat?

The sticky, glue-like saliva on their tongue helps them feed on termites, ants, beetles, larvae and ant eggs. They dig out prey using the forefeet, shovelling soil back, inserting their tongue into termite mounds or onto prey, and retracting it into their snout.

▶ How do they move?

Mainly terrestrial, they do climb trees and swim. They bow their front legs and tuck the long claws under, in a shuffling walk. They use the tail as a prehensile limb to climb.

▶ How do they live?

They are mostly solitary.

▶ How do they communicate?

They hiss when disturbed. They also emit a strong musky secretion, which could be a territorial marking.

▶ Young ones

They have one or, rarely, two offspring after a pregnancy of 65-70 days. The newborn are six inches long with soft scales that harden in a few days. They start an insectivorous diet when a month old, but suckle for four months.

▶ Threats and conservation

Hunting as a delicacy by tribes and the demand for their scales in the Far East has pushed the Chinese Pangolin into IUCN's Critically Endangered list.

Grey–brown scales

Ear flaps

Naked tail tip

ANWARUDDIN CHOUDHURY

Chinese Pangolin, near Guwahati, Assam

Family: Manidae
Indian Status: Uncommon
Social Unit: Solitary; mother and offspring
Size: HBL: 54-79 cm, Wt: 2-7 kg
Best Seen At: Nowhere commonly seen

Chinese Pangolin

This is a critically-endangered, smaller, north-eastern species found over a larger area in South-East and Far Eastern Asia. Like the Indian

Indian Pangolin

Family: Manidae
Indian Status: Uncommon
Social Unit: Solitary; mother and young
Size: HBL: 60-70 cm, Wt: 9-11 kg
Best Seen At: Mudumalai WLS, Tamil Nadu; Bandipur NP, Karnataka

This is a large, Old World anteater that has a faint pinkish white skin covered on the back by a suit of 11-18 rows of dirty yellow scales. Unlike in African Pangolins, the scales are covered with reddish brown hair, and the skin can be seen only on its lower body and face. The scale colours vary in yellow and red overtones, depending on the soil it burrows in. Its nose is rounded, with large nostrils, which have flaps that can close. The tail is long and ends in a scale.

Pangolins hiss sharply if confronted and then curl into a ball, tuck away their soft parts under scales and become very difficult to 'unroll'. Without teeth, this is their main defence mechanism.

They are found in urban cultivation, grasslands and forests through most of India except deserts, the high Himalayas and the North-East.

Bronzed overlapping scales

Reddish hair on scales

No ear flaps

Long tail covered to tip with scales

SANJAYAN KUMAR

Indian Pangolin, Parambikulam WLS, Kerala

Pangolin, it has a tubular snout, muscular tail, massive forefeet and claws, and a body covered on the back with overlapping scales. The tongue protrudes 8-10 cm beyond its lips. A shorter tail and very pronounced ear flap tell it apart from the Indian Pangolin. The mother may curl herself around the offspring or sweep it under the belly, using the tail to protect it. She carries her young hanging from her tail for the first few days. It is found in grasslands, forests, bamboo groves and agricultural areas in the North-East.

TREE SHREW JAWBONE AND TRACKS

Lower Jaw

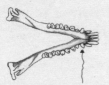

Prominent grooming incisors

Tracks

Front Hind

Squirrel or Tree Shrew?

When on trees, tree shrews can look like squirrels with long snouts: Madras Tree Shrew, Damoh Dist., Madhya Pradesh

Where they live

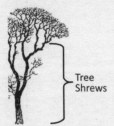

Tree Shrews

INDIAN TREE SHREWS **AT A GLANCE**

NUMBER OF SPECIES **3**

BIGGEST **NORTHERN TREE SHREW**

Tree Shrews

A Madras Tree Shrew on its hind legs, peering from the fork of a tree, Damoh Dist., Madhya Pradesh

R.P. MISHRA/WTI

SMALLEST	MOST COMMON	MOST ENDANGERED	ACTIVITY
NICOBAR TREE SHREW	**MADRAS TREE SHREW**	**NICOBAR TREE SHREW**	⚙

▶What is a tree shrew?

Tree shrews look more like squirrels than shrews, but do not have the cheek whiskers of squirrels, so you can tell them apart easily. Despite their name, they are also not as tree-dwelling as squirrels (except the Nicobar Tree Shrew). They do not jump in trees, or jerk their tails like squirrels. All 19 tree shrews of the world are found only in Asia and are identified by their long snout, large eyes, large ears with unique ear flap, a whisker-less face and a bushy tail.

▶What do they eat?

They are both insectivorous and frugivorous. They eat insects, other arthropods, fruit, bird chicks, even rodents, and drink water regularly.

▶How do they move?

They often stand up on two legs for better visibility of the surrounds. When climbing, they use their claws for gripping and their tail to balance.

▶How do they live?

Tree shrews are solitary, or in pairs during courtship and mating.

▶How do they communicate?

They express themselves with aggressive squeals, screams indicating danger, and chatters when disturbed. They scent-mark boulders, branches, even offspring,

▶Young ones

Females have between 1-4 young ones every year with a pregnancy periods of 46-56 days. The young get little maternal care and they sleep in nests separate from the mother's resting place.

▶Threats and conservation

Tree shrews suffer from habitat loss and domestic predators like cats.

Tail longer than head and body

Dark brown coat

MANIS H CHANDI

Nicobar Tree Shrew, Little Nicobar, Andaman & Nicobar Islands

Small size; tree-living

Family: Tupaiidae
Indian Status: Rare
Social Unit: Solitary; pairs
Size: HBL:13.5-19 cm, Wt: 80-170 g
Best Seen At: Nowhere commonly seen

Nicobar Tree Shrew

This is an reddish brown tree shrew, with paler underparts, nose, neck and limbs. Its tail is longer than the head and body, Nearly fully tree-dwelling and active in the day, it often feeds among birds. It is found in forests in Little and Greater Nicobar Islands.

Madras Tree Shrew

KALYAN VARMA

Also called the Southern Tree Shrew, this is a chocolate-brown shrew with pale markings around the eyes and a white shoulder stripe. Its upper parts are speckled yellow and brown near the shoulder, while underparts are greyish white. It is found in rocky areas in forests in peninsular and southern India.

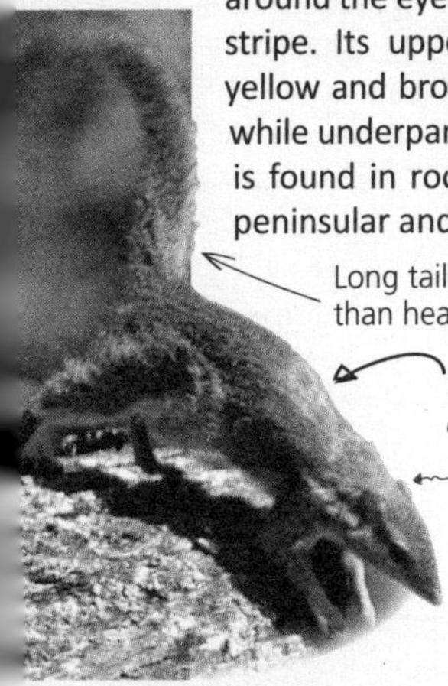

Long tail, shorter than head and body

Reddish brown coat

Hairy ears

Southern Tree Shrew, Biligiri Rangaswamy Temple WLS, Karnataka

Family: Tupaiidae
Indian Status: Uncommon
Social Unit: Solitary
Size: HBL:17.5-20 cm, Wt:160 g
Best Seen At: Nowhere commonly seen

Greyish brown coat

Buff or orange underparts

DHRITIMAN MUKHERJEE

Northern Tree Shrew, Nagaland

Northern Tree Shrew

Also known as the Malay Tree Shrew, it has an olive-brown or greyish brown coat (not much of red in it) and buff or orange underparts. The long, furry tail is equal to its head-and-body length. It feeds its young in a nest that it visits only once in two days! It is found in forests, plantations, bamboo groves and gardens in north-east India and the eastern Himalayas.

Family: Tupaiidae
Indian Status Uncommon
Social Unit: Solitary; mother and offspring
Size: HBL:17-23 cm, Wt:160 g
Best Seen At: Nowhere commonly seen

SHREWS AND MOLES FOREFEET AND TRACKS

MAYUKH CHATTERJEE (ADAPTED FROM WWW.ANIMALDIVERSITY.UMMZ.UMICH.EDU)

Mole (*top*) and shrew (*above*) forefoot

Mole (*top*) and shrew (*above*) tracks

Where they live

Shrews, Moles

INDIAN INSECTIVORES **AT A GLANCE**

NUMBER OF SPECIES **28**

BIGGEST **SHORT-TAILED MOLE**

Shrews and Moles

Hill Shrew in the forests of
Vazachal, Kerala

P.P. MOHANDAS

SMALLEST
**PYGMY WHITE-
TOOTHED SHREW**

MOST COMMON
**HOUSE
SHREW**

MOST ENDANGERED
**MILLER'S, JENKIN'S
& NICOBAR SHREWS**

ACTIVITY
**SHREWS,
MOLES**

▶What is an insectivore?

Shrews are small, mouse-like mammals. They live under fallen leaves, fallen logs, rock crevices (even underground); some species are semi-aquatic. A shrew is often mistaken for a rodent. It has a long, pointed snout (not the short muzzle of mice) and depressed conch-shaped ears (not the mice's perky triangular ears). Territorial by nature, they keep away rats and mice.

Moles are small, ancient mammals that hunt voraciously, helped mainly by their sense of smell. They live underground, rarely coming above ground. They have very small eyes, a streamlined shape, reversible hair and powerful digging limbs.

▶How do they move?

Both moles and shrews have a 'plantigrade' locomotion: they place the entire palm/sole on the ground when walking. They have five digits on each foot. Shrews scurry quickly with a jerky start-stop motion, feeding or searching for food, sniffing the air and then feeding again. Moles are slow movers on ground, but they tunnel quickly with modified forefeet to shovel earth.

▶What do they eat?

Shrews feed on small invertebrates, and sometimes on amphibians, reptiles, fish, vegetable matter and small rodents. Mainly nocturnal, they eat up to their body weight or more daily. Many species hoard food. Moles feed on earthworms, beetles, grubs, seeds and nuts.

▶How do they communicate?

Shrews communicate by a series of clicks and twitters. Moles are mostly silent, with some vibrational and chemical communication.

▶Young ones

The pregnancy period is about a month and 1-8 young are born. When led out, the young latch on to the mother's fur and siblings so tightly that one can pick up a mother and her entire caravan off! Moles have short life cycles. The pregnancy period lasts only 35 days. The young attain adulthood in 6-9 months and live to about three years.

▶Threats and conservation

They are threatened due to habitat loss and use of pesticides and insecticides close to their habitats.

Caravanning: A White-toothed Shrew characteristic

Asian Grey Shrew

Family: Soricidae
Indian Status: Locally Common
Social Unit: Unknown
Size: HBL: 6–9 cm
Best Seen At: North Indian farmlands

Medium-sized with a brownish grey back and pale yellowish grey underside, it is also called the Grey Woodland Shrew. It has a dark brown tail, prominent ears and three upper teeth. It feeds on an omnivorous diet of insects, seeds and fruits. It is found in fields, forests, farm and open land in Himachal Pradesh, Uttarakhand, Assam, Meghalaya, Mizoram, Manipur and Arunachal Pradesh.

ANWARUDDIN CHOUDHURY

Brownish grey back ↘

Asian Grey Shrew, Ranga RF, Lakhimpur, Assam

SIMILAR SPECIES are the **Kelaart's Long-clawed Shrew** (Kerala, Tamil Nadu); **Miller's Andaman Shrew, Andaman Spiny Shrew, Jenkin's Andaman Shrew, Nicobar Spiny Shrew** (all on Andaman & Nicobar Islands); **Gueldenstaedt's White-Toothed Shrew, Pale Grey Shrew, Kashmir White-Toothed Shrew/Dusky Shrew, Horsfield's Shrew** (Jammu & Kashmir); **South-East Asian Shrew** (the North-East).

House Shrew

Family: Soricidae
Indian Status: Common
Size: HBL: 10–16 cm
Best Seen At: Nowhere commonly seen

The common shrew of India, it is also called the Grey Musk Shrew because of the odour it leaves about the house. It is greyish brown, has a short, thick tail tapering to a point, and large, pink ears. This shrew is very vocal, and keeps away insects from the home. Active just after dusk, it has acute hearing but poor eyesight. It lives in burrows near homes, and in and around sewers throughout India.

Grey fur ↘

Large shrew ↘

JOYA THAPA

House Shrew, Simtham, Sikkim

Pygmy White-toothed Shrew

Family: Soricidae
Indian Status: Common
Size: HBL: 3–3.5 cm
Best Seen At: Nowhere commonly seen

SIMILAR SPECIES are Day's Shrew (Tamil Nadu) and Anderson's/Yellow-Throated Shrew (Himachal Pradesh, Uttarakhand, Rajasthan, Gujarat, Madhya Pradesh, Maharashtra and Karnataka).

One of the smallest terrestrial mammals in the world, it weighs just over two grams. It has a velvety, dark greyish brown coat with silvery brown below, large pink ears and a long tail mixed with white hair. It is found in forests all over India, except dry areas of Gujarat and Rajasthan, and Jammu & Kashmir.

Very small size, grey–brown fur on back

Large ears

Long tail with white hair

MANUEL RUEDI

Pygmy White-toothed Shrew, photo from outside India

Sikkim Large-clawed Shrew

Family: Soricidae
Indian Status: Occasional
Size: HBL: 7–9.5 cm
Best Seen At: Nowhere commonly seen

SIMILAR SPECIES are Highland/Hill Shrew (Tamil Nadu, Kerala, Karnataka); Tibetan Shrew, Eurasian Pygmy/Tiny Shrew; Flat-Headed Kashmir Shrew (Jammu & Kashmir); Blanford's Long-Tailed/Arboreal Brown-Toothed Shrew, Indian Long-Tailed Shrew, Hodgson's Brown-Toothed Shrew (Sikkim, West Bengal, Uttarakhand); Himalayan Water Shrew (Himachal Pradesh, Sikkim, West Bengal), Elegant Water Shrew (Arunachal Pradesh, Sikkim), Assam Mole Shrew (North-East).

This shrew is a large, burrowing shrew with large feet and claws and a short tail. The shrew is dark brown above and pale brown on the underside. It is mainly nocturnal, but is at times seen at dawn or dusk. Native to the Himalayas, it is found in mountain forests, scrub and open rocky areas eastwards from Kumaon in Uttarakhand to Sikkim and northern West Bengal, Assam and Arunachal Pradesh.

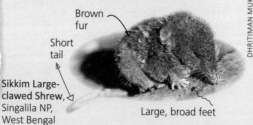

Brown fur

Short tail

Large, broad feet

DHRITIMAN MUKHERJEE

Sikkim Large-clawed Shrew, Singalila NP, West Bengal

Short-tailed Mole

Family: Talpidae
Indian Status: Occasional
Social Unit: Solitary
Size: HBL: 10–16 cm
Best Seen At: Nowhere common; seen in forest areas of Assam

Also called the Eastern or Himalayan Mole, this mole is covered with dense, black, glossy, velvety fur, except for its pinkish nose pad and large shovel-like forefeet. Its fur is flexible and can lie in any direction, helping it to scurry backwards and forwards in low burrows, without soil sticking to it. It does not shovel earth out of its burrows, so it does not leave telltale molehills. This territorial mole was once thought to be found only in the hills, but it is, in fact, a forest creature. It lives in black vegetable mould areas where the original forest cover has been destroyed in the Himalayas in Assam, Arunachal Pradesh, Mizoram, Meghalaya and Sikkim.

Dense black fur

Short, black tail

ANWARUDDIN CHOUDHURY

Short-tailed Mole, Lakhimpur, Assam

White-tailed Mole

Family Name: Talpidae
Indian Status: Rare
Social Unit: Solitary
Size: HBL: 8-11 cm
Best Seen At: Namdapha NP, Arunachal Pradesh; Balphakram NP, Meghalaya

This rare mole looks very much like the Short-tailed Mole but it is smaller and its tail is longer, widening slightly into a club shape towards the tip. The tip has white hair, giving it the name 'White-tailed Mole'. It spends time outside its burrow during the night, foraging on the forest floor. It sets territories of 100–200 sq. m. It inhabits hills and grassy and forested plains, and has been recorded from Arunachal Pradesh, Assam and Meghalaya.

Broad, paddle-like forefeet

Short, dense velvety fur

Longer white tail

TAMO DADA

White-tailed Mole, Namdapha NP, Arunachal Pradesh

HEDGEHOG PAW BONES AND TRACKS

Front

Hind

Front foot

Hind foot

Where they live

Hedgehogs

INDIAN
HEDGEHOGS
AT A GLANCE

NUMBER
OF SPECIES **3**

BIGGEST
**LONG-EARED
HEDGEHOG**

Hedgehogs

Indian Long-eared Hedgehog,
Churu, Rajasthan

VIJAY KUMAR

SMALLEST
**MADRAS OR
BARE-BELLIED
HEDGEHOG**

MOST COMMON
**INDIAN
HEDGEHOG**

MOST RARE
**MADRAS
HEDGEHOG**

ACTIVITY

▶What is a hedgehog?

Hedgehogs are small insectivorous mammals with large external ears, and small spines covering their back, which do not shed like a porcupine's. They are both fossorial (burrow-dwelling) and terrestrial. They hunt by using their sense of smell. The hedgehog seizes its prey with its teeth, half curled into a ball, with its spines erect. When the prey strikes back, it gets impaled on the spines.

▶How do they move?

The Indian Hedgehog scurries at great speed when capturing prey. It can curve its back and prick with its spines but does not leave them in a predator's body like a porcupine.

▶What do they eat?

They eat insects, frogs, snakes, spiders, scorpions, lizards, and fruits. They like dung beetles and Jujube fruits that have fallen ripe.

▶How do they communicate?

They do not call out except for a sharp hiss when cornered.

▶Young ones

Females bear one or two young. Male Collared hedgehogs have a dancing ritual that lasts many days before mating. The young are born naked in burrows, with soft spines that harden in a couple of days.

▶Threats and conservation

No major threat is known, though roadkills are reported.

Pale frosted spines

White face mask

NIRAV BHATT

Indian Hedgehog, Surendranagar, Gujarat

Indian Hedgehog

Family: Erinaceidae
Indian Status: Uncommon
Social Unit: Solitary
Size: HBL: 14-23 cm, Wt: 300-450 g
Best Seen At: Desert NP, Rajasthan

It has a masked face due to greyish white hairs on its forehead and cheeks. Its spines, arranged in 16-18 sections, have a pale tip, giving it a frosted look, and the name of Pale Hedgehog. It burrows less than the Collared Hedgehog and curls up under a Jujube bush, the fruit of which it eats. If food or water is scarce, it curls up in a burrow and sleeps for many days. It is found in dry and rocky habitats in Rajasthan and Gujarat (Kutch).

Desert Hedgehog

Family: Erinaceidae
Indian Status: Uncommon
Social Unit: Solitary
Size: HBL: 14-17.5 cm, Wt: 400-500g
Best Seen At: Desert NP, Rajasthan

A small, dark hedgehog with long legs and ears, it is also known as the Collared or Long-eared Hedgehog. The spines are dark, its belly and tail are black, giving it a brownish look. Its legs have sharp, visible claws. Males are known to eat other males and females sometimes eat their young. It lives in a burrow that it also uses to aestivate (sleep) in very hot summers or hibernate in very cold winters. It is found in semi-desert, scrub and desert areas in Rajasthan, Gujarat (Kutch) and Uttar Pradesh.

SACHIN RAI

Dark spines

Long ears

No white on face

Desert Hedgehog, Ranthambore NP, Rajasthan

Reddish spines

PUNNEN KURIAN VENKADATHU

Bare-bellied Hedgehog, Kumarakom, Kerala

Bare-bellied Hedgehog

Family: Erinaceidae
Indian Status: Uncommon
Social Unit: Solitary
Size: Unknown
Best Seen At: Nowhere commonly seen

Earlier this was thought to be a subspecies of the Indian Hedgehog, but recently it has been described as a separate species. Also known as the Madras Hedgehog, it is more reddish in appearance than the Indian Hedgehog. It is found in dry scrub and rocky hills in Tamil Nadu, Andhra Pradesh and Kerala.

RODENT SKULLS

Squirrels

Giant Squirrel

Porcupine

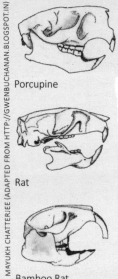

Rat

Bamboo Rat

MAYUKH CHATTERJEE (ADAPTED FROM HTTP://GWENBUCHANAN.BLOGSPOT.IN)

Where they live

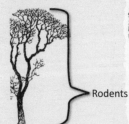

Rodents

INDIAN
RODENTS
AT A GLANCE

NUMBER
OF SPECIES **105**

BIGGEST
**INDIAN
CRESTED
PORCUPINE**

Rodents

Red Flying Squirrel pokes its head out of its nest hole, Lansdowne, Uttarakhand

SMALLEST	MOST COMMON	MOST ENDANGERED	ACTIVITY
PYGMY GERBIL	**HOUSE MOUSE, HOUSE RAT**	**MALABAR SPINY DORMOUSE**	**MURIDS** ☾☀ **SQUIRRELS** ☾☀ **PORCUPINES** ☾

▶ What are Rodents?

Rodents are a group of mammals, all with a single pair of incisors in both jaws. These teeth, adapted for cutting, grow continuously through life. The incisors are often visible in the field even in small rodents.

India has hamsters and voles in the Himalayas, gerbils and jirds in the desert, bamboo rats in the North-East, bandicoots and mice in the plains and spiny dormice in the Western Ghats.

Porcupines are known by their quills. Squirrels are medium- to large-sized rodents with long, bushy tails. Rodents also include rats, mice, hamsters, voles, lemmings, and gerbils. Totalling around 1,326 species in the world, they are found throughout the world, except certain islands and Antarctica. They are mostly small (10-80 cm), with long tails and short limbs. They are all terrestrial, but some live in trees and caves. They can be diurnal (active at daytime) or nocturnal (active at night). Hamsters are small rodents with short tails and limbs. While marmots live in colonies in complex underground tunnel systems and are diurnal, hamsters live solitarily or in small groups in burrows in sand and are nocturnal. Gerbils and Jirds are long- and furry-tailed rodents adapted to semi-dry regions and deserts, and live in colonies.

Voles are small, cylindrical rodents living a fossorial (burrowing) lifestyle in colder climates. Metads or soft, furred field rats are medium-sized South Asian species with characteristics of both house rats and wood rats, but they are not found in human habitation.

▶ How do they move?

Most rodents are quadrupedal (four-footed), but some like gerbils show bipedality (using two feet). They have speeds ranging from 10.3 kmph to 17.1 kmph on land. Giant squirrels are mainly arboreal but are known to take giant leaps of up to 20 m with outspread limbs,. On ground, gerbils are the giant leapers, clearing 1 1.5 m in a leap when alarmed.

The most evolved locomotion is that of flying squirrels, which glide from a higher to a lower branch. A squarish skin flap forms a parachute when the squirrel opens all four legs and gains speed as it falls. The tail stabilizes it in flight and slows it down on landing, when raised. They can glide for 50 m or more.

▶ What do they eat?

Rodents are largely herbivorous (they are much more grain-eating

Largest rodents

Porcupines are the largest rodents of the subcontinent, with thick and stiff modified hair, known as quills. Here, an Indian Porcupine, Eravikulam NP, Kerala

SANDESH KADUR

and fruit-eating), but some may be carnivorous too. The Indian Crested Porcupine eats tubers, roots, stems, leaves and tree bark, but it also raids crops of potato, groundnut and maize. Indian Flying Squirrels eat fruit, leaves and plant parts. Palm squirrels eat seeds in the wild along with flowers, leaves and insects. Near human habitation, it turns omnivorous, even eating cooked food.

Gerbils eat grain, roots, leaves and grass, and may be crop pests. They also eat insects, eggs and nestlings of ground birds, as well as smaller rodents.

Rats and mice eat grain. Cannibalism (the young being eaten) is not uncommon.

▶ How do they communicate?

The palm squirrels' call is one of the commonest voices with a scolding chatter, repeated frequently. Giant squirrels in forests have a loud rattling call too. Both the Hoary-bellied and Orange-bellied Squirrels have a very loud, cackling cry. Flying squirrels are very vocal at night.

Marmots utter a sharp whistling scream in alarm, warning others to get back into burrows.

▶ Young ones

The pregnancy period in rats is 18-30 days and litter size can vary between 1–22. Most squirrels build dreys or large nests of twigs and leaves high up in trees, or nest in tree hollows. Most rodents have burrows, or they breed in crevices, rock overhangs and human environments (drainpipes, irrigation ditches and sewers). For the Northern Palm Squirrel, pregnancy is of 40-42 days, with an average litter of three young ones. Among the marmots, 2-4 young are born in spring. Porcupine pregnancy is about 112 days with 2-4 young. In wood mice, pregnancy is 25-26 days; the litter is on average five. The soft-furred mice have 2-7 litters a year with 1-8 young per litter.

Rats are known for the number of offspring they have. The Indian Bandicoot may produce up to 70 young a year. The Black Rat can produce 6–7 litters a year with 13-14 young in a litter, and pregnancy

40%

of all mammals worldwide and more than 25 per cent in India are rodents!

only 21-29 days. The House Mouse has an even shorter pregnancy of 8-21 days and up to 12 young are born in a litter in underground nests.

SOS!

Rats emit ultrasonic calls as pup distress calls. Here, a Roof Rat, Upper Nilgiris, Tamil Nadu

▶ Threats and conservation

The main threat facing rodents is the lack of awareness of their true status. All rats and mice are in Schedule V of the Wildlife Protection Act, labelled as Vermin, except the Malabar Spiny Dormouse. This clumping of endangered, threatened and abundant species has made them all seem harmful to humans, but 27 per cent of all rodents globally need protection, only given to rodents such as squirrels, porcupines and marmots. Ecological threats to rodents include loss of habitat including the cutting down of large trees, introduction of non-native species, hunting for the pot in some tribal communities, and disease.

Family: Hystricidae
Indian Status: Common
Social Unit: Solitary; groups of 2-4
Size: HBL: 60-90 cm, Wt: 11-18 kg
Best Seen At: Bandipur NP, Karnataka

Indian Crested Porcupine

The commonest and largest of Indian porcupines, this heavy rodent is covered with long black and white quills and a crest of spines flowing from the forehead to the middle of its back. Its short tail ends in a bunch of thick white quills. In central and southern India, a form called the 'Red Porcupine' has quills with a rusty tinge. When it senses danger, it erects the quills on its back and rattles its tail quills menacingly. If the danger persists, it rushes backwards into its attacker, leaving quills embedded in its flesh. In big cats, this can lead to death. It is found in rocky hillsides, forests, open countryside, thick bush and tall grass throughout India except the North-East.

Multi-banded black and white quills

Long crest of black hairs

Visible tail of white quills

Indian Crested Porcupine, Craigmore, Nilgiris, Tamil Nadu

Himalayan Crestless Porcupine

Family: Hystricidae
Indian Status: Occasional
Social Unit: Solitary; groups of 2-4
Size: HBL: 45-75 cm, Wt: 8 kg
Best Seen At: Orang NP, Assam

Also called Hodgson's Porcupine, it can be told apart from the Indian Porcupine by its smaller size, shorter crest, small tail instead of a visible tail with white quills, and thinner body quills. The quills on its back have one dark band while the Indian Porcupine's have more than two. It does not rattle its tail quills like the Indian Porcupine does. It inhabits forests and forest fringes with rocky outcrops in Arunachal Pradesh, Assam, Meghalaya, Sikkim, West Bengal, Mizoram and Nagaland.

Double-banded black and white quills

Very short crest

Short tail

DHRITIMAN MUKHERJEE

Himalayan Crestless Porcupine, Manas NP, Assam

Asiatic Brush-tailed Porcupine

Family: Hystricidae
Indian Status: Rare
Social Unit: Groups of 6-8
Size: HBL: 38- 52 cm, Wt: 1.5-4 kg
Best Seen At: Nowhere commonly seen

NCF CAMERA TRAP/COURTESY APARAJITA DATTA

The smallest of Indian porcupines, it lacks the long body quills of the other species. The first third of its long, scaly tail is spineless and the rest covered in quills that seem beaded due to rice-grain-sized thick bits on them. It is nocturnal and lives underground. It inhabits forests, especially with cane, bamboo and palms, in Assam, Arunachal Pradesh and Meghalaya.

Short, spiny quill

Greyish colour

Long tail with swatch of quills at the tip

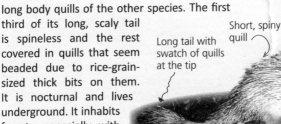

Asiatic Brush-tailed Porcupine, Namdapha NP, Arunachal Pradesh

Family: Sciuridae
Indian Status:
Locally Common
Social Unit: Groups of
pairs to families of 10-15
Size: HBL: 45-67 cm,
Wt: 4-9.2 kg
Best Seen At: Ladakh,
Jammu & Kashmir

Himalayan Marmot

Marmots are some of the world's highest living, large-bodied ground squirrels. The southernmost of these is the common marmot of the Himalayas, the Himalayan Marmot, the size of a domestic cat. It has short, coarse fur, varying from pale buff to rust, with some black hair on its back. Its has a short black-tipped brown tail. Its winter burrows, used to hibernate for six or seven months, can be as deep as 10 m. During hibernation they wake up once a month to pee or poo. They lose half their body weight during hibernation. They live in the Himalayas from Ladakh in Jammu & Kashmir through Himachal Pradesh, Uttarakhand, Sikkim and Arunachal Pradesh.

Short, coarse, rust fur with no black saddle

Short, black tipped tail

DHRITIMAN MUKHERJEE

Himalayan Marmot, Ladakh, Jammu & Kashmir

Family: Sciuridae
Indian Status: Occasional
Social Unit: Pairs or
family groups
Size: HBL: 45.5-55.5 cm,
Wt: 3-5 kg
Best Seen At: Zanskar,
Ladakh, Jammu & Kashmir

Long-tailed Marmot

A golden marmot with a long and bushy tail, it has coarse black hair spread like a saddle on its back over a base of yellow-buff or rich gold. The underparts are a rich orange-gold. The tail is more than half of the body length and a very large part of its tip is black. Eye patches of the male are larger than those of the female. It is active in the day and lives partly underground. It hibernates for half the year and comes out of its burrow only in spring. It is often seen basking on rock faces or standing like a sentry by its burrow. It lives above the treeline, mountain meadows and scrub, particularly where there is dwarf juniper, in Zanskar in Ladakh and Gilgit in Jammu & Kashmir, and in Sikkim.

Rich golden fur with black saddle

Long, black tipped tail

DHRITIMAN MUKHERJEE

Long-tailed Marmot, Zanskar, Jammu & Kashmir

Giant Squirrels

Family: Sciuridae
Indian Status: Locally Common to Occasional
Social Unit: Solitary; pairs
Size: HBL: 25-51 cm, Wt: 1.2-3 kg

There are four species of giant squirrels (the world's largest squirrels) in South and South-East Asia, of which three are found in India.

The common one is the **INDIAN** or **MALABAR GIANT SQUIRREL**, with a maroon and black back and cream/buff underparts. Rarely descending to the forest floor, they build many globe-shaped nests, for sleeping and as a nursery. They make shrill sounds, especially when mobbing predatory birds. They often sleep draped over a branch, with tails falling over. They inhabit the tree canopies in forests and dry scrub in south and central India. **Best Seen At:** Tamil Nadu; Andhra Pradesh; Kerala

Cream face

Maroon saddle on black body; maroon ears

N.A. NASEER

Black tail →

Indian Giant Squirrel, Vazhachal, Kerala

Grizzled tail ↑

The smallest of India's giant squirrels, the **GRIZZLED** or **GIANT SQUIRREL**, is brownish grey with pale hair tips, giving it a grizzled look. It feeds on young leaves, pollen and bark. It inhabits forests and mango orchards in the eastern slopes of the Western Ghats in Kerala and Tamil Nadu. **Best Seen At:** Chinnar WLS, Kerala

CHAITRA-RAJESH

Grizzled Squirrel, Cauvery WLS, Karnataka

Dark brown or black back and face ↗

Long, thick, black tail ↙

A black and buff eastern forest squirrel, the **MALAYAN** or **BLACK GIANT SQUIRREL** feeds on nuts, seeds, leaves, flowers, tree bark and fruit pulp. It does not store food. It inhabits montane forests in Sikkim, northern West Bengal, and the North-East. **Best Seen At:** Kaziranga NP, Assam

DHRITIMAN MUKHERJEE

Malayan Giant Squirrel, Kaziranga NP, Assam

Giant Flying Squirrels

Family: Sciuridae
Indian Status: Common to Rare
Social Unit: Solitary
Size: HBL: 30-49 cm
Wt: 2.2-2.7 kg

DHRITIMAN MUKHERJEE

Thick, long tail, darker at tip

Red coat

Black eye ring

Red Giant Flying Squirrel, Berajan, Assam

P.O. NAMEER

Grizzled grey back

Long, grey tail

Indian Giant Flying Squirrel

BRIJ KISHOR GUPTA

Yellow head patch extends as stripe on back

Orange tail, black-tipped

Dark chestnut upper body

Bhutan Giant Flying Squirrel, Gangtok, Sikkim

The **RED GIANT FLYING SQUIRREL** is large, and chestnut-red to reddish brown with big, liquid brown eyes. It glides up to 100 m, making a noise like rushing wind. It is found in forests through the Himalayas and in Assam, Meghalaya, Arunachal Pradesh and Manipur. **Best Seen At:** The Himalayas

The **INDIAN GIANT FLYING SQUIRREL** has a drabber coffee-brown to grey coat, grizzled with white. Between 7:30pm and 11:30pm is its most active gliding time. It is found in forests, forest edges and cardamom plantations across India, except in the Himalayas and the North-East. **Best Seen At:** Anamalais, Tamil Nadu

Large and chestnut-brown with pale reddish-brown or yellow undersides, the **BHUTAN** or **GRAY'S GIANT FLYING SQUIRREL** has a yellow patch on its crown, going down its back. It lives in forests in Sikkim, northern West Bengal and Arunachal Pradesh. **Best Seen At:** Darjeeling, West Bengal

The **WOOLLY FLYING SQUIRREL** has long silken (not woolly!) hair and a blue-grey coat. It does not hibernate and prefers rocky caves to trees in forests and grasslands from Jammu & Kashmir to Sikkim. **Best Seen At:** Nowhere commonly seen

SIMILAR SPECIES are the **Namdapha Flying Squirrel** (Arunachal Pradesh); **Spotted Giant Flying Squirrel** (east Arunachal Pradesh); **Hodgson's Flying Squirrel**, **Grey-Headed Flying Squirrel** (Sikkim, northern West Bengal and Arunachal Pradesh).

Small Flying Squirrels

Family: Sciuridae
Indian Status:
Locally Common to Rare
Social Unit: Solitary;
pairs
Size: HBL: 21.4–33.7 cm,
Wt: 240-733 g

The **KASHMIR FLYING SQUIRREL** is a small and dark flying squirrel that seems grizzled grey because it has short black hairs along with longer, pinkish buff ones. Its underside is cream. This squirrel can be distinguished from the large flying squirrels by its shorter flat and feathery brown tail, broad at the base and narrowing to a black tip. Its muzzle is longish. It often shelters in roofs of village houses. When eating nuts, it bores a neat square hole in them which is a telltale clue of this squirrel. It is found in Jammu & Kashmir, Himachal Pradesh and Uttarakhand. **Best Seen At:** Nowhere commonly seen

Flat, feathery, brown tail, tip black

SYED AMIR AMIR

Kashmir Flying Squirrel, Kishtwar, Jammu & Kashmir

The **TRAVANCORE FLYING SQUIRREL** is a small, dark brown or reddish flying squirrel with yellowish white undersides. This colour extends to the cheeks, and white hairs fringe its wing membrane. Almost fully a canopy dweller, it is found in forests, forest edges and plantations in the Western Ghats of Tamil Nadu, Kerala, Karnataka and possibly Goa. **Best Seen At:** Anamalai WLS, Tamil Nadu

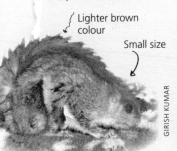

Lighter brown colour

Small size

GIRISH KUMAR

Travancore Flying Squirrel, Periyar NP, Kerala

Small, grey and white, the **Parti-coloured Flying Squirrel** has brown hairs only on the back. The remaining upper body is grey, and underside is white (except the tail). The tail is also grey, and darker under. It makes very high-pitched sounds, which are used to detect it. It is found in forests and near human habitation in Arunachal Pradesh, Meghalaya, Manipur, Nagaland, Sikkim, northern West Bengal, and Assam. **Best Seen At:** Kaziranga NP, Assam

SIMILAR SPECIES: Hairy-footed Flying Squirrel (Sikkim, northern West Bengal, the North-East).

Black base to ears

ANJAN TALUKDAR

Parti-coloured Flying Squirrel, Kaziranga NP, Assam

Family: Sciuridae
Indian Status: Common
Social Unit: Solitary; pairs
Size: HBL: 18-23 cm
Best Seen At: Kaziranga NP, Assam

Hoary-bellied Squirrel

Uniform greyish white back

Also called the Irrawaddy Squirrel, this is small and brown with a pale grey underside, a buff belly and a reddish-brown tinge at the base of its limbs. The back hairs have two light rings of yellow, giving it a grizzled look. It has a long tail, as long as head and body length, without a dark tip. It is found near human habitation where the Pallas's Squirrel (*below*) is not found. It lives halfway up tree canopies in riverine and mixed forests and near inhabitation in Sikkim, north West Bengal and north-east India.

G.S. BHARDWAJ

Hoary-bellied Squirrel,
Kaziranga NP, Assam

Family: Sciuridae
Indian Status: Uncommon to Locally Common
Social Unit: Solitary/pairs
Size: HBL: 21.7-22.7 cm, Wt: 359-375 g
Best Seen At: Borajan WLS; Assam

Pallas's Squirrel

Bright red venter

Olive-brown grizzled upper coat

A medium-sized olive-brown grizzled squirrel, the Pallas's or Red-bellied Squirrel has reddish, maroon, orange-brown or creamy undersides. The paws are dark-coloured and a dark band may divide the reddish underside into two halves. The long olive-brown tail is equal to head and body. Adult females build nests on the outer branches of trees, with three layers of leafy twigs, smaller twigs, and leaves and bark linings. This squirrel is found in forests throughout north-east India.

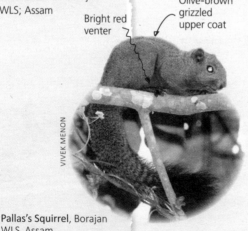

VIVEK MENON

Pallas's Squirrel, Borajan
WLS, Assam

Himalayan Striped Squirrel

Family: Sciuridae
Indian Status: Locally Common
Social Unit: Solitary; pairs; small groups
Size: HBL: 12.9-13.9 cm, Wt. 49.4-51.8 g
Best Seen At: Manas and Kaziranga NPs, Assam

This small, striped squirrel has a black stripe down its back from nape to tail, flanked by two pale stripes, which in turn have two broader black stripes on each side and again two more pale, yellower ones. Very arboreal, it can freeze in the middle of frenzied dashes by spreadeagling its body and tail onto a tree trunk. It is found in forests and near human habitation in Sikkim, northern West Bengal, Arunachal Pradesh, Manipur, Assam, Mizoram and Nagaland.

Thick yellow lateral stripes from eye to base of tail

VIVEK MENON

Himalayan Striped Squirrel, Manas NP, Assam

Orange-bellied Himalayan Squirrel

Family: Sciuridae
Indian Status: Locally Common
Social Unit: Solitary; pairs
Size: HBL: 18-19.4 cm, Wt. 172-180 g
Best Seen At: Sikkim

A shy, common species similar to the Pallas's Squirrel, this medium-sized squirrel has a chunky body, short limbs, small ears and a pointed snout. The thick and soft hairs of the coat are brown at the base, yellow in the middle and black at the tip. It nests in tree holes close to the ground in forested hills and foothills in northern West Bengal and north-east India, north of River Brahmaputra.

SIMILAR SPECIES are **Perny's Long-Nosed Squirrel** and **Asian Red-Cheeked Squirrel** found in Assam, Arunachal Pradesh, Manipur and Nagaland.

Grey dorsal coat, orange underside

Orange-bellied Himalayan Squirrel, Sikkim

BISWAPRIYA RAHUT

Common Striped Squirrels

Family: Sciuridae
Indian Status: Very Common to Rare
Social Unit: Solitary, pairs; larger feeding groups
Size: HBL: 12-16 cm
Wt: 99-117.5g

Three pale buff stripes

Red stripe through tail

Three-striped Squirrel, Kabini, Karnataka

KALYAN VARMA

Five pale buff stripes on back

Bottlebrush grey tail

Five-striped Squirrel, Ranthambore NP, Rajasthan

VIVEK MENON

Darker back with three pale lines

AMRIT MENON

Ruddy face

Jungle-striped Squirrel, Chalakudy, Kerala

The common squirrel of south India, the **THREE-STRIPED** or **INDIAN PALM SQUIRREL** is small, grey-brown or olive-brown with a pale underside. It has three pale parallel lines on its back. Its bushy, black-and-white peppered tail has a bold reddish brown line down it. Active in the day and partly arboreal, it is found in forests, scrub, grasslands and human habitation. **Best Seen At:** South Indian towns

This common squirrel of north India, the **FIVE-STRIPED** or **NORTHERN PALM SQUIRREL** is nearly a copy of its southern cousin except that it has five pale stripes on its greyish brown/olive-brown body. The tail looks like a grey bottlebrush. Bold and curious, it repeats shrill, birdlike calls up to 10 times, along with tail jerks. It is found in urban, rural and forested areas very commonly in north India (also in the North-East, and Andaman & Nicobar). **Best Seen At:** northern Indian towns

Smaller and darker than the two above, the **JUNGLE-STRIPED SQUIRREL** has three pale dull stripes on its fur. It has been known to eat both crops, such as coconut flowers and paddy, and insects such as termites, caterpillars and beetles. It is found in the Western Ghats of Maharashtra, Goa, Karnataka, Kerala and Tamil Nadu. **Best Seen At:** Nowhere commonly seen

A **SIMILAR SPECIES** is the Dusky Striped Squirrel (Western Ghats of Karnataka, Kerala and Tamil Nadu).

Voles

Family: Muridae
Status: Common
Social Unit: Solitary
Size: HBL: 10-12 cm

The **SILVERY MOUNTAIN VOLE** has a longer tail and larger rounded ears than most other voles. It is silvery grey with dense, velvet fur and a long, bicoloured tail – grey above and white below. This bold rodent visits homes and campsites. It is often seen with the Royle's Pika and Long-tailed Marmots. It lives in rock crevices and because it is not adapted to live underground, does not burrow much. It has been recorded from Jammu & Kashmir in mountain meadows and rocky areas above the treeline. **Best Seen At:** Nowhere commonly seen.

Prominent rounded ears

KRISHNAPRIYA TAMMA

Silvery Mountain Vole, Great Himalayan NP, Himachal Pradesh

The **STOLICZKA'S VOLE** is similar in look to the Silvery Mountain Vole except that it is a bright reddish-brown vole with white or slaty grey underparts. A plateau dweller, it constructs burrow systems that are not very deep. It is found in northern Ladakh (Jammu & Kashmir) and Sikkim in mountain meadows and rocky areas near wetlands. **Best Seen At:** Nowhere commonly seen

Bright reddish-brown fur

DHRITIMAN MUKHERJEE

SIMILAR SPECIES are True's Sub-Alpine Kashmir Vole, Muree or Coniferous Kashmir Vole; Scully's Mountain Vole; Royle's Mountain Vole, Kashmir Mountain Vole; White-tailed Mountain Vole; Thomas's Short-tailed Vole, Sikkim Mountain Vole; Pere David's Red-Backed Vole, Blyth's Mountain Vole; Grey Hamster and Ladakh Hamster. These are all found in Ladakh in Jammu and Kashmir, and in Himachal Pradesh.

Stoliczka's Vole, Ladakh, Jammu & Kashmir

Gerbils & Jirds

Family: Muridae
Indian Status: Locally Common to Uncommon
Social Unit: Colonies
Size: HBL: 7.5-18.8 cm

The **INDIAN GERBIL** is a large biscuit-coloured rodent with a white underside. It has a peculiar long tail that is two-coloured (cream along the sides, and grey on top and bottom), ending in a tuft of blackish brown hairs. It is different from other gerbils in its long, naked ears and naked soles. It is a nocturnal and very territorial animal, living in separate burrow systems within a loose colony. It can eat its own babies. It is found east to the River Ganges delta in north India, in dry areas in western and southern India, including deserts, open, barren land, grasslands and rocky areas. **Best Seen At:** Rann of Kutch, Gujarat

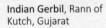

Long ears; long hind feet

Long, bicoloured tail with brown hair tuft

Indian Gerbil, Rann of Kutch, Gujarat

ARPIT DEOMURARI

JUGAL KISHOR TIWARI

The **INDIAN DESERT JIRD** or **DESERT GERBIL** is greyish brown and has a peppering of black on the rump and yellowish grey on the belly. These jirds are diurnal and less aggressive than gerbils and live in colonies close to one another. They inhabit uncultivated, barren land with many bushes in Rajasthan and Gujarat. **Best Seen At:** Desert NP, Rajasthan

Shorter, single-coloured tufted tail

Short hind feet; haired sole, long foreclaws

Indian Desert Jird, Rann of Kutch, Gujarat

The **LITTLE INDIAN HAIRY-FOOTED GERBIL** is smaller than the Pygmy Gerbil and can be told apart by its reddish buff fur. Its eyes look wide open because of the stiff hair surrounding them, and the soles of its feet are hairy – both adaptations for living in sand dunes. It eats salty vegetation, insects and seeds as well. This burrowing gerbil is active by night. It is found in Rajasthan and Gujarat in sand dunes. **Best Seen At:** Desert NP, Rajasthan

A **SIMILAR SPECIES** is the **Pygmy Gerbil** (Rajasthan and Gujarat).

Head of Little Indian Hairy-footed Gerbil *(left)* showing characteristic white patches behind ears; and head of Sand-coloured Rat *(right)* without them

Malabar Spiny Dormouse

Family: Muridae
Indian Status: Rare
Social Unit: Colony
Size: HBL: 13-14 cm
Best Seen At: Kalakkad–Mundanthurai NP, Tamil Nadu

A unique forest mouse with no similar species, the Malabar Spiny Dormouse has spiny and light brown fur and cream underparts. It has a long and bushy tail. Living in tree hollows, it is also called the Pepper Rat as it is a pest in pepper plantations. It inhabits forests in the Western Ghats in Kerala, Tamil Nadu and Karnataka.

Light brown, spiny fur

KALYAN VARMA

Malabar Spiny Dormouse, Vazhachal RF, Kerala

Long-tailed Mice

Family: Muridae
Indian Status: Uncommon to Locally Common
Social Unit: Unknown
Size: HBL: 6-10.5 cm

SANJAY MOLUR

The medium-sized **INDIAN LONG-TAILED TREE MOUSE** or **PALM MOUSE** is identified by its very long tail. It body colour is fawn or light brown – brighter in north, duller in south India. It builds its nest high up in tree branches or in tree holes in forests and near human habitation across India, except high Himalayas and coasts. **Best Seen At:** Nowhere commonly seen

Yellow underparts
Palm Mouse, Madikeri, Kodagu, Karnataka

A yellowish brown field mouse, the **LONG-TAILED FIELD MOUSE** or **EUROPEAN WOOD MOUSE** looks like the House Mouse but its feet are white and the tail brown on top and pale grey at bottom. Nocturnal and burrowing, they store food in burrows shared by many mice. They are found in mountain forests, scrub and grasslands in the Himalayan foothills and the North-East. **Best Seen At:** Himachal Pradesh

KRISHNAPRIYA TAMMA

Long, bicoloured tail

Large circular ears

Long-tailed Field Mouse, Great Himalayan NP, Himachal Pradesh

SIMILAR SPECIES are Pencil-tailed Tree Mouse (North-East); Fukien/South China Wood Mouse (North-East); Miller's Wood Mouse (Jammu & Kashmir, Himachal Pradesh, Uttarakhand); Wroughton's Wood Mouse (Jammu & Kashmir); and Nilgiri Long-tailed Mouse (Karnataka, Tamil Nadu).

House Mouse

Family: Muridae
Indian Status: Abundant
Social Unit: Solitary; groups of 2-3
Size: HBL: 5.2-10 cm
Best Seen At: Homes throughout India

A small rodent with a short, blunt nose, the House Mouse comes in all shades of brown, from sandy to reddish-brown, with slightly whitish or paler underparts. The tail, which is always longer than the head and body, may be lighter below or wholly dark, while the feet may be white, or dark with white toes. Common in agricultural land and human habitation, kitchens and grain storehouses, throughout the country.

SANJAY MOLUR

Brown fur

Some white on feet; or wholly white

Tail longer than head-and-body

House Mouse, Madikeri, Kodagu, Karnataka

Little Indian Field Mouse

Family: Muridae
Indian Status: Common
Social Unit: Solitary; groups of 2-3
Size: HBL: 5.6-6.3 cm
Best Seen At: Paddy fields through India

This is a small greyish brown field mouse, much like a miniature House Mouse. It differs most markedly in its white underparts and lower limbs. Its eyes are large and so are the rounded ears. Its burrows are 30-40 cm in flat fields. It is found in croplands, paddy fields and dry forests throughout India.

KARTIK SHANKAR

Dark brown back; light brown underside

Little Indian Field Mouse, Bengaluru, Karnataka

SIMILAR SPECIES are **Bonhote's Mouse** (Western Ghats); **Spiny Field Mouse** (peninsular India); **Fawn-Coloured Mouse** (Sikkim, North-East, Anadamans), **Wroughton's Mouse** (Peninsular India); **Sikkim Mouse** (Sikkim, northern West Bengal; North-East); **Harvest Mouse** (North-East); **Elliot's Brown Spiny Mouse, Pygmy Field Mouse** (throughout India); **Cooke's Mouse** (Wetsern Ghats, Assam, Nagaland), **Kashmir Birch Mouse** (Gilgit, Jammu & Kashmir) and **Crump's Mouse** (Assam, Manipur, Bihar).

Bamboo Rats

Family: Muridae
Indian Status: Least Uncommon to Uncommon
Social Unit: Groups of 2–3
Size: HBL: 15-35 cm

A relatively large rodent with a blunt face, big teeth and a short tail, the **BAY** or **LESSER BAMBOO RAT** has a reddish brown body. It has dense, soft fur that hangs down like a cloak over the body. The chunky face is blunt. It has a habit of living under bamboo clumps. It is found in montane forests and bamboo patches in Assam, Manipur, Meghalaya, Mizoram, northern West Bengal and Bihar. **Best Seen At:** Nowhere commonly seen

The **HOARY BAMBOO RAT** is much larger than the Bay Bamboo Rat and has grey fur tipped with white, giving it a grizzled or greyish white look. It is found in the foothills and mountainous areas in Arunachal Pradesh, Manipur, Meghalaya, Mizoram, Nagaland and Tripura. **Best Seen At:** Khasi Hills, Meghalaya.

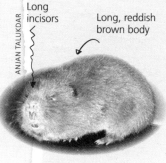

Long incisors

Long, reddish brown body

ANJAN TALUKDAR

Bay Bamboo Rat, Doigurung, Golaghat, Assam

Soft-Furred Field Rat

Family: Muridae
Indian Status: Common
Social Unit: 2-3
Size: HBL: 10-15.5 cm
Best Seen At: Throughout India in open fields

A medium-sized field rat, with soft grey fur that is pale but grizzled, its tail is dark grey on top and paler, almost white below and is equal to, or shorter than, the head and body in length. It has very prominently rounded ears and eyes. It is a poor burrower and makes its home in cracks in the soil or embankments. It is found in fields and open country, cultivated areas, gravelly grounds or grassy embankments throughout India, north to Himachal Pradesh and east to West Bengal.

SIMILAR SPECIES are the **Kondana Rat**, (endemic to Pune, Maharashtra) and **Sand-coloured Rat** (Gujarat and Rajasthan).

Grizzled, grey body

Two-coloured tail with rings

KARTIK SHANKAR

Soft-furred Field Rat, Upper Nilgiris, Tamil Nadu

Family: Muridae
Indian Status:
Uncommon to Common
Social Unit: Solitary;
groups of 4-5
Size: HBL: 11.4-19.5 cm

Brown tail,
pale below

Brown dorsal;
white venters

KRISHNAPRIYA TAMMA

Bush Rats

The **WHITE-TAILED WOOD RAT** is an adaptable rat easily told apart by its two-coloured tail. It is brownish grey on the back with a paler underside, but what makes it different from other rats is the brown tail, which two-thirds of the way down is covered with long white hairs. This rat builds its nest in tree hollows, but often in boulder crevices too. It is found in forests, scrub jungle and open country north up to Madhya Pradesh, and east to Bihar and West Bengal. **Best Seen At:** Parambikulam and Peechi WLSs, Kerala

White-tailed Wood
Rat, Kurnool, Andhra
Pradesh

A reddish or yellow-brown rodent, the **INDIAN BUSH RAT** has a long tail, brownish above and yellowish grey below. Its ears are very large and conch-like, and hairy on the outside. It burrows under thick bush and makes unique pathways from its burrow to its foraging ground. It is arboreal as well as terrestrial and raids crop fields and coffee estates. Found in peninsular India, east to western Assam in grasslands and scrub forests. **Best Seen At:** Keoladeo Ghana NP, Rajasthan.

Reddish
fur

Large, conch-
shaped ears

SANJAY MOLUR

SIMILAR SPECIES are the **Kutch Rock Rat** (many different places in India) and **Ellerman's Rat** (Salem district, Tamil Nadu).

A burrowing rat of hilly forests, the **MANIPUR RAT** has dense and coarse, brown fur with a paintbrush-like texture. The tail, as long as the head and

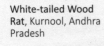

Indian Bush Rat, Bengaluru,
Karnataka

Brown tail
with yellow
underside

body, has a short white tip. Not an agricultural pest, it is found in hills and foothills, oak and evergreen forests, scrub, and riverine meadows south of River Brahmaputra in Assam, Nagaland and Manipur.

India is home to half a dozen species of soft, densely furred, high-altitude rats that are all richly coloured on their backs, while the underside is white or very pale. The tail is slightly longer than the head and body. The **CHESTNUT RAT** has chestnut-brown to reddish upper parts and clear white underparts. Its flexible tail is two-coloured with a dark tip. It is found in forests, and forests edges from the western Himalayas to Assam and Arunachal Pradesh. **Best Seen At:** Nowhere commonly seen

Large body size

Flat spines; grey coat

URAIPORN PIMSAI

Manipur Rat

Reddish brown back

KRISHNAPRIYA TAMMA

Long, flexible tail with dark tip

Chestnut Rat, Siju WLS, Meghalaya

SIMILAR SPECIES are Bower's Rat (Assam, Meghalaya); **Kenneth's White-toothed Rat** (Assam, Nagaland, Manipur); **Millard's Large-toothed Rat** (West Bengal, Assam, Arunachal Pradesh); **Hume's Manipur Bush Rat** (Assam, Manipur); **Edward's Noisy Rat** (West Bengal, Garo Hills, Arunachal Pradesh, Nagaland); **Smoke-bellied Rat** (Sikkim, West Bengal); **Mishmi Rat** (Arunachal Pradesh); **White-bellied Rat/Himalayan Niviventer** (Jammu & Kashmir, Sikkim, West Bengal); **Lang Bian Rat** (probably Arunachal Pradesh); **Tennaserim Rat** (probably Mizoram) and **Chinese/ Confucian White-bellied Rat** (Arunachal Pradesh, Nagaland).

Bandicoot Rats

Family: Muridae
Indian Status: Common to Very Common
Social Unit: 2-3
Size: HBL: 14-34 cm
Best Seen At: South India (Large Bandicoot); Kolkata, West Bengal (Lesser Bandicoot); North Indian farms (Short-tailed Bandicoot)

A large dark brown, nearly black, rat with coarse fur, the **LARGE BANDICOOT RAT** at first sight makes people go 'Ew!'. It is dark overall and the underside is only slightly greyer. It lives in a single burrow system that has large openings on the surface. It is found alongside human habitation and farms, except in deserts and mountains, throughout India. **Best Seen At:** South India

Pointed muzzle

Dark grey to black fur

Long tail

Large Bandicoot Rat, Kottayam, Kerala

PUNNEN KURIAN VENKADATHU

The **LESSER BANDICOOT RAT** or **INDIAN MOLE RAT** is recognized by its browner rather than black colouration, and a dark tail that is shorter than its head-and-body length. Its undersides are greyish; its face is more rounded, with round pinkish ears. Its burrow system has up to a dozen openings, plugged with loose soil. It grunts often and is very aggressive. It is found near human habitation and crop fields, pasture, wasteland, vegetation near wetlands or waterbodies, and flooded paddy fields throughout India. **Best Seen At:** Kolkata, West Bengal

Round pinkish ears

Brown fur

Lesser Bandicoot Rat, Kodagu, Karnataka

SANJAY MOLUR

The **SHORT-TAILED BANDICOOT RAT** is a smaller, dull brown or pale brown rat with a lighter grey underside. Its chunky body has a short dark tail. Crop damage by this rat is immense because it feeds on the underground parts of the plants. It is found in cultivated fields and gardens in urban areas, plantations, scrub, grasslands and pastures in the north Indian plains. Best Seen At: **North Indian farms**

Blunt muzzle

Chunky body; light grey brown fur

Short-tailed Bandicoot Rat, Kolkata, West Bengal

SUMIT SEN

Common Rats

The most common rat in the world, the **HOUSE RAT** or **BLACK RAT**, variously known as the Roof or Ship Rat, is a medium-sized dark brown rat with many distinct subspecies. It is recognized by the flat spines in the fur on its back. It is found in all habitats, in homes and forests throughout India, except cold deserts.
Best Seen At: All over India

The **BROWN RAT**, also called the **NORWAY RAT** or **SEWER RAT**, is a large, dark brown rat with lighter underparts and feet, small ears, and a tail that is always shorter than its head-and-body. It is more terrestrial and less of a climber than the House Rat, and frequents wet areas as well. It is found in sewers, ports along the coast, the banks of rivers and forests in coastal states and islands.
Best Seen At: Ports

SIMILAR SPECIES are the **White-footed Himalayan Rat** (from Kumaon to North-East); **Himalayan Rat** (Himalayan foothills, from Jammu & Kashmir to Arunachal Pradesh); **Indo-Chinese Forest Rat** (Sikkim, Arunachal Pradesh, Meghalaya, Andaman & Nicobar Islands); **Ranjini's Rat** (Thiruvananthapuram Distt, Kerala); **Sahyadris Forest Rat** (Western Ghats); **Oriental House Rat** (the North-east, Andaman & Nicobar Islands); **Miller's Nicobar Rat** (Andaman & Nicobar Islands); **Andamans Archipelago Rat** (Andaman Islands) and **Car Nicobar Rat** (Nicobar Islands).

Family: Muridae
Indian Status: Common to Abundant
Social Unit: Groups of 2-3
Size: HBL: 14-25 cm;
Best Seen At: All over India (Black Rat); Ports (Brown Rat)

KARTIK SHANKAR

White underparts

Tail shorter than head-and-body length

House or Black Rat, Upper Nilgiris, Tamil Nadu

Brown, coarse fur

Blunt face

DHRITIMAN MUKHERJEE

Tail shorter than head-and-body length

Brown Rat, Narcondom Island, Andaman & Nicobar Islands

TAIL TYPES IN BATS

Sheath-tailed

Free-tailed

Evening bats

MEASURING BATS

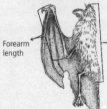

Forearm length

Head and body length

Right wing
(Underside view)

Where they live

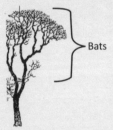

Bats

INDIAN BATS
AT A GLANCE

NUMBER
OF SPECIES **123**

LARGEST
**LARGE
FLYING FOX**

Bats

Fulvous fruit bats at a cave roost, Dholpur, Rajasthan

ANSAR KHAN

SMALLEST	MOST COMMON	MOST ENDANGERED	ACTIVITY
INDIAN PYGMY BAT	**INDIAN FLYING FOX**	**PETER'S TUBE-NOSED & WROUGHTON'S FREE-TAILED BAT**	**BATS** ☾

▶ What are bats?

The only mammals capable of true flight, bats are found the world over except in Antarctica. They roost in caves, on trees, in rock crevices, or in empty buildings during the day, coming out only at night to take to the sky. When roosting, they prefer to hang upside down, although some cling to rocky surfaces like geckos on a wall. Most bats find their way around by echolocation, a technique of producing high-frequency sounds that bounce back to them off obstacles. Here are the different types of bats.

● **Fruit bats:** All fruit bats are medium to large in size, have furred bodies, long snouts, simple nose and ears, and no tail (or a small tail).

● **Mouse-tailed bats:** Found in dry areas, the three mouse-tailed bats found in India are small insectivorous bats with a long and slender mouse-like tail that hangs partially free from the thigh membrane.

● **Tomb or Sheath-tailed bats:** The six tomb bats, found all over India, are small and strong-smelling, with dog-like heads and eyes that shine in the dark and a tail that is enclosed in a sheath.

● **Free-tailed bats:** They have wrinkled lips, medium-sized fleshy ears and a thick tail that is free-hanging.

● **False vampires:** The two Indian species of this carnivorous bat family are tailless, with tall oval ears and a simple nose leaf.

● **Horseshoe bats:** The 17 species of Indian horseshoe bats have a complex nose leaf, with a horseshoe-shaped projection around nostrils.

● **Leaf-nosed bats:** Closely related to horseshoe bats, the 14 species of Indian leaf-nosed bats are small, insect-eating cave-roosters.

● **Evening bats:** There are many kinds of small insect-eating bats grouped together as evening bats. They are small bats with dense woolly or wavy fur and relatively broad wings.

The three long-eared Indian bat species have long (as long as head and body), oval ears set close together on the forehead and a long tail. Pipistrelles and serotines are small- or medium-sized bats with broad wings. They lack a nose leaf and exaggerated ears. As a group they have the same rapid, erratic flight and are the first bats out in the evening. Yellow House Bats are similar to serotines, with smaller ears and a pointed tragus. Flat-headed or Bamboo Bats are two serotine-like bats with a broad and flattened head gently sloping to the nostrils.

Despite being among the smallest bats (the size of a large moth), the Painted Bats are the easiest to

What is a nose leaf?

Bats make clicking sounds and receive their echoes, which help them in their locomotion and to avoid obstacles. They have unique folds and flaps on their nose called 'nose leafs' which help them receive the echoes.

GABOR CSORBA

Fruit Bat

Indian Flying Fox hanging by its claws. Note the large size, furry body and long dog-like muzzle.

SANDESH KADUR

Lesser False Vampire Bat

It shows large ears and specialized nose leafs, typical of a creature depndent on echolocation.

BANDANA AUL & SARAVANAKUMAR

Schneider's leaf-nosed Bat

Note the very large ears and the ornate nose leafs.

CHAITRA-RAJESH

Nicobar Flying Fox

Medium-sized and brownish, the Nicobar Flying Fz is a furit-eater.

BANDANA AUL

Rufous Horseshoe Bat

Note the complex horseshoe-shape on nose leaf and the noticeably large ears.

P.O. NAMEER

Mouse-tailed bat: Note the long, naked tail

Wrinkle-lipped Free-tailed Bat: Note the thick ears and wrinkled lips, which give it its name

recognize because of their distinctive coat. However, these bats are well camouflaged in dead banana leaves or other ingenious hiding places such as abandoned nests of weaver birds.

▶ How do they move?

The distinguishing feature of bats is the fact that they fly. Some of them drop down and then flap away; others flutter weakly while most bats fly strongly. The forelimbs of bats have modified bones and a large 'patagium' or skin-like membrane stretching from shoulder to ankle. It also extends between the hind legs and encloses the tail fully or partially. This helps bats to achieve true flight, unique among mammals.

Long-eared Bat
Note the very long ears.

In caves or on the ground, bats can crawl using their hind feet, and wrists and thumbs of the forefeet. Many fruit bats can move around trees using the claw on their thumbs.

▶ What do they eat?

Bats (Order Chiroptera) are broadly divided into Megachiroptera and Microchiroptera. While these names suggest large and small bats, the main difference is in their diets. Fruit-eating bats feed by perching on trees and gnawing on fruit and flowers, often in cropland and large orchards. Some of them are useful pollinators. The insectivorous bats catch flying insects or pick them off foliage or the ground and can eat up to a third of their body weight, or hundreds of insects a day. A few, for e.g., false vampires, are carnivorous and eat small mammals and reptiles, and the Fulvous Fruit Bat catches fish.

▶ How do they communicate?

Bats may well be among the most vocal mammals but most sounds are not audible to the human ear. Some clicks, screeches and calls can be heard but most are ultrasonic. These calls are used to find their way about, to avoid obstacles, to detect small prey and also to communicate with each other. Chemical signalling is also used by bats to recognize roost-mates. The sense of smell of fruit-eating bats is essential for them to locate ripe fruits and flowers. Bats can also see very well, and use touch and sight to add to their hearing and chemical communication.

▶ Young ones
Bats generally have a single young each year, although twins are known. The young call constantly after birth for the mothers to recognize them in large roosts. Some species carry them around while feeding whereas others leave them at the roost. In about three months, young bats become independent.

▶ Threats and conservation
Fruit bats are useful to humans in pollinating several plants, and they are also an efficient and cheap pest-control mechanism. However, bats are threatened by habitat loss, ill-treatment and diseases. Bat roosts are often disturbed and bats smoked or driven away, especially from man-made constructions because of the guano (droppings), or their odour which may be unpleasant. Fruit bats get electrocuted by high-tension power lines if they roost on them. A new threat to bats is wind-energy mills in which they get caught.

Only 27 Indian bats are listed as threatened by IUCN; however, only two bats are protected in India (Salim Ali's Fruit Bat and Wroughton's Free-tailed Bat). Even more worryingly, all fruit bats are listed as Vermin in the Indian Wildlife Protection Act. India needs to conduct long-term detailed studies of its bats.

Identifying Bat Families

FAMILY	TAIL	EARS	MUZZLE
FRUIT BATS	Small or absent	No tragus (small prominent bit on inner side of ear)	Simple; no nose leaf.
MOUSE-TAILED BATS	Thin, long, naked, main part free of membrane	Membrane joins ears above forehead; tragus present	No nose leaf
TOMB BATS	Tip emerges from middle of membrane	Variable; tragus present	Simple; no nose leaf
FALSE VAMPIRES	Absent	Large, joined over forehead; tragus present	Long, erect nose leaf
HORSESHOE BATS	Enclosed in membrane	Large,; no tragus	Complex nose leaf
LEAF-NOSED BATS	Enclosed in membrane	Large; no tragus	Complex nose leaf;
FREE-TAILED BATS	Thick, free of membrane	Thick and fleshy; small tragus	Broad, no nose leaf, wrinkled lips
EVENING BATS	Long, enclosed in membrane	Simple; tragus present	Simple; no nose leaf

Family: Pteropodidae
Indian Status: Abundant
Social Unit: Roosts of
100s, even 1000s
Size: HBL: 19.8-30 cm
Best Seen At: All over
India

Indian Flying Fox

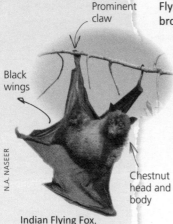

Prominent claw

Black wings

N.A. NASEER

Chestnut head and body

Indian Flying Fox,
Wayanad, Kerala

Possibly the best known bat in India, the Indian Flying Fox or Indian Fruit Bat has a chestnut-brown head with large black, pointed ears and huge black wings that it often folds over its tan or orange belly. The back is blackish brown with few pale hair. It has a long hairy snout with visible nostrils. It constantly grooms itself and sprinkles urine on itself to keep cool in summer. It flies out about half an hour after sunset to feed. It takes in only the juice and discards chewed fruit.

It is found on large trees near human habitation along roads and avenues, as well as near cropland and waterbodies in peninsular India and in Jammu & Kashmir, Himachal Pradesh, Uttarakhand, Sikkim, Arunachal Pradesh, Assam and Manipur.

Family: Pteropodidae
Indian Status: Locally
Common
Social Unit: 10-15 to
hundreds, even thousands
Size: 17-40 cm
Best Seen At: Car Nicobar
Island, Andaman & Nicobar
Islands

Black-Eared Flying Fox

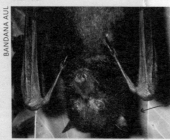

BANDANA AUL

Black face and ears

Black-eared Flying Fox,
Camorta, Andaman & Nicobar Islands

This medium-sized island bat, also called Blyth's Flying Fox, has variable fur ranging from dark brown – almost black – to a golden tawny, with the back sprinkled with grey hairs. It is not easily disturbed when at roost. It prefers roosting in mangroves and riverbank vegetation, or near the coast,. It is found in the Andaman and Nicobar Islands.

SIMILAR SPECIES are the **Island Flying Fox**, the **Nicobar Flying Fox** and the **Large Flying Fox**, all found in the Andaman and Nicobar Islands.

Salim Ali's Fruit Bat

Family: Pteropodidae
Indian Status: Rare
Social Unit: Low hundreds
Size: HBL: 10.2-10.9 cm
Best Seen At:
Kardana Coffee Estate, Chinnamannur, Tamil Nadu

This bat has short, soft and dark brown fur on its back. The fur is less on the belly and throat. The lower back, elbows and forearms are chestnut. Its ears are brown ovals without a hairy or pale fringe. It is tailless on the outside. It is partial to eating figs. This cave-dwelling bat is found in mountain broadleaved forests interspersed with plantations in Periyar TR, Kerala, and Kalakkad–Mundanthurai TR and Kardana Coffee Estate, High Wavy Mountains, in Tamil Nadu.

Salim Ali's Fruit Bat, Meghamalai WLS, Tamil Nadu

CHAITRA–RAJESH

Chocolate-brown body with grizzling

Short snout

Other Fruit Bats

Family: Pteropodidae
Indian Status: Very Common to Rare
Social Unit: Commonly 2-3-4; small groups; large colonies up to 100s
Size: HBL: 7.6-14.7 cm

The **Fulvous Fruit Bat** is a robust bat with long legs. It has fine, tawny-brown fur on the back and a grey belly. The ears are long and the tail is short. Their eyes reflect orange in torchlight. Very noisy and smelling of fermented fruit, they roost in mixed colonies although young ones roost singly. Easily disturbed, they fly out in a large group. They inhabit caves, tunnels, disused buildings and, rarely, trees throughout India except deserts and high mountains. **Best Seen At:** Kanheri Caves, Mumbai, Maharashtra.

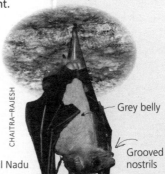

CHAITRA–RAJESH

Grey belly

Grooved nostrils

Fulvous Fruit Bat, Madurai, Tamil Nadu

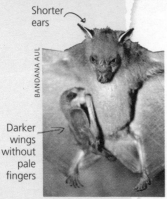

Brown head and body

Tawny collar and grey belly in females

The soft, silky and brown-furred **Greater Short-nosed Fruit Bat** has large, fur-lined coffee-brown ears with pale borders and dark brown wings marked by pale 'fingers'. These bats in northern India are larger than in the south. The male constructs a tent from stems to shelter itself, females and pups during the breeding season. It is found in farmland, forests and on roofs as well, throughout India except deserts and the high Himalayas.

Greater Short-nosed Fruit Bat, Cliffs Bay, Andaman & Nicobar Islands

Shorter ears

Darker wings without pale fingers

The **Lesser Short-nosed Fruit Bat** has much shorter ears with a slight or no pale border. It is largely a hill forest species but is also found near human habitation in Gujarat, Karnataka, Kerala, Madhya Pradesh, Maharashtra, Meghalaya, Odisha, Uttar Pradesh, West Bengal and in the Andamans and Nicobar Islands.

Lesser Short-nosed Bat, Cliffs Bay, Andaman & Nicobar Islands

Slightly smaller than the Fulvous Fruit Bat, the **Lesser Dawn Bat's** fur is dark brown on the back and mottled, greyish brown below. It makes a clapping noise with its wings as it flies. Largely cave-roosting, it also known to roost in village hut roofs. It is found patchily in Uttarakhand, Andaman archipelago, Tamil Nadu, Karnataka, Andhra Pradesh, Assam, Manipur, Meghalaya, Mizoram, Nagaland and Sikkim. **Best Seen At:** Muroor Caves, Karnataka

Dark ears, no borders

Wings without 'fingers'

Long muzzle

Thinly furred underside

Lesser Dawn Bat, Baratang Island, Andaman & Nicobar Islands

BANDANA AUL

A small, uniformly brown tailless bat, the **Blanford's Fruit Bat** has long fur, and two buff spots on its chin. It is found in bamboo and pine and oak forests in Uttarakhand, West Bengal, Sikkim, Mizoram and Arunachal Pradesh.

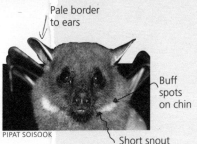

Pale border to ears

Buff spots on chin

Short snout

PIPAT SOISOOK

Blanford's Fruit Bat

SIMILAR SPECIES are the **Ratnaworabhan's Fruit Bat** and the **Greater Long-nosed Fruit Bat** or **Hill Fruit Bat** (West Bengal and the North-East).

Mouse-tailed Bats

Family: Rhinopomatidae
Indian Status: Common
Social Unit: Groups of 1–10, up to 3,000
Size: HBL: 5.5-8.4 cm

The **Greater Mouse-tailed Bat** is grey-brown and has short fur only on its head and upper body. If disturbed, it crawls along the roof, crab-like, before taking flight. Its flights, in late evening, are weak and fluttering, with frequent glides. It lives in caves, tunnels, vacant buildings and crevices in dry areas including deserts, in Gujarat, Rajasthan, Madhya Pradesh and Maharashtra. **Best Seen At:** Tughlakabad Fort, Delhi

Long (shorter than forearm) naked tail

Brown fur on upper part of body

ANOOP K.R.

Greater Mouse-tailed Bat, Jaisalmer, Rajasthan

A smaller version of the above-mentioned bat, the **Lesser Mouse-tailed Bat** has a longer tail, a distinct grey belly and a weak flight too. The colonies of both these bats are known by a strong, pungent odour. It lives in caves, tunnels, disused buildings, and crevices in Delhi, Uttar Pradesh, Rajasthan, Gujarat, Madhya Pradesh, Tamil Nadu, Arunachal Pradesh, Karnataka, Odisha, Bihar and West Bengal. **Best Seen At:** Around Qutab Minar, Delhi

A **SIMILAR SPECIES** is the **Small Mouse-tailed Bat** (Tamil Nadu and Rajasthan).

Tail longer than forearm

Brown fur on upper part of body

MANOJ P.

Lesser Mouse-tailed Bat, Gokarna, Karnataka

Wroughton's Free-tailed Bat

Family: Molossidae
Indian Status: Rare
Social Unit: Groups of 2-15
Size: HBL: 8.7-9.9 cm
Best Seen At: Barapade Caves, Karnataka

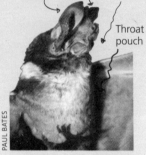

Ears connected on top of head

Large size

Moustache on wrinkled lips

Throat pouch

PAUL BATES

Wroughton's Free-tailed Bat, Barapade Cave, Karnataka

A large, glossy, chocolate-brown species, this bat has large ears that are connected to each other with a membrane, on top of its head. It has a distinct grey collar on its underside, which is lighter brown.

It has hairs resembling a small moustache beneath circular nostrils. It is found in ceilings of caves in forested valleys and plateaus. This bat is known from two locations: one, in Barapade Caves in Belgaum District of Karnataka and second, from Phrang Karuh Cave, near Nongtrai village in Meghalaya.

Other Free-tailed Bats

Family: Molossidae
Indian Status: Common
Social Unit: Variable; from ones and twos to roosts of hundreds and thousands
Size: HBL: 6.1-7.7 cm

A medium-sized, noisy bat, the **Egyptian Free-tailed Bat** is buff to dark brown on top and paler under. It has a short, thick tail free of the membrane. It has hairy feet. Its roosts smell unpleasant. It is found in cliffs, boulder overhangs, crevices in old buildings, rock faces and caves in Rajasthan, Gujarat, Maharashtra, Madhya Pradesh, Karnataka, Kerala, and Tamil Nadu. **Best Seen At:** Aurangabad, Maharashtra

SIMILAR SPECIES are the **Wrinkle-lipped Free-tailed Bat** (scattered in Punjab, Rajasthan, Maharashtra, Goa, Tamil Nadu, Karnataka, Andhra Pradesh and Meghalaya) and the **European Free-tailed Bat** (West Bengal).

Large, unconnected, fleshy ears with square tragus

Wrinkled lips

GABOR CSORBA

Egyptian Free-tailed Bat

Tomb Bats

Family: Emballonuridae
Indian Status: Locally Common
Social Unit: Variable; tens, hundreds, thousands
Size: HBL: 6.7-10.5 cm

A small, brown, strong-smelling bat, the **Long-winged Tomb Bat** have males that are reddish brown, have a pouch and a circular gland on the chest but no beard. Females are darker with no throat ('gular') pouch or gland. Wings are attached to ankles. It comes out in the early evening and lives in caves, ruins, trees and even house roofs. It has a strong smell. **Best Seen At:** Khandala Caves, Elephanta Island, Maharashtra

Reddish brown males

Long-winged Tomb Bat

The **Naked-rumped Tomb Bat** also has a throat pouch and a circular gland on the chest but no beard. Its lower back and abdomen are bare. It is found in rock crevices, deserted buildings, step wells and tombs in dry areas in peninsular India. **Best Seen At:** Step wells in Ahmedabad

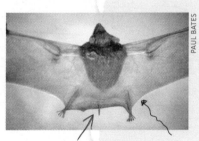

Naked rump | Wings attached to bone

Naked-rumped Tomb Bat, Bhuj, Gujarat

This **Black-bearded Tomb Bat** is easily recognized by its hairy chin. Its underside is paler than its back. Easily disturbed, it even flies out in daylight. It is found in hilly areas and forests, caves, ruins and even urban areas except in the north-west, North-East and the high Himalayas. **Best Seen At:** Champa Baoli, Mandu, Madhya Pradesh

SIMILAR SPECIES are the **Egyptian Tomb Bat** (Gujarat, Rajasthan), the **Theobald's Tomb Bat** (Madhya Pradesh, Karnataka) and the **Pouch-bearing Tomb Bat** (patchily found, including the Andamans).

Beard and throat pouch

Wings attached to ankles

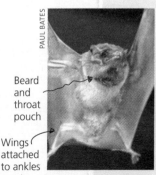

Black-bearded Tomb Bat, Mandu, Madhya Pradesh

False Vampires

Family: Megadermatidae
Indian Status: Common to Locally Common
Social Unit: Groups of 15-20 to hundreds
Size: HBL: 5.4-9.5 cm

PAUL BATES

Large, grey bat with pale belly

Greater False Vampire Bat, Bhuj, Gujarat

The **Greater False Vampire Bat** is large and mouse-grey with paler undersides. Its tall nose leaf resembles two joined ovals. A silent flier, it emerges an hour after sunset. It is unique among Indian bats in eating vertebrates (frogs, rodents and small birds) as well as insects. It is found in caves, forests and houses across India, except the high Himalayas and deserts. **Best Seen At:** Kanheri Caves, Mumbai, Maharashtra

P.O. NAMEER

Brownish bat, smaller size

Ears joined at base

Lesser False Vampire Bat, Parambikulam WLS, Kerala

The **Lesser False Vampire** is a smaller version of the Greater False Vampire, but is deep brown with thicker ears. It flies very close to the ground for a few hours after dark without hunting, feeding only later at night. It is found in the Western Ghats, Andaman Islands and the North-East in caves and disused houses, wells and tree hollows. **Best Seen At:** Barapade Caves, Karnataka

Rufous Horseshoe Bat

Family: Rhinolophidae
Indian Status: Common
Social Unit: Colonies of 100s **Size:** HBL: 4.2-6.6 cm
Best Seen At: Mahabaleshwar, Khandala & Kanheri Caves, Maharashtra

Small size, dense fur

ADITYA JOSHI

This medium-sized bat has dense fur ranging from orange to reddish brown in winter and dull brown to grey in summer. It emerges after sunset, flying below canopy level, sometimes low at bush level, for the first hour catching prey while flying. Then after rest, it swoops on insects, 'flycatcher' style. It lives in caves, tunnels, wells, temples and tree hollows in wet forests in peninsular India and the North-East.

Horseshoe-shaped nose leaf

Rufous Horseshoe Bat, near Pune, Maharashtra

SIMILAR SPECIES are the Greater Horseshoe Bat (Jammu & Kashmir, Himachal Pradesh, Uttarakhand, West Bengal, Sikkim, Arunachal Pradesh, Nagaland); Lesser Horseshoe Bat (Jammu & Kashmir); Blyth's Horseshoe Bat (across India), Big-eared Horseshoe Bat (Uttarakhand, West Bengal, Arunachal Pradesh, Meghalaya); Lesser Woolly Horseshoe Bat (Maharashtra, Andhra Pradesh, Karnataka, Kerala); Pearson's Horseshoe Bat (West Bengal, Sikkim, Manipur, Meghalaya, Uttarakhand); Dobson's Horseshoe Bat (Arunachal Pradesh, Mizoram, Andaman Islands); Chinese Rufous Horseshoe Bat (Himachal Pradesh, Uttarakhand, West Bengal, Sikkim, Arunachal Pradesh, Nagaland, Meghalaya); Intermediate Horseshoe Bat (West Bengal, Arunachal Pradesh, Nagaland, Meghalaya, Andaman & Nicobar Is.); Thai Horseshoe Bat (Meghalaya); Least Horseshoe Bat (Uttarakhand, West Bengal, Arunachal Pradesh, Meghalaya, Andhra Pradesh, Odisha, Karnataka); Little Nepalese Horseshoe Bat (Arunachal Pradesh, Meghalaya); Andaman Horseshoe Bat (Andaman Is.); Woolly Horseshoe Bat (Uttarakhand, West Bengal, Meghalaya, Nagaland); Trefoil Horseshoe Bat (West Bengal, Assam); Mitred Horseshoe Bat (Bihar) and Shortridge's Horseshoe Bat (north India).

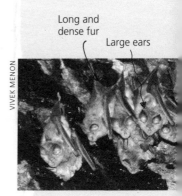

Long and dense fur
Large ears

VIVEK MENON

Greater Horseshoe Bat

Fulvous Leaf-nosed Bat

Family: Hipposideridae
Indian Status: Locally Common
Social Unit: Few to 200+
Size: HBL: 4-5 cm
Best Seen At: Ajanta and Ellora Caves, Maharashtra

This bat is similar to the Dusky Leaf-nosed Bat but with larger ears, smaller wings and a longer forearm. It is late-evening bat with a fluttering low flight, and feeds on cockroaches and beetles. It is found across peninsular India, the Andamans Islands, and northern India in cooll damp caves and disused buildings close to water.

Large ears

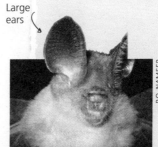

P.O. NAMEER

Fulvous Leaf-nosed Bat,
Parambikulam WLS, Kerala

Other Leaf-nosed Bats

Family: Hipposideridae
Indian Status: Common to Rare
Social Unit: Few individuals to several hundred colonies
Size: HBL: 3.8-10.6 cm

A small bat with small forearms, brownish black, naked wings and body fur varying from golden to dark brown to grey, the **Dusky Leaf-nosed Bat** is a late-evening bat flies low with rapid wing beats.

It is found in deep wells, wall crevices, disused buildings, thatch roofs, tree hollows, seashore caves and disused mines in Madhya Pradesh, Kerala, Maharashtra, Karnataka, Tamil Nadu, Odisha. **Best Seen At:** Konark Temple, Odisha

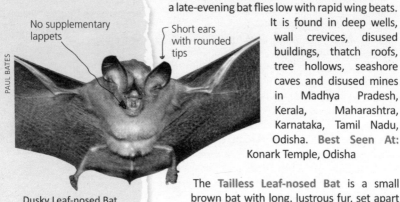

No supplementary lappets

Short ears with rounded tips

PAUL BATES

Dusky Leaf-nosed Bat, Chennai, Tamil Nadu

The **Tailless Leaf-nosed Bat** is a small brown bat with long, lustrous fur, set apart from all other leaf-nosed bats by its very short tail. The ears are round like saucers. There are two records of it in West Bengal and Meghalaya. It inhabits caves and tree hollows in forests.

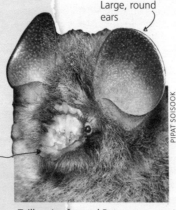

Large, round ears

PIPAT SOISOOK

Distinctive nose leaf with two additional leaflets

Tailless Leaf-nosed Bat

A medium-sized species, the **Schneider's Leaf-nosed Bat** varies from grey to orange-brown. It has small ears and its nose leaf has three additional leaflets. It leaves its roost about 10 minutes after sunset and hunts in small parties of 10-15 bats. It is largely found in southern India but is also recorded in Gujarat, Maharashtra, Odisha and Uttarakhand. It roosts in caves, tunnels, disused buildings, and hill crevices in forested and hilly areas. **Best Seen At:** Elephanta Caves, Maharashtra

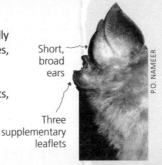

Short, broad ears

Three supplementary leaflets

Schneider's Leaf-nosed Bat, Parambikulam WLS, Kerala

The largest of the leaf-nosed bats, the **Great Himalayan Leaf-nosed Bat** is identified by the four supplementary leaflets on its nose leaf. It has dark brown wings and membranes against a grey-brown body with soft, long fur. It circles around trees, close to the ground or around bushes, like flying foxes, and hunts shortly after sunset. It is not easily disturbed at roost sites, which are caves or in old or disused buildings in bamboo and other forests in central and eastern Himalayas. **Best Seen At:** Mussoorie, Uttarakhand

Long grey-brown fur; large size

Four supplementary leaflets

Great Himalayan Leaf-nosed Bat

The **Kelaart's Leaf-nosed Bat** is a large, leaf-nosed bat. The fur varies greatly from cream to orange or red. It is an early evening bat that can predate high in the air or rush out and leap forth around vegetation. It can eat hard-bodied insects such as beetles. It inhabits caves and ruins in wet and hilly forests in Rajasthan, central and south India, West Bengal, Odisha and Meghalaya. **Best Seen At:** Kolar, Vijayanagar, Karnataka

SIMILAR SPECIES are the **Geoffroy's Trident Bat** (Rajasthan); **Horsfield's Leaf-Nosed Bat** (North-East, Andaman Is.); **Cantor's Leaf-Nosed Bat** (central, western, southern India); **Diadem Leaf-Nosed Bat** (Nicobar Is.); **Andersen's Leaf-Nosed Bat** (North-East, south India, Nicobar Is.); **Least Leaf-Nosed Bat** (Uttarakhand to Arunachal Pradesh); **Khajuria's Leaf-Nosed Bat** (Madhya Pradesh); **Kolar Leaf-Nosed Bat** (Karnataka) and **Nicobar Leaf-Nosed Bat** (Nicobar Is.).

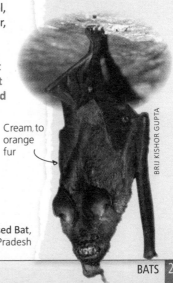

Cream to orange fur

Kelaart's Leaf-nosed Bat, Bandhavgarh, Madhya Pradesh

Myotis Bats

Family: Vespertilionidae
Indian Status: Common to Rare
Social Unit: Small groups up to 8
Size: HBL: 4.1-4.7 cm

The **Hodgson's Bat** is a rare, medium-sized tree bat of striking colouration. It has a yellowish back, sides and undersides, and a cinnamon throat. Its wings are orange with black markings along the wing bones. It roosts in trees, often camouflaged in decaying leaves or flowers of the same colour as itself. It is mainly a tree- or bush-roosting bat, but sometimes roosts in caves. It is found in northern India, north-eastern India and the Himalayan foothills.

Orange fur

GABOR CSORBA

Hodgson's Bat

The **Nepalese Whiskered Bat** is a small bat that has a lip with a hairy whisker-like fringe. Its hair is russet-brow, and it has small ears and feet. It often roosts in rolled-up banana leaves at the centre of the plant. It is found in valleys and mountains of northern and eastern India.

SIMILAR SPECIES are the **Lesser Mouse-eared Bat** (north India); **Whiskered Bat** (north and east India); **Siliguri Bat** (Uttarakhand, northern West Bengal, Sikkim, Meghalaya); **Mandelli's Mouse-Eared Bat** (Uttarakhand, West Bengal, Sikkim, Meghalaya) ; **Kashmir Cave Bat** (Jammu & Kashmir, Meghalaya); **Hasselt's Bat** (earlier in West Bengal); **Horsfield's Bat** (southern India); **Water Bat** (Meghalaya); **Hairy-Faced Bat** (West Bengal, Nagaland); **Peyton's Whiskered Bat** (Karnataka, Tamil Nadu).

Flat head

Dark brown fur with pale hair tips

PIPAT SOISOOK

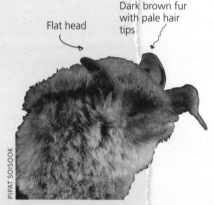

Nepalese Whiskered Bat

Pipistrelles

Family: Vespertilionidae
Indian Status: Common to Occasional
Social Unit: solitary; small groups; hundreds
Size: HBL: 3.3-6.4 cm

The small **Indian Pipistrelle** is a brown bat, chocolate or chestnut on top and beige below. Its wings, membranes and tip of the muzzle are naked and black. Though it inhabits dense vegetation, it also flies into houses for insects and roosts in bamboo thatch roofs. It is found throughout India except in Rajasthan. it roosts in tree holes, under the bark, in disused buildings in forested areas and towns. **Best Seen At:** Mumbai (Maharashtra), Bengaluru (Karnataka)

Almost identical to the Indian Pipistrelle, the **Indian Pygmy Bat** is slightly smaller, darker, and with squarish ears. The fur ranges from dark yellow to brown or even dark blackish brown. It is one of the first bats to come out at dark with a slow, erratic flight. It inhabits the same places as the Indian Pipistrelle throughout India except in the high Himalayas and deserts.

SIMILAR SPECIES are the **Javan Pipistrelle** (Jammu & Kashmir to Arunachal Pradesh, the North-East, Madhya Pradesh, Andhra Pradesh); **Kelaart's Pipistrelle** (south, central, eastern and western India); **Dormer's Bat** (across India except in high Himalayas); the **Common Pipistrelle** (Jammu & Kashmir, Assam); **Mount Popa Pipistrelle** (Jammu & Kashmir, Bihar, North-East); **Japanese Pipistrelle** (Andhra Pradesh, Arunachal Pradesh, Meghalaya, Uttar Pradesh); **Kuhl's Pipistrelle** (West Bengal, Assam, Megahlaya); **Black Gilded Pipistrelle** Meghalaya), **Chocolate Pipistrelle** (all over India); **Thomas's Pipistrelle** (West Bengal, Assam) and **Savi's Pipistrelle** (Meghalaya).

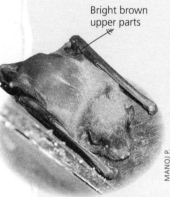

Bright brown upper parts

MANOJ P.

Indian Pipistrelle, Kumarakom, Kerala

Darker fur

Squarish ears

Small size

MANOJ P.

Indian Pygmy Bat, Kumarakom, Kerala

Great Evening Bat

Family: Vespertilionidae
Indian Status: Rare
Social Unit: Unknown;
large groups outside
India
Size: FA: 7–7.7 cm
Best Seen At: Mawsmai
Cave, Meghalaya

Among the biggest of the evening bats, it is large and grey-brown with black wings. Its long tail sticks partially out and its ears are broad and rounded off. It is found in Meghalaya and Assam. It inhabits caves at 1,500 m, in oak forests.

Large and
broad ears

Large size

Grey–brown fur

GABOR CSORBA

Great Evening Bat

Common Serotine

Family: Vespertilionidae
Indian Status:
Uncommon
Social Unit: Ones and
twos; small groups
Size: HBL: 8 cm
Best Seen At: Nowhere
commonly seen

This is a large, dark brown bat with a pale buff belly and throat. Its ears are dark and long. It has a long tail. It has a straight, even, slow flight, and makes constant clicks and squeaks. It hibernates in tree hollows. It lives in the Himalayan foothills from Jammu & Kashmir to Nagaland. It inhabits hollow trees and caves.

Long,
pointed ears
with ridges

Thick,
swollen
muzzle

SIMILAR SPECIES are the **Bobrinskii's Serotine** (Jammu & Kashmir); **Sombre Bat** (West Bengal); **Bottae's Serotine** (Jammu & Kashmir) and **Thick-eared Bat** (Meghalaya).

PAUL BATES

Common Serotine

Asiatic Greater Yellow House Bat

Family: Vespertilionidae
Indian Status: Common
Social Unit: Between one and fifty
Size: HBL: 6.7-9.3 cm
Best Seen At: Towns and cities all over India

Easily known by its yellow-brown back and bright yellow underside, this bat is heavy, with a long tail. It has a low, straight, silent flight, and is not shy of light when roosting. It is found across India except in Jammu & Kashmir and the high Himalayas. It roosts in old buildings, hollow trees and palm fronds.

SIMILAR SPECIES: **Lesser Yellow House Bat** (peninsular India except North-East and Rajasthan), **Parti-Coloured Bat** (Jammu & Kashmir), **Yellow Desert Bat** (Himachal Pradesh, Uttar Pradesh, West Bengal, Bihar); **Hairy-Winged Bat** (Kerala, Tamil Nadu, North-East); **Harlequin Bat** (North-East); **Tickell's Bat** (different parts of India).

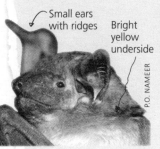

Small ears with ridges
Bright yellow underside

P.O. NAMEER

Asian Greater Yellow House Bat, Choolannur, Kerala

Painted Bat

Family: Vespertilionidae
Indian Status: Uncommon
Social Unit: Solitary; pairs
Size: HBL: 4.5-4.8 cm
Best Seen At: Banana groves, Kerala

This bat has bright orange and black wings and long, dense fur also bright orange on the back. It flies with an up and down flutter like a moth. It hangs upside down among dead leaves, especially of plantain trees. It is found in dry forests, banana groves and fields in Kerala, Karnataka, Tamil Nadu, Andhra Pradesh, Maharashtra, Goa, Rajasthan, Sikkim, West Bengal, Assam and Odisha.

SIMILAR SPECIES are the **Hardwicke's Forest Bat** (North-East); **Papillose Bat** (West Bengal); **Lenis Woolly Bat**, **Eastern Barbastelle** (the Himalayas); **Kachin Woolly Bat** (Meghalaya).

Bright orange fur on back
Black and orange wings

MANOJ. P.

Painted Bat, Pambadi, Kerala

Flat-headed Bat

Family: Vespertilionidae
Indian Status: Occasional
Social Unit: Multi-male–multi-female
Size: HBL: 3.4–4.6 cm,
Best Seen At: Sirsi, Karnataka

Flat head and traingular ears

Pale golden brown on upper half

This is a very small bat with triangular ears and dark brown wings. It has a golden head, throat and back; the lower back and belly are dark brown. It lives in bamboos, entering the stem through slits made by insect larvae. Fleshy pads and balls on its feet help it to cling and move inside the smooth bamboo. It inhabits bamboo forests in the Western Ghats, Andaman & Nicobar Islands and the North-East.

BANDANA AUL & SARAVANAKUMAR

Flat-headed Bat, Mayabunder, Andaman & Nicobar Islands

A **SIMILAR SPECIES** is the **Greater Flat-Headed Bat** (Mizoram).

Grey Long-eared Bat

Family: Vespertilionidae
Indian Status: Occasional
Social Unit: Small groups
Size: HBL: 4.7-5.3 cm
Best Seen At: Nowhere commonly seen

A small, dark buff or cream bat, it has very large an ears. This is a slow-flying, early-evening bat that hovers in front of bushes in search of food. It is found in the forests and mountains of Jammu & Kashmir.

IMRE DOMBII

Very long, translucent ears

Very large size

SIMILAR SPECIES are the **Brown Long-Eared Bat** (Jammu & Kashmir, Uttarakhand, Himachal Pradesh, West Bengal, Meghalaya) and **Hemprich's Long-Eared Bat** (Jammu & Kashmir, Himachal Pradesh).

Grey Long-eared Bat

Round-eared Tube-nosed Bat

Family: Vespertilionidae
Indian Status: Locally Common
Social Unit: 2-5
Size: HBL: 3.8-5 cm
Best Seen At: Khasi Hills, Meghalaya

A small reddish brown bat with rounded ears, it has an orangish back and paler underside. It has a slow flight, at times skimming close to the ground. It is found in forests and hilly plantations (especially cardamom). Recorded from West Bengal, Meghalaya, Mizoram, Sikkim, Andaman and Nicobar, Andhra Pradesh and Tamil Nadu.

SIMILAR SPECIES are the **Nicobar Long-fingered Bat** (Nicobar Islands, Katrnataka, Tamil Nadu); **Sanborn's Long-fingered Bat** (North-East); **Scully's Tube-nosed Bat** (Himalayas); **Greater Tube-nosed Bat** (Himalayas); **Hutton's Tube-nosed Bat** (Jammu & Kashmir, Uttarakhand, West Bengal, Assam); **Little Tube-nosed Bat** (Sikkim, Meghalaya); **Rainforest Tube-nosed Bat** (Meghalaya); **Jaintia Tube-nosed Bat** (Meghalaya); **Peter's Tube-nosed Bat** (Uttarakhand).

Rounded ears

Orangish fur on back

Tube nose

BANDANA AUL

Round-eared Tube-nosed Bat, Trinket Island, Andaman & Nicobar Islands

Schreiber's Long-fingered Bat

Family: Vespertilionidae
Indian Status: Rare
Social Unit: Colonies
Size: HBL: 4.7-6.5 cm
Best Seen At: Robber's Cave, Mahabaleshwar, Maharashtra

A small evening bat with long, dense fur varying from russet to dark brown, this bat has small, rounded ears. Its typical position at rest, with its wings folded back, gives it the name of Bent-winged Bat. It lives in huge colonies, but hunts solitarily. Recorded from Maharashtra, Tamil Nadu, Uttarakhand, West Bengal, Sikkim, Meghalaya and Arunachal Pradesh, it inhabits caves in hilly and forested areas.

Russet brown fur

Long wings

PAUL BATES

Schreiber's Long-fingered Bat, Maharashtra

Whales and dolphins *(top)* and shark *(bottom)* faces, showing absence and presence of gills

Whales and dolphins *(top)* and shark *(bottom)* tails, showing horizontal and vertical tail flukes

Difference between whale *(top)* and shark *(bottom)* skin

VASUNDHARA KANDPAL

Where they live

Whales, Dolphins, Porpoises

INDIAN CETACEANS **AT A GLANCE**

NUMBER OF SPECIES **25-29**

BIGGEST **BLUE WHALE**

Whales & Dolphins

Indo-Pacific Bottlenose
Dolphin surfaces,
showing blowhole

VIVEK MENON

SMALLEST	MOST COMMON	MOST ENDANGERED	ACTIVITY
FINLESS PORPOISE	INDO-PACIFIC HUMPBACK DOLPHIN	SOUTH ASIAN RIVER DOLPHIN	☀ ☾☀

▶What is a Cetacean?

Whales and dolphins belong to the order Cetacea, which evolved around 60 million years ago when the dinosaurs had just died out. Earlier, biologists thought Cetaceans were fish – till the 18th century when it was discovered that they were mammals as they were warm-blooded, gave birth to their young, and breathed through lungs and not gills.

Lobtailing or tail-slapping is the slapping of the water with the tail before submerging; Here, a Sperm Whale lobtails

Going by their external features, fish and Cetaceans can be easily differentiated as Cetaceans have horizontal tail flukes compared with the vertically aligned tail fins of fish. Most Indian Cetacean species are marine (living in oceans), some live in estuaries and tidal creeks, and one species inhabits rivers. Some, such as the Ganges River Dolphin, are native to India, while others such as the Humpback Whale are found all over the world. Ranging from the mammoth Blue Whale – the world's largest living creature – to the small dolphins, the order Cetacea includes some of the most fascinating, social and intelligent creatures.

▶Whales, dolphins and porpoises

All three are Cetaceans, but whales are generally the largest, dolphins smaller, and porpoises the smallest. Porpoises and dolphins are told apart close up by the spade-shaped teeth of the former and the conical

Spy Hopping

Spy hopping is rising above eye level from the water and scanning the horizon by rotating the head. Here, an Irrawaddy Dolphin in Chilika Lake, Odisha Lake, Odisha

Roll Play

Rolling is the act of exposing their nostrils for breathing and then arching their back to submerge. Here, a Sperm Whale rolls.

ones of the latter. With exceptions, dolphins generally have longer beaks, and are more acrobatic and larger.

▶How do they move?

Cetaceans have evolved to lead a marine life, and are adapted to swim and dive. This includes the reduction of the body's surface area by 23 per cent compared to other mammals (reducing drag), and increase in oxygen storage capacity to allow them to dive for long hours underwater. Flukes are the key to their locomotion as they provide hydro-dynamic thrust and flippers aid movement in all directions. Baleen whales, despite their size, can reach top speeds of 48 km per hour, although normally they cruise at 19-22.5 km per hour. The Sei is one of the fastest baleen whales, reaching speeds of 55.5 km per hour, about the same as a much smaller bottlenose dolphin.

▶How do they eat?

Gangetic River Dolphins, the Irrawaddy Dolphin and the Finless Porpoise eat fish and shrimp, largely from riverbeds. The Irrawaddy Dolphin is known to spit water as a

Breaching

This is a leap that takes the whole body out of water. Here, an Indo-Pacific Bottlenose Dolphin, Ashtamudi Port, Kerala

DIPANI SUTARIA

hunting strategy to confuse or stun fish, which is a unique predatory technique. Squids, octopus and fish from the seabed or around reefs form the diet of the Indo-Pacific Bottlenose and Humpback Dolphins. Rough-toothed dolphins have a diet similar to other small dolphins but may take large dolphinfish. Narrow-beaked dolphins, like the Long-beaked Common Dolphin and the Pan-tropical Spotted Dolphin, eat small fish and crustaceans and krill.

Humpbacks use both bubble-feeding (forcing large schools of fish up by blowing bubbles under them, and then eating them in one go) and lunge-feeding to get at krill and small fish, while Blue Whales gulp-feed almost entirely on krill. Fins and Sei use both lunge- and gulp-feeding for krill, crustaceans, fish and squid. The Bryde's and Minke Whales feed on both fish and plankton more by gulp feeding. Pilot Whales, beaked whales, Dwarf and Pygmy Sperm Whales eat squid, but fish and crustaceans too, as do Orcas. Pygmy and false killer whales eat squid, fish and dolphins. Risso's Dolphins eat squids, octopus and krill.

▶How do they communicate?

The South Asian River Dolphin can be quite vocal, with continuous echolocating clicks and a loud, sneeze-like blow. Calls of marine dolphins have been connected to feeding as well as their 'community', travelling resting and breeding.

Sperm Whale mother and child

Generally, these Cetaceans emit whistles, pulsed calls including clicks and noisy sounds. The clicks are high frequency and can range from 120–140 Hertz. Special calls between separated dolphin mothers and calves and complex humpback songs are examples of evolved communication in Cetaceans.

▶Young ones

Dolphins generally have a pregnancy period of about a year to one-and-a-half years and bear a single young. Humpbacks, Fins, Sei, Bryde's and Minke Whales have their young after around a year's pregnancy. Blue Whales have a shorter pregnancy period of 6–8 months. Pilot Whales and Orcas have a gestation of 15–18 months. False Killer Whales have pregnancies of 11–16 months. Pygmy and Dwarf Sperm Whales have short pregnancies of about seven months.

▶Threats and conservation

River dolphins are threatened by fishing, toxic contamination, catching of fish fingerlings and crustacean larvae, increased number of vehicles in rivers and decreased water flow due to damming of rivers.

Larger oceanic cetaceans are threatened by pollution, habitat destruction, over-fishing, climate change and underwater noise pollution. Very little has been done for Cetacean conservation in India.

Social Circuit

Humpback Dolphins can be very socially active. Here, two dolphins playfully rub beaks and bodies, Cochin Port, Kerala

VIVEK MENON

DIVYA PANICKER

Dorsal fins of dolphins

Fraser's Dolphin

Risso's Dolphin

Rough-toothed Dolphin

Bottlenose Dolphin

Pan-tropical Dolphin

Long-snouted Spinner Dolphin

Short-snouted Spinner Dolphin

Striped Dolphin

Indo-Pacific Humpback Dolphin

Common Dolphin

Irrawaddy River Dolphin

Ganges River Dolphin

Breaching

Killer Whale

Fin Whale

Minke Whale

Sei Whale

Sperm Whale

Bryde's Whale

Whales' blows

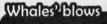

Blue Whale

Minke Whale

Fin Whale

Sei Whale

Humpback Whale

South Asian River Dolphin

Family: Platanistidae
Indian Status: Locally Common
Social Unit: Solitary; pairs; small group of up to 10
Size: HBL: 2.2- 2.6 m, Wt.: 70-90 kg
Best Seen At: Vikramshila WLS, Bihar; Kaziranga NP, Assam

The only true freshwater cetacean in India, this endangered dolphin is easily recognized by its long beak sticking out of water. Its mouth curves upwards at the end of its snout in a menacing leer. Its flexible neck enables it to turn its head at right angles! It has large, paddle-shaped flippers and a low hump-like fin on the back. Its stocky body may vary from slate-blue to muddy brown. The eyes are small and this is the only Cetacean without a crystalline eye lens, making it blind. Very active and vocal, it is known to swim on its side a few inches above the riverbed. It is found in the rivers Ganges and Brahmaputra and their tributaries, in the Sunderbans and in the Beas in Punjab.

Long, 'toothed' beak'

Short, triangular 'hump'-like fin on back

Broad flippers

South Asian River Dolphin

ALL ILLUSTRATIONS: VASUNDHARA KANDPAL

Indo-Pacific Humpback Dolphin

Family: Delphinidae
Indian Status: Common
Social Unit: Small pods of 3-7; up to 25 animals
Size: HBL: 1.8-3 m, Wt.: 250-280 kg
Best Seen At: Calicut (Kozhikode) coast, Kerala

A large dolphin, lead-grey with a pink-tinged underside, flippers and flukes, and spotting on its body sometimes, it has a characteristic hump with a small fin on its back. Its mouth line is straight, the beak moderately long. It breaks out of the water at an angle, breathes with its beak, arches its back, lifts its flukes in the air, then flops back. It is found in shallow coastal and estuarine waters, as well as mangroves, from Gujarat to Kerala and Andhra Pradesh to the Andaman Islands.

Short, triangular fin on large 'hump'

Medium-sized beak

Broad flippers, rounded tip

Lead-grey to greyish blue upper side, pale pinkish underside

Indo-Pacific Humpback Dolphin

Finless Porpoise

Family: Phocoenidae
Indian Status: Locally Common
Social Unit: Solitary/pairs, groups of up to 17
Size: HBL: 1.2-2 m
Wt: 70-100 kg
Best Seen At: Nowhere commonly seen

One of the smallest cetaceans in the world, this is the only porpoise found in Indian waters. Its body is pale blue or grey-blue like the Ganges River Dolphin's, but it does not have a long-toothed snout. It has no fin on its back. Its flippers are long and tapering. The tail fluke is deeply notched. This porpoise does not normally come out of the water, but 'spy-hops', holding itself vertically and lifting its head clear of the water surface. It is found mainly in estuarine and coastal waters with a sandy bottom, in shallow bays and mangroves on the east and west coasts, from Mumbai to Odisha, and Lakshadweep. It has been recently seen in the Gulf of Kutch.

No fin on back, but a ridge

Large, blunt melon head

Finless Porpoise

Paler underside

No beak, pale lip

Broad flipper, narrower at base

Irrawaddy Dolphin

Family: Delphinidae
Indian Status: Occasional
Social Unit: 2-3, occasionally 10-15
Size: HBL: 1.7-2.75 cm,
Wt.: 90-130 kg
Best Seen At: Chilika Lake, Odisha

This is a blunt-headed, beakless, 'beluga-like' dolphin varying from dark blue-grey to pale blue, with a lighter underside. It has long and broad flippers with a curved, trailing edge, and a tail with broad flukes notched in the middle. It rarely comes out of the water, shooting water out by spitting. It has a smooth, slow roll and breaches occasionally in a low fashion. It inhabits coastal waters and estuaries, creeks and mangrove habitats, especially river mouths on the eastern coast of India, from Chennai to West Bengal, including the Sunderbans.

Small, triangular fin on back

Large, blunt melon head

Broad, notched fluke

Long, broad flippers

No beak

Irrawaddy Dolphin

Indo-Pacific Bottlenose Dolphin

Family: Delphinidae
Indian Status: Occasional
Social Unit: 5–15 individuals; large congregations known
Size: HBL: Up to 2.6 m, Wt.: Up to 230 kg
Best Seen At: Malvan coast, Maharashtra

One of the commonest dolphins globally, it is large, stocky and a drab grey. It has a short, distinct beak. A tall fin on the back is darker than the rest of its body. The underside is paler and, in some, spotted. Its flippers are moderately long. The tail is thick and flukes notched with curved, trailing edges. Friendly and active, it swims close to boats and is said to help fishermen drive shoals of fish into their nets. It is found in shallow coastal waters on the continental shelf and near islands. It has been recorded off both coasts, from Maharashtra through Karnataka, Goa, Kerala and Lakshadweep, and Tamil Nadu to West Bengal.

Dark cape and grey body

Short beak and crease between beak and head

Broad, notched fluke

Dark, slim and long flippers

Indo-Pacific Bottlenose Dolphin

Long-beaked Common Dolphin

Family: Delphinidae
Indian Status: Common
Social Unit: 10-30; concentrations of 100-500
Size: HBL: 1-2.5 m, Wt: Up to 240 kg
Best Seen At: Nowhere commonly seen

Easily recognized by the hourglass pattern on its body, this dolphin's back is brownish, black or purplish, with a yellow or tan patch on both sides. Its undersides are white or creamy. It has a dark circle around its eyes and a dark stripe from flipper to jaw. The fin on its back is tall and pointy. Large pods of these acrobatic, boisterous dolphins are seen with other dolphins in open waters, from Goa to Kerala and Lakshadweep, and Odisha to Andaman & Nicobar Islands.

Dark, tall, hooked or triangular fin

Dark beak with crease

Dark cape

Tan or yellow patch

Grey tail

Long-beaked Common Dolphin

ALL ILLUSTRATIONS: VASUNDHARA KANDPAL

Long-snouted Spinner Dolphin

Grey with a creamy white underside, this has a very long, dark-tipped beak with a prominent crease where it joins the forehead, a large, triangular fin on its back, and long flippers. It throws itself in the air up to 3 m, then twists on a vertical axis up to seven times. It is the only dolphin in Indian waters that spins; others somersault and dive. Large schools of these can be seen churning the water into a frothy foam. Inhabiting warm waters near islands and coasts, it has been recorded off both coasts from Maharashtra through Karnataka, Kerala, Tamil Nadu, Lakshadweep and Andhra Pradesh.

Family: Delphinidae
Indian Status: Locally Common
Social Unit: 5-200; sometimes up to 1,000
Size: HBL: 1.75-2.4 m, Wt: 45-75 kg
Best Seen At: Nowhere commonly seen

Tall fin on back

Dark grey stocky body with white patch on belly or whole underside

Long-snouted River Dolphin

Small, dark flippers

Very long, thin, dark beak

Pan-tropical Spotted Dolphin

Its grey or blue body is heavily spotted and older dolphins may be covered in bubble-like spots. It has a dark fin and small convex flippers. The beak is white-tipped (unlike the fully black beak of Spinner Dolphins) and it has white lips. An active, energetic swimmer that jumps about a lot in water, it sometimes breaches, making high leaps and falling back after a moment of being motionless in air. It is found in warm waters off West Bengal, Lakshadweep Islands, the Bay of Bengal and the Arabian Sea.

Family: Delphinidae
Indian Status: Uncommon
Social Unit: 50-1,000
Size: HBL: 1.6-2.6 m, Wt: 90-120 kg
Best Seen At: Nowhere commonly seen

Dark, hooked fin on back

Dark grey cape

White-tipped dark beak

Pan-tropical Spotted Dolphin

Small, dark flippers

Rough-toothed Dolphin

Family: Delphinidae
Indian Status: Uncommon
Social Unit: 10-20; occasionally up to 50 individuals
Size: HBL: 2.1-2.6 m, Wt: 90-160 kg
Best Seen At: Nowhere commonly seen

Long beak with white lip and chin

Sloping forehead

Dark, hooked fin on back

Dark large flippers

Pinkish white underside

Rough-toothed Dolphin

Unlike most beaked dolphins, this dolphin's beak does not have a crease separating it from the forehead. Its head has a unique conical shape that, combined with its white lips and throat, makes it easy to recognize. Another unique feature: its almond-shaped teeth. There are yellowish or pink blotches on its underbelly, while the fin on its back is set at an angle of 45 degrees to its body. This species swims fast just beneath the water surface and rarely surfaces. When it does, it pops out in a low arc. It is found in deep offshore and warm waters, beyond the continental shelf off Tamil Nadu and Nicobar Islands.

Risso's Dolphin

Family: Delphinidae
Indian Status: Uncommon
Social Unit: Groups of 10-30; sometimes 100s
Size: HBL: 2.6-4 m Wt: 300-500 kg
Best Seen At: Nowhere commonly seen

Bulging forehead

Very tall fin on back

No beak

Dark, long sickle-shaped flippers

Risso's Dolphin

This dolphin is identified by its dome-shaped forehead with a crease that runs from the centre to the mouth line. It is almost beakless, with younger ones having a short beak. It has a white mouth line. Its body is heavily scarred with white streaks and varies from very dark grey (juveniles) to almost white or pale grey (adults), with paler undersides. It comes half out of the water before slapping its head back in. It feeds on deep water squid, using echolocation and a variety of clicks to navigate. It is found in deep offshore and continental shelf waters off Kerala, Lakshadweep, Tamil Nadu and Nicobar Islands.

Short-finned Pilot Whale

Family: Delphinidae
Indian Status: Uncommon
Social Unit: 10–50
Size: HBL: 3.6-6.5 m, Wt: 1,500-3,500 kg
Best Seen At: Nowhere commonly seen

It looks a lot like the False Killer Whale. It has an off-white belly patch on a dark grey body, a W-shaped grey patch on its throat, and a grey or white diagonal stripe from its eye to the fin on its back. Very social, this night-feeder travels in large pods and is often seen with other Cetaceans, especially the Bottlenose Dolphin. It has a strong blow and is easily identifiable as it approaches ships in large numbers.

It is found in deep waters off the continental shelf and has been recorded off West Bengal, Lakshadweep Islands, the Andamans, Maharashtra and Tamil Nadu (Tuticorin port).

Broad base to fin

Bulbous head

Short-finned Pilot Whale

Off-white belly patch

Greyish white on throat

Melon-headed Whale

Family: Delphinidae
Indian Status: Uncommon
Social Unit: 100-500 up to 2,000
Size: HBL: 2.1-2.7 m, Wt: 160-275 kg
Best Seen At: Nowhere commonly seen

A dark, small dolphin with a torpedo-shaped body, it gets its name from its rounded head. Its fin is tall and more hooked. The flippers are pointed. Its narrow face is unique with its dark mask and white lips, and a dark cape running across its back, giving it a bandit-like look! Along with the Pilot and Killer Whales, this species belongs to a group of smaller-toothed whales known as 'blackfish'.

Closely related to dolphins, it is alternately classified as whale or dolphin. It makes shallow leaps out of the water. Little seen, travels in large numbers and is found in deep waters in Andhra Pradesh, Tamil Nadu and Nicobar Islands.

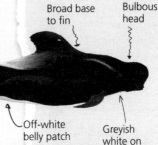

Tall, hooked fin in older animals

Dark cape till mid-body

Melon-shaped head

White belly patch (not often visible)

Pointed flippers

White lips

Melon-headed Whale

Family: Delphinidae
Indian Status: Rare to Uncommon
Social Unit: 3-50 individuals
Size: HBL: 4-9.8 m, Wt: 1,100-5,500 kg

Killer Whales

Probably the best known whale because of its appearance in films and marine shows, the **KILLER WHALE** is black and white with a huge fin on the back that in males may be as long as 1.8 m. Its jet-black body has a white oval patch behind the eye and a grey saddle patch behind the fin. It has a white chest, white side patches and rounded flippers. Males are larger and heavier than females and have taller, straighter fins on the back. Younger ones may show tan or yellow colouration in the white patches. A very inquisitive, acrobatic species, the Killer Whale often approaches boats and humans. It has a low blow but displays other whale-like behaviour such as lobtailing, breaching, flipper-slapping, and speed swimming. It is found in most marine habitats including near the shore off Gujarat, Goa, Tamil Nadu, Andaman & Nicobar Islands, and Lakshadweep Islands. **Best Seen At:** Nowhere commonly seen

Huge fin on the back

White oval patch behind eye

Large, rounded paddle flippers

White patches on the underside

Killer Whale

A rare, large and active whale, the **FALSE KILLER WHALE** is uniformly dark grey in colour. It has a slightly grey or off-white 'W' on its chest, a large fin on its back and a unique flipper that is set very far forward on the body with a clear elbow. This whale has a long slender head unlike the Pilot Whale, and is larger than the Melon-headed and Pygmy Killer Whale. An active swimmer, it is known to feed on smaller Cetaceans. It frequently swims with its mouth open, exposing its sharp teeth. It has been recorded off the coast of Maharashtra, Kerala, Tamil Nadu and the Andaman & Nicobar Islands. It prefers deep, warm, offshore waters, but is also known to move into shallow water on occasion. **Best Seen At:** Nowhere commonly seen

Narrow, tapered head (not bulbous like the Melon-headed Whale)

Curved sickle fin

False Killer Whale

Pointed, long flipper with an 'elbow'

Fully grey body; no markings

Sperm Whales

The most easily recognizable large whale, the **SPERM WHALE** has a big, square head, a shrivelled prune-like purple-brown body, short flippers and no fin on its back. It has a triangular hump on the back and a row of knuckles between the hump and tail. Unlike any Cetacean, it blows an angled blow of water from the left side of its nose. It inhabits deep open oceans off Gujarat, Karnataka, Maharashtra, Kerala to Tamil Nadu, Puducherry, Andaman & Nicobar Islands and Lakshadweep. **Best Seen At:** Nowhere commonly seen

Family: Physeteridae (Sperm Whale); Kogiidae (Pygmy Sperm Whale & Dwarf Sperm Whale)
Indian Status: Uncommon
Social Unit: Sperm Whale: 1-50; Pygmy Sperm Whale: 3-6, up to 10; Dwarf Sperm Whale: 1-2, up to 10
Size: HBL: 2.7-18 m, Wt: Pygmy Sperm Whale: 300-680 kg; Sperm Whale: Up to 70,000 kg; Dwarf Sperm Whale: 135-275 kg

The **PYGMY SPERM WHALE**, with its squarish head, is possibly a close cousin of the Dwarf Sperm Whale. It is steel-grey, with a pale or pinkish underside, a tiny fin on the back, a prominent false gill and broad flippers. When rising to the water surface, it may drop back without arching out, a unique habit. Like squids, it releases a red or brown ink jet if startled. It lives in deep outer continental shelves and beyond, and warm temperate waters. Only a few records from Kerala, Andaman & Nicobar Islands, and Andhra Pradesh. **Best Seen At:** Nowhere commonly seen

THE DWARF SPERM WHALE and the identical-looking Pygmy Sperm Whale (except the tall fin) can be confused with sharks because of the shape of their jaw, small sharp teeth and false gill behind the eye. But their blowhole and bulky bodies show they are whales. Recorded from Andhra Pradesh, Tamil Nadu and Kerala, it is found in deeper waters than the Pygmy Sperm Whale. **Best Seen At:** Nowhere commonly seen

Row of knuckles and hump on back
Square head
Sperm Whale
Stubby flippers

Small hooked fin
Grey body
Pygmy Sperm Whale
Pale belly
White markings on face

Larger fin on back
Dwarf Sperm Whale

Beaked Whales

Family: Ziphiidae
Indian Status: Uncommon
Social Unit: 1-25 (Cuvier's); 1-12 (Blainville's Beaked Whale)
Size: HBL: 5.5-7 m, Wt: 2,500-3,500 kg (Cuvier's Beaked Whale)
Social Unit: 1-12
Size: HBL: 4.5-7 m

Beaked whales are medium to large Cetaceans that live in deep ocean trenches and are rarely seen above water. All have a fewer number of teeth and females have no teeth at all. The most abundant of all beaked whales, the **CUVIER'S BEAKED WHALE** is recognized by its goose-beak shaped mouth and a gently sloping forehead. Its colour varies from pale brown to cream to purplish black and red, making identification difficult. It rarely breaches, and has an indistinct blow. Its head may be exposed while swimming. It has been recorded only twice off Tamil Nadu, and Lakshadweep. It prefers deep waters (deeper than 200 m), especially near a steep sea slope and around oceanic islands.
Best Seen At: Nowhere commonly seen

Goose-beaked mouth with two conical teeth in lower jaw

Small fin on back

Cuvier's Beaked Whale

Variable colour from cream to brown to purple but with whitish scarring

A slightly smaller beaked whale, the **BLAINVILLE'S BEAKED WHALE** can be identified only at close range by its large, single-lobed and flattened teeth. Its dark bluish grey body has a lighter patch on the underside and a large number of scars all over. A series of shallow dolphin-like dives is followed by a slightly longer, deeper dive from which it emerges with its beak pointing skywards. It has been recorded only off Nicobar Islands and inhabit deep continental slope waters. **Best Seen At:** Nowhere commonly seen

Dark grey upper parts, heavily scarred

Goose-beaked mouth with flat teeth

Blainville's Beaked Whale

Pale underparts

Minke Whale

The smallest and most common of the large whales, it is dark grey or slaty brown above, and white or pale grey-brown under. It has a sharp triangular head with a pointed snout. Most have a white band on the flipper. It can be easily spotted by its triangular snout, with which it breaks out of the water surface. It starts blowing as soon as the snout emerges but the low, indistinct blow is a 2-3 m spray, easy to miss. It inhabits temperate waters and only two records are confirmed from Kakinada in Andhra Pradesh, and Lakshadweep.

Family: Balaenopteridae
Indian Status: Uncommon
Social Unit: 1-3; can reach up to 100
Size: HBL: 6.7-10.7 m, Wt: 2,000-2,700 kg
Best Seen at: Nowhere commonly seen

Dark body

Triangular head

Minke's Whale

Flipper may have white band

White or pale undersides

Humpback Whale

A large, energetic whale with distinctive flippers, head and tail, the Humpback is one of the world's best-known whales. It has a slender head (almost crocodilian) with a single ridge and a large splash guard. Its flippers are the longest in any whale, nearly one-third of the body. Its body is blue-black or dark grey with whitish patches on the underside. The broad blue-black tail flukes have frayed edges and white patches. It is known to leap clear of the water and land on its back in the water. It is one of the top vocalizers among aquatic mammals. Males sing without break for as long as 35 minutes, and all day till other whales join in. It is found in Gujarat, Maharashtra, Tamil Nadu and Kerala in warm waters in winter, and cold waters in summer.

Family: Balaenopteridae
Indian Status: Rare
Social Unit: 1-3 commonly; up to 15 in feeding concentrations
Size: HBL: 11-16 m, Wt: 30,000-34,000 kg
Best Seen At: Nowhere commonly seen

Small fin set on hump on back

Dark body, scarred with barnacles

Narrow head

Long, arm-like flipper with white underside

Humpback Whale

Sei Whale

Family: Balaenopteridae
Indian Status: Uncommon
Social Unit: 5-6, up to 100
Size: HBL: 13.5-14.5 m, Wt: 22,000-38,000 kg
Best Seen At: Nowhere commonly seen

A bluish grey whale, the Sei (pronounced as 'say') has a tall and slender sickle-shaped fin on the back. It has small, dark flippers and a small tail. The dark grey body has whitish brushstrokes on its upper half. The Sei Whale's underside is pale and mottled with white scars, and there is a single ridge on its head. Its blowhole and the fin on its back are both visible during its shallow dive. When diving and breaching, its head comes out almost kissing the water surface. In a breach, its belly flops back into water, and in a dive its back and the fin on its back are visible for longer. Its short blow rises up to 3 m. It has been recorded off Gujarat, Kerala and Tamil Nadu.

One ridge

Bluish grey body

Tall, sickle-shaped fin on the back

Small, dark flippers

Mottled, scarred, pale underside

Sei Whale

Bryde's Whale

Family: Balaenopteridae
Indian Status: Uncommon
Social Unit: 1-2, groups up to 30
Size: HBL: 12.2-12.5 m, Wt:15,000-16,000 kg
Best Seen At: Nowhere commonly seen

ALL ILLUSTRATIONS: VASUNDHARA KANDPAL

A smoky-grey or brown tropical whale with blue-grey, purplish or creamy grey undersides, the Bryde's (say *broo-dees*) Whale has three longitudinal ridges on its head – a unique feature among rorqual whales. Their large tail flukes have whitish undersides. It breaches fairly regularly, at times leaving the water almost vertically, showing three-quarters of its body as it does. Its back arches before it flops back into water. It comes quite close to ships and boats unlike the shyer and more sedate Sei. Its indistinct and thin blow can rise up to 4 m. It has been recorded a dozen times in the Bay of Bengal, Tamil Nadu, Lakshadweep and Kerala. It prefers warm waters off both the east and west coasts.

Smoky grey body

Erect, sickle shaped fin

Three ridges

Large, tall, dark flippers

Mottled and scarred, pale underside

Bryde's Whale

Fin Whale

The second largest whale in the world after the Blue Whale, this whale is easily recognizable, if seen on its right side because of its bicoloured lip. The lower lip is dark grey on the left side and white on the right, A ridge joins the backswept fin to the tail flukes, giving it the name of Razorback. Its blow is a visible tall, narrow column of spray up to 6 m in height. At first, its head emerges out of water, then it rests with only its back showing, and then it blows. Then, it arches and dives. During breaching, its body breaks the surface at around 45° and re-enters with a loud splash. It is found off the east and west coasts in deep offshore waters.

Family: Balaenopteridae
Indian Status: Uncommon
Social Unit: 3-7, up to 100
Size: HBL: 19-26 m, Wt.: 60,000-90,000 kg
Best Seen At: Nowhere commonly seen

Backswept, low fin on back

Dark brown or black body

Pointed head

Fin Whale

Right side has white jaw and grey V-shaped mark

Blue Whale

This whale is the largest living creature on earth. It is uniformly blue-grey, with some mottling. The under-body is the same colour as the back. The head appears U-shaped like a submarine. The rear of the body is elongated, ending in a deep tailstock. The fin on its back is tiny, perched way back, almost on the tailstock and the flipper is large. When diving, the Blue Whale comes out of the water at a shallow angle, back visible horizontally, blows a tall columnar spout and dives back. Its back is visible for longer, the tiny fin on its back coming out just before it sinks downwards. It inhabits cold waters and open seas off both coasts in the Indian Ocean, usually found in the top 100 m of the sea.

Family: Balaenopteridae
Indian Status: Uncommon
Social Unit: 1-4, more in feeding concentrations
Size: HBL: 20-27 m, Wt: 113,000-150,000 kg
Best Seen At: Nowhere commonly seen

Blue-grey body, mottled look

Broad head, stocky appearance

Blue Whale

Dugong

Manatee

Dugong Skull

The Dugong's flipper looks like this inside!

MAYUKH CHATTERJEE (ADAPTED FROM WWW.INKART.NET)

Rounded back *(top)* showing no fin and flukes that are visible at sea *(above)*

Where they live

 Dugongs

INDIAN
DUGONGS
AT A GLANCE

NUMBER
OF SPECIES **1**

ACTIVITY
✿

Dugongs

Dugong, Neil Island,
Andaman & Nicobar Islands

VARDHAN PATANKAR

▶What are manatees and dugongs?

The order Sirenia includes the marine dugongs and manatees, which look somewhat like a cross between a walrus and a dolphin. Not only are Sirenians the only completely vegetarian marine mammals but they are also thought to be closely related to the elephant!

Dugongs have only six vertebrae while most other mammals have seven. Dugongs are found in the oceans of East Africa, Asia and

to move faster through the water. They can stay for long periods at their seagrass feeding beds. They are known to move over relatively long distances, making daily and seasonal movements.

▶What do they eat?

Dugongs have a big appetite for seagrass. Their presence in marine areas can be known by the snake-like trails of feeding in seagrass beds. Unlike turtles that eat only the blades, dugongs dig up seagrass

VARDHAN PATANKAR

Dugong, Neil Island, Andaman & Nicobar Islands

Australia, while the manatees inhabit the Americas and West African waters. Dugongs have a notched tail whereas manatees have a rounded tail.

▶How do they move?

Dugongs are strong swimmers, and they use their tail flukes and flippers

beds and eat the tubers too. Often they have been seen to choose both highly nutritious and easily digestible food rather than bulk-feed on less nutritious plants.

▶How do they communicate?

Dugongs are known to chirp, trill and whistle.

▶Young ones

Dugongs have a long lifespan (with as many as 70 years on record), with a very low reproductive rate. They invest a very long time in nurturing their young one and so the period between two births of young ones may be between three to seven years. Pregnancy is between 13–15 months. The single calf born is fully dependent on the mother for as long as 14–18 months.

▶Threats and conservation

The dugong is possibly the most threatened marine mammal in India. Its seagrass beds are reducing and there is disturbance due to increased boat and ship movements. In the Andaman & Nicobar Islands, they were common till the 1950s, but numbers have dropped. Now they seem limited to four sites near the Andaman Islands and three around the Nicobar Islands.

Family: Dugongidae
Indian Status: Rare
Social Unit: 2-54
Size: HBL: 2.5-3 m, Wt: 250-420 kg
Best Seen At: Gulf of Mannar, Tamil Nadu

Dugong

The Sea Cow or Dugong is a very large marine mammal that looks like a dolphin in its general body shape. It has a streamlined or spindle-shaped torso, flat and deeply notched or indented tail flukes, and flippers instead of forelimbs. The body colour is brownish grey above, and whitish or dirty flesh colour below. The face of the Dugong is more like that of a seal or walrus. Males have a pair of tusk-like incisors that stick out. The eyes and ear openings are small. The young are paler and with smoother skin.

Dugongs are secretive, unlike their cousins, the manatees, who can get close to boats. Dugongs live in seagrass pastures in coastal or near-shore waters. They have been recorded off Gujarat, Kerala, Tamil Nadu, Karnataka, and Andaman and Nicobar Islands.

Dark grey back

Many scars on the back

Tail with a notch in the middle

Pale grey underside

Broad paddle-shaped flipper

Broad muzzle

Dugong

VASUNDHARA KANDPAL

Contributors & Acknowledgements

GENERAL REVIEWERS

Ajith Kumar
Course Director, P.G.
Prog. In Wildlife Biology &
Conservation, NCBS
ajith@ncbs.res.in

P.O. Nameer
Associate Professor (W)
and Head; CWS, College
of Forestry, Kerala Agri.
University
nameerpo@gmail.com

SUBJECT REVIEWERS

Gabor Csorba, Deputy
Head, Dept. of Zoology,
Curator of Mammals,
HNHM, Hungary
csorba@nhmus.hu

Goutam Narayan
Ecosystems India;
gn@ecosystems-india.org

Gopinathan Maheswaran
ZSI (Zoological Survey of
India) – Birds Section
gmaheswaran@yahoo.
com

Kumaran Sathasivam
Naturalist and author
kumaran.sathasivam@
gmail.com

Nikolai Formozov
Prof., Moscow State
University, Russia
formozov@list.ru

Nita Shah
Conservation biologist
nitashah.india@gmail.
com

Paul Bates, Director,
Harrison Institute, UK
pjjbates2@hotmail.com

Raman Sukumar
Prof., IISc (Indian Institute
of Science) – CES
rsuku@ces.iisc.ernet.in

M.K. Ranjitsinh
IAS (Retd.), Former
Chairman, WTI
mkranjitsinh@gmail.com

Surendra Varma
Scientist, ANCF (Asian
Nature Conservation
Foundation)
varma@ces.iisc.ernet.in

Yash Veer Bhatnagar
Sr. Scientist, NCF (Nature
Conservation Foundation)
yash@ncf-india.org

RESEARCH & PRODUCTION TEAM

Amrit Menon
Project officer, WTI
amrit@wti.org.in

John Kunjukunju
Senior Executive
Assistant, WTI
john@wti.org.in

Mayukh Chatterjee
Manager, WTI
mayukh@wti.org.in

Radhika Bhagat
Manager – Wildlife Aid,
WTI
radhika@wti.org.in

Sharada Annamaraju
Freelance writer and
editor
Sharada.annamaraju@
gmail.com

Sheetal P. Navgire
Wildlife Conservation
Trust
bluefalcon.28@gmail.
com

Smita Bodhankar
Warnekar
Project Officer, WTI
smita@wtiy.org.in

Sujai Veeramachaneni
Ecologist; formerly with
WTI
vsujai80@gmail.com

Vasundhara Kandpal
Formerly Project Officer,
WTI
vmisanthrope@gmail.
com

PHOTOGRAPHERS & CONTRIBUTORS

- A.M.A Nikon; nixon@wti.org.in
- Aamir Amir; aamirktw11@gmail.com
- Aditya Joshi
  aditya4wildlife@gmail.com
- Aishwarya Maheshwari
  aishwaryamaheshwari@gmail.com
- Ajith Kumar; ajith@ncbs.res.in
- Amrit Menon; amrit@wti.org.in
- Anil Kumar Chhangani
  chhanganiak@yahoo.com
- Aniruddha Majumder
  aniruddha_majumder@yahoo.com
- Aniruddha Mookerjee
  jhampanm@gmail.com
- Anjan Sangma
  anjansangma@wti.org.in

- Anjan Talukar; *anjan@wti.org.in*
- Anoop K.R.; *dullforester@gmail.com*
- Ansar Khan; *ansarknp@gmail.com*
- Anwaruddin Choudhury
  acbadru56@gmail.com
- Aparajita Datta
  aparajita@ncf-india.org
- Arpit Deomurari
  deomurari@gmail.com
- Ashok Kumar; *ashok@wti.org.in*
- Bandana Aul
  bandana_aul@rediffmail.com
- Biswapriya Rahut
  bishwapriya@gmail.com
- Brij Kishor Gupta
  brijkishor68@yahoo.com
- Dhritiman Mukherjee
  dhritiman2000@yahoo.com
- Dipani Nitin Sutaria
  dipani.sutaria@gmail.com
- Divya Panicker; *divya145@gmail.com*
- Dushyant Parasher
  dushyantparasheer@yahoo.com
- G.S. Bhardwaj
  gobindsagarbhardwaj@gmail.com
- Gabor Csorba; *csorba@nhmus.hu*
- George B. Schaller; *gbs.kms@att.net*
- Girish Kumar
  girishnature@yahoo.com
- Gopinathan Maheswaran
  gmaheswaran@yahoo.com
- Goutam Narayan
  gn@ecosystems-india.org
- Imre Dombi; *imreka@freemail.hu*
- Intesar Suhail; *n.suhail@yahoo.com*
- Jose Louies; *jose@wti.org.in*
- Jugal Kishor Tiwari
  cedoindia@yahoo.com
- Joya Thapa; *joyathapa@gmail.com*
- K.M.B Prasad
  kmb.prasad@gmail.com
- Kalyan Varma; *kalyan@rtns.org*
- Kamolika Roy Chowdhury
  kamolika76@gmail.com
- Karma Sonam
  karma@ncf-india.org
- Kartik Shanker; *kshanker@gmail.com*
- Kripaljyoti Mazumdar
  kripaljyoti@gmail.com
- Krishnapriya Tamma
  priya.tamma@gmail.com
- M.K. Ranjitsinh
  mkranjitsinh@gmail.com
- Manish Chandi
  manishchandi@yahoo.com
- Manoj Dholakia
  pqcindia@gmail.com
- Manoj P; *manojp_iv@gmail.com*
- Mansoor Nabi Sofi
  mansoor@wti.org.in
- Manuel Ruedi
  manuel.ruedi@ville-ge.ch
- Mark Bibby; *mbibby255@aol.com*
- Mayukh Chatterjee
  mayukh@wti.org.in
- Mohit Agarwal
  mohit.aggarwal@asianadventures.in
- N.A. Naseer; *naseerart@gmail.com*
- Narayan Sharma
  narayansharma77@gmail.com
- Nicole Duplaix
- Nirav Bhatt
  birdwatchernrb@gmail.com
- P.O. Nameer; *nameerpo@gmail.com*
- Paul Bates; *pjjbates2@hotmail.com*
- Pipat Soisook; *pipat66@gmail.com*
- Prabal Sarkar

Contributors & Acknowledgements

- *prabalsarkarindia@gmail.com*
- Pranav Chanchani
  chanchanipranav@gmail.com
- Praveen Mohandas
  praveen.p.mohandas@gmail.com
- Punnen Kurian Venkadathu
  pkvenkadath@gmail.com
- Radhika Bhagat
  radhika@wti.org.in
- R.P Mishra; *rajendra@wti.org.in*
- Rajesh Puttaswamaiah
  rajesh.bp@hotmail.com
  & Chaitra Ramaiah
  chaitra.mr@gmail.com
- Ramakrishnan A.
  ram.wildlifer@gmail.com
- Ramith M.; *ramith@wti.org.in*
- Rathin Barman
  rathinbarman@yahoo.com
- Riyaz Ahmed; *riyaz@wti.org.in*
- S. Goutham; *goutham@wti.org.in*
- Sachin Rai
  sachin@landofthewild.com
- Sandesh Kadur; *sandesh@felis.in*
- Sanjayan Kumar
  sanjayankumarifs@gmail.com
- Sanjay Molur; *herpinvert@gmail.com*
- S. Sathyakumar; *ssk@wii.gov.in*
- Sashanka Barbaruah
  sashb@hotmail.com
- Siddharth Rao; *sidsrao@gmail.com*
- Som B. Ale; *sale1@uic.edu*
- Sumanta Kundu
  sumanta1979@gmail.com
- Sunil Kyarong; *sunil@wti.org.in*

- Sunita Khatiwara
  sunitak@ncbs.res.in
- Suresh Elamon
  yeselamon@gmail.com
- Sushovan Roy
- Sumit Sen; *sumitsen@gmail.com*
- Tamo Dadda
  tamodadda@gmail.com
- Tanushree Srivastava
  tanushrees@ncbs.res.in
- Ulrike Streicher; *u.streicher@hust.vn*
- Uraiporn Pimsai
  u.pimsai@gmail.com
- Vardhan Patankar
  vardhan@ncf-india.org
- Vasundhara Kandpal
  vmisanthrope@gmail.com
- Vijay Kumar; *vykumar@gmail.com*
- Vivek R. Sinha; *vivarati@gmail.com*
- Yash Veer Bhatnagar
  yash@ncf-india.org

ACKNOWLEDGEMENTS

There are many whom I must thank for assisting in converting the much loved book *Indian Mammals: A Field Guide* into a more easily accessible book for young readers.

Not in alphabetical order, but in order of hard work, I must thank Vatsala Kaul Banerjee, my terribly hard-working editor, and Pow Aim Hailowng for most of the concept and textual modifications, Amrit Menon and John Kunjukunju for technical and administrative assistance, all the photographers who make the book what it is and the talented artists from within WTI who helped with the illustrations (Mayukh, Radhika, Sheetal and Vasundhara). Thank you, Team!

Index

COMMON NAME		LATIN NAME	PG.NO
	Diadem Leaf-nosed	*Hipposideros diadema nicobarensis*	211
	Dobson's Horseshoe	*Rhinolophus yunanensis*	209
	Dormer's	*Scotozous dormer*	213
	Dusky Leaf-nosed	*Hipposideros ater*	210
	Eastern Barbastelle	*Barbastella leucomelas*	215
	Egyptian Free-tailed	*Tadarida aegyptiaca*	206
	Egyptian Tomb	*Taphozous perforates*	207
	European Free-tailed	*Tadarida teniotis*	206
	Flat-headed	*Tylonycteris pachypus*	216
	Fulvous Fruit	*Rousettus leschenaultii*	203
	Fulvous Leaf-nosed	*Hipposideros fulvus*	209
	Geoffroy's Trident	*Asellia tridens murraiana*	211
	Greater False Vampire	*Megaderma lyra*	208
	Greater Flat-headed	*Tylonycteris robustula*	216
	Greater Horseshoe	*Rhinolophus ferrumequinum*	209
	Greater Long-nosed/Hill Fruit	*Macroglossus sobrinus sobrinus*	205
	Greater Mouse-tailed	*Rhinopoma microphyllum*	205
	Greater Short-nosed Fruit	*Cynopterus sphinx*	204
	Greater Tube-nosed	*Murina leucogaster*	217
	Great Evening	*Ia io*	214
	Great Himalayan Leaf-nosed	*Hipposideros armiger*	211
	Grey Long-eared	*Plecotus austriacus*	216
	Hairy-faced	*Myotis annectans*	212
	Hairy-winged	*Harpiocephalus harpia*	215
	Hardwicke's Forest	*Kerivoula hardwickii*	215
	Harlequin	*Scotomanes ornatus*	215
	Hasselt's	*Myotis hasseltii*	212
	Hemprich's Long-eared	*Otonycteris hemprichii*	216
	Hodgson's	*Myotis formosus*	212
	Horsfield's	*Myotis horsfieldii*	212
	Horsfield's Leaf-nosed	*Hipposideros larvatus leptophyllus*	211
	Hutton's Tube-nosed	*Murina huttoni huttoni*	217
	Indian Flying Fox	*Pteropus giganteus*	202
	Indian Pipistrelle	*Pipistrellus coromandra*	213
	Indian Pygmy	*Pipistrellus tenuis*	213

COMMON NAME		LATIN NAME	PG.NO
	Nicobar Flying Fox	*Pteropus faunulus*	202
	Nicobar Leaf-nosed	*Hipposideros nicobarule*	211
	Nicobar Long-fingered	*Miniopterus pusillus*	217
	Painted	*Kerivoula picta*	215
	Papillose	*Kerivoula papillosa*	215
	Parti-coloured	*Vespertilio murinus*	215
	Pearson's Horseshoe	*Rhinolophus pearsonii*	209
	Peter's Tube-nosed	*Murina grisea*	217
	Peyton's Whiskered	*Myotis peytoni*	212
	Pouch-bearing Tomb	*Saccolaimus saccolaimus*	207
	Rainforest Tube-nosed	*Murina pluvialis*	217
	Ratnaworabhan's Fruit	*Megaerops niphanae*	205
	Round-eared Tube-nosed	*Murina cyclotis*	217
	Rufous Horseshoe	*Rhinolophus rouxii*	208
	Salim Ali's Fruit	*Latidens salimalii*	203
	Sanborn's Long-fingered	*Miniopterus magnater*	217
	Savi's Pipistrelle	*Hypsugo savii austenianus*	213
	Schneider's Leaf-nosed	*Hipposideros speoris*	210
	Schreiber's Long-fingered	*Miniopterus schreibersii*	217
	Scully's Tube-nosed	*Murina tubinaris*	217
	Shortridge's Horseshoe	*Rhinolophus shortridgei*	209
	Siliguri	*Myotis siligorensis*	212
	Small Mouse-tailed	*Rhinopoma muscatellum*	205
	Sombre	*Eptesicus tatei*	214
	Tailless Leaf-nosed	*Coelops frithii*	210
	Thai Horseshoe	*Rhinolophus siamensis*	209
	Theobald's Tomb	*Taphozous theobaldi*	207
	Thick-eared	*Eptesicus pachyotis pachyotis*	214
	Thomas's Pipistrelle	*Hypsugo cadornae*	213
	Tickell's	*Hesperoptenus tickelli*	215
	Trefoil Horseshoe	*Rhinolophus trifoliatus*	209
	Water	*Myotis daubentonii*	212
	Whiskered	*Myotis mystacinus*	212
	Woolly Horseshoe	*Rhinolophus luctus*	209

Index

Index

COMMON NAME		LATIN NAME	PG.NO
Jackal, Golden		Canis aureus	130
Jird		Meriones hurrianae	188
	Indian Desert, see Gerbil	Tatera indica	188
Khur	See Wild Ass, Asiatic, Indian	Equus hemionus khur	66
Kiang	See Wild Ass, Tibetan	Equus kiang	67
Langur			45-47
	Capped	Trachypithecus pileatus	45
	Chamba/Kashmir	Semnopithecus ajax	47
	Golden	Trachypithecus geei	45
	Himalayan	Semnopithecus schistaceus	47
	Nilgiri	Semnopithecus johnii	46
	Northern Plains	Semnopithecus entellus	47
	Phayre's Leaf/ Spectacled monkey	Trachypithecus phayrei	44
	South-eastern	Semnopithecus priam	47
	South-western	Semnopithecus hypoleucos	47
	Terai	Semnopithecus hector	47
Leopard			115-117
	Common	Panthera pardus	115
	Indo-Chinese Clouded	Neofelis nebulosa	117
	Snow		116
Linsang, Spotted		Prionodon pardicolor	126
Lion, Asiatic		Panthera leo	114
Loris			39
	Bengal Slow	Nycticebus bengalensis	39
	Grey Slender	Loris lydekkerianus	39
Lynx, Eurasian		Lynx lynx	120
Macaque			40-46
	Arunachal	Macaca munzala	42
	Assamese	Macaca assamensis	42
	Bonnet	Macaca radiata	41
	Crab-eating/ Long-tailed	Macaca fascicularis	43
	Lion-tailed	Macaca silenus	46
	Northern Pig-tailed	Macaca leonina	43
	Rhesus	Macaca mulatta	40
	Stump-tailed	Macaca arctoides	44
Markhor		Capra falconeri	92
Marmot			180
	Himalayan	Marmota himalayana	180

COMMON NAME		LATIN NAME	PG.NO
	Indian/Red	*Muntiacus muntjak*	77
Nilgai, see *Blue Bull*		*Boselaphus tragocamelus*	86
Otter			140-141
	Asian/Oriental Small-clawed	*Aonyx cinerea*	141
	Eurasian	*Lutra lutra*	140
	Smooth-coated	*Lutrogale perspicillata*	140
Panda, Red		*Ailurus fulgens*	137
Pangolin			158-159
	Chinese	*Manis pentadactyla*	158
	Indian	*Manis crassicaudata*	159
Pika			154-155
	Forrest's	*Ochotona forresti*	155
	Indian/Royle's	*Ochotona roylei*	154
	Ladakh	*Ochotona ladacensis*	155
	Large-eared	*Ochotona macrotis*	155
	Moupin's	*Ochotona thibetana*	155
	Nubra	*Ochotona nubrica*	155
	Plateau	*Ochotona curzoniae*	155
Porcupine			178-179
	Asiatic Brush-tailed	*Atherurus macrourus*	179
	Himalayan Crestless/Hodgson's	*Hystrix brachyura*	179
	Indian Crested	*Hystrix indica*	178
Porpoise			225
	Finless	*Neophocaena phocaenoides*	225
Rat			191-195
	Andamans Archipelago	*Rattus stoicus*	195
	Bay Bamboo	*Cannomys badius*	191
	Black/House Rat	*Rattus rattus*	195
	Bower's	*Berylmys bowersi*	193
	Brown	*Rattus norvegicus*	195
	Car Nicobar	*Rattus palmarum*	195
	Chestnut	*Niviventer fulvescens*	193
	Confucian White-bellied/ Chinese	*Niviventer confucianus*	193
	Edward's Noisy	*Leopoldamys edwardsi*	193
	Ellerman's	*Cremnomys elvira*	192
	Himalayan	*Rattus pyctoris*	195
	Himalayan Niviventer/White-bellied	*Niviventer niviventer, Niviventer niviventer lepcha*	193
	Hoary Bamboo	*Rhizomys pruinosus*	191

Index

COMMON NAME		LATIN NAME	PG.NO
	Assam Mole	*Anourosorex squamipes*	169
	Day's	*Suncus dayi*	168
	Dusky/Kashmir White-toothed	*Crocidura pullata*	167
	Eastern	*Euroscaptor micrura*	169
	Elegant Water	*Nectogale elegans*	168
	Eurasian Pygmy/Tiny	*Sorex minutus*	168
	Flat-headed Kashmir	*Sorex planiceps*	168
	Gueldenstaedt's White-toothed	*Crocidura suaveolens (gueldenstaedti)*	167
	Highland/Hill	*Suncus niger*	168
	Himalayan Water	*Chimarrogale himalayica*	168
	Hodgson's Brown-toothed	*Soriculus caudatus*	168
	Horsfield's	*Crocidura horsfieldi*	167
	House	*Suncus murinus*	167
	Indian Long-tailed	*Soriculus leucops*	168
	Jenkin's Andaman Shrew	*Crocidura Jenkinsi*	167
	Kelaart's Long-clawed	*Feroculus feroculus*	167
	Miller's Andaman	*Crocidura andamanensis*	167
	Nicobar Spiny	*Crocidura nicobarica*	167
	Pale Grey	*Crocidura perigrisea*	167
	Pygmy White-toothed	*Suncus etruscus*	168
	Sikkim Large-Clawed/Himalayan	*Soriculus nigrescens*	168
	South—East Asian	*Crocidura fuliginosa*	167
	Tibetan	*Sorex thibetanus*	168
Sheep			
	Argali	*Ovis ammon*	97
	Greater Blue	*Pseudois nayaur*	93
	Urial	*Ovis orientalis*	96
Squirrel			181-186
	Asian Red-cheeked	*Dremomys rufigenis rufigenis*	185
	Bhutan/Grey's Giant Flying	*Petaurista nobilis*	182
	Black Giant	*Ratufa bicolor*	181
	Dusky-striped	*Funambulus sublineatus*	186
	Five-striped/Northern Palm	*Funambulus pennantii*	186
	Grey-headed Flying	*Petaurista caniceps*	182
	Grizzled Giant	*Ratufa macroura*	181

Index

COMMON NAME		LATIN NAME	PG.NO
	Silvery Mountain	*Alticola argentatus*	187
	Stoliczka's Mountain	*Alticola stoliczkanus*	187
	Thomas's Short-tailed	*Alticola stracheyi*	187
	True's/Sub-alpine	*Hyperacrius fertilis*	187
	White-tailed Mountain	*Alticola albicauda*	187
Weasel			142-143
	Back-striped	*Mustela strigidorsa*	143
	Himalayan Stoat/Ermine	*Mustela erminea*	142
	Pale/Altai/Mountain	*Mustela altaica*	142
	Siberian	*Mustela sibirica*	142
	Yellow-bellied	*Mustela kathiah*	143
Whale			229-235
	Blainville's Beaked	*Mesoplodon densirostris*	232
	Blue	*Balaenoptera musculus*	235
	Bryde's	*Balaenoptera edeni*	234
	Cuvier's Beaked	*Ziphius cavirostris*	232
	Dwarf Sperm	*Kogia sima*	231
	False Killer	*Pseudorca crassidens*	230
	Fin	*Balaenoptera physalus*	235
	Humpback	*Megaptera novaeangliae*	233
	Killer	*Orcinus orca*	230
	Melon-headed	*Peponocephala electra*	229
	Minke	*Balaenoptera acutorostrata*	233
	Pygmy Sperm	*Kogia breviceps*	231
	Sei	*Balaenoptera borealis*	234
	Short-finned Pilot	*Globicephala macrorhynchus*	229
	Sperm	*Physeter macrocephalus*	231
Wild Ass			66-67
	Asiatic, Indian	*Equus hemionus*	66
	Tibetan	*Equus kiang*	67
Wild Dog		*Cuon alpinus*	131
Wild Pig			100-101
	Indian	*Sus scrofa*	100
	Pygmy Hog	*Porcula salvania*	101
Wild Buffalo		*Bubalus arnee*	84
Wild Yak		*Bos mutus*	85
Wolf, Grey	Indian	*Canis lupus*	130
	Tibetan	*Canis lupus chanco*	130